I0125172

TALES FROM THE VALLEY OF DEATH

Reflections from psychotherapy on the fear of death

Ross G. Menzies & Rachel E. Menzies

AUSTRALIANACADEMIC**PRESS**

First published 2019 by:
Australian Academic Press Group Pty. Ltd.
www.australianacademicpress.com.au

Copyright © Ross G Menzies & Rachel E Menzies 2019 .

Copying for educational purposes
The *Australian Copyright Act 1968* (Cwlth) allows a maximum of one chapter or 10% of this book, whichever is the greater, to be reproduced and/or communicated by any educational institution for its educational purposes provided that the educational institution (or the body that administers it) has given a remuneration notice to Copyright Agency Limited (CAL) under the Act.
For details of the CAL licence for educational institutions contact:
Copyright Agency Limited, 19/157 Liverpool Street, Sydney, NSW 2000.
E-mail info@copyright.com.au

Production and communication for other purposes
Except as permitted under the Act, for example a fair dealing for the purposes of study, research, criticism or review, no part of this book may be reproduced, stored in a retrieval system, or transmitted in any form or by any means electronic, mechanical, photocopying, recording or otherwise without prior written permission of the copyright holder.

A catalogue record for this book is available from the National Library of Australia

ISBN   9781925644357   (paperback)
ISBN   9781925644364   (hardback)
ISBN   9781925644371   (ebook)

Disclaimer
Every effort has been made in preparing this work to provide information based on accepted standards and practice at the time of publication. The publisher and author, however, make no representations or warranties with respect to the accuracy or completeness of the contents of this book and specifically disclaim any implied warranties of merchantability or fitness for a particular purpose. It is sold on the understanding that the publisher is not engaged in rendering professional services and neither the publisher nor the author shall be liable for damages arising herefrom. If professional advice or other expert assistance is required, the services of a competent professional should be sought.

Publisher and editor: Stephen May
Cover illustration: Morgan Lawrence
Cover design: Luke Harris, Working Type Studio
Page design and Typesetting: Australian Academic Press
Printing: Lightning Source

For Helen and Colin, my mother and father, who gave me the finest chance to build a life — RGM

For Lachlan, with whom I'm deeply fortunate to share my moments on earth, however briefly — REM

Contents

Ross G. Menzies

Ross Menzies completed his undergraduate, masters and doctoral degrees in psychology at the University of NSW. He is currently Professor of Psychology in the Graduate School of Health, University of Technology Sydney (UTS). In 1991, he was appointed founding Director of the Anxiety Disorders Clinic at the University of Sydney, a post which he held for over 20 years. He is the past NSW President, and twice National President, of the *Australian Association for Cognitive Behaviour Therapy* (AACBT). He is the editor of Australia's national CBT journal, Behaviour Change, and has trained psychologists, psychiatrists and allied health workers in CBT around the globe. Professor Menzies is an active researcher with nearly three decades of continuous funding from national competitive sources. He currently holds over $AUS7 million in research funding. He has produced 9 books and more than 200 journal papers and book chapters and was the President and Convenor of the *8th World Congress of Behavioural and Cognitive Therapies* (WCBCT).

Rachel E. Menzies

Rachel Menzies completed her honours degree in psychology at the University of Sydney, taking out the Dick Thompson Thesis Prize for her work on the dread of death and its relationship to Obsessive Compulsive Disorder (OCD). She published her first paper on death fears in *Clinical Psychology Review* as an undergraduate student, and followed this by convening a symposium on the topic at the *8th World Congress of Behavioural and Cognitive Therapies* in Melbourne in 2016. Her manuscript on death anxiety and compulsive behaviour was the lead paper in the first edition of the *Australian Clinical Psychologist*. Her subsequent work on fear of death and psychopathology has been published in several leading international journals, and she can regularly be heard on national radio, popular podcasts and relevant public events (e.g. *The Festival of Death and Dying*). In 2017, she gave her first invited plenary address on death anxiety, and an invited workshop, at the *47th Congress of the European Association of Behavioural and Cognitive Therapies* (EABCT). In 2018 she was the lead editor of *Curing the Dread of Death: Theory, Research and Practice* published by Australian Academic Press. She has just completed an invited workshop tour on the dread of death across seven cities for the *Australian Association for Cognitive Behaviour Therapy* (AACBT). This is her second book on death anxiety and its impact on mental health.

Part 1

Theoretical Issues

Rachel E. Menzies

Chapter 1

Cultural responses to death anxiety

'Sorrow has entered my heart! I am afraid of death.'

— *The Epic of Gilgamesh,* 2100 BC

'The great leveller, Death: Not even the gods can defend a man, not even one they love, that day when fate takes hold and lays him out at last'

—The Odyssey, 8th Century BC

The dread of death is a problem nearly as old as time itself. From the ancient laments about death immortalised in the epic poems of Babylon and Greece to the desperate attempts at bodily preservation in the Egyptian mummification rituals, fears of death are hardly a modern invention. In fact, themes of mortality and our efforts to cope with death can be perceived as the common thread underlying much of human history and culture. Our awareness of our own mortality, arguably a cognitive capacity unique to our species, has been famously referred to by William James as 'the worm at the core' of human existence, lingering in the shadows of our daily lives. Unsurprisingly, then, human societies have employed an array of cultural tools in order to combat this fear of death across the ages, including using art, ritual, literature, religion poetry, philosophy, music and theatre to deal with the ever-present dread of death.

Myth and Ritual

Many ancient myths reveal a fixation on themes of death. For instance, when one reviews the mythology of ancient Greece, for which extensive written evidence is available, themes of mortality and ageing can be seen to riddle this ancient belief system. On the surface, much of Greek myth appears to emphasise the inevitability of death, despite the desperate attempts of individuals to escape it. For example, the goddess responsible for choosing the timing and manner of each individual's death was known as *Atropos*, 'the inevitable'. It is also the immortality of 'the deathless gods' that is their defining feature, and it is this immortality which separates them from humankind. Although the Greek gods famously fall in love with many unsuspecting (and often unwilling) mortals, even they cannot prevent the eventual death of their beloved humans. The goddess Aphrodite herself is said to grieve the mortality of one of her mortal lovers, lamenting: 'Old age will soon enfold you, remorseless, the same for everyone, for it stands one day at the side of all human beings, deadly, dispiriting – even the gods abhor it' (Homer, Cashford, 2003, p. 95). The mythology of ancient Greece is also teeming with examples of mortals who have tried and yet failed to cheat death. Most notably, the mythical musician Orpheus was famously unsuccessful in his quest to rescue his beloved wife Eurydice from the underworld after her death.

While these and other ancient myths emphasised the inescapable nature of death, many rituals appear to offer the hope of immortality. One such ritual is that of Egyptian burial rites, or mummification, which serves as a vivid example of the attempt to cheat death. The process of mummification was incredibly lengthy and intricate, centering on elaborate mortuary procedures. Spanning 70 days, the process involved removing organs, casting spells to prevent decay, and various techniques to ensure the corpse remained lifelike in appearance, such as filling the body cavity with sawdust or inserting artificial eyes. These Egyptian mummification rituals represent a desperate and ambitious attempt to prevent any decay of the body and thus ensure the successful revival of the individual in the afterlife. The Egyptian belief in the immortality of their pharaoh, such that each pharaoh is viewed as a literal incarnation of their predecessor, highlights a similar desire to elude the inevitable.

Of course, the Egyptians were not the only early society to deny their mortality. Despite the emphasis on the inescapable nature of death in the ancient Greek myths, a closer examination of their rituals reveals some interesting loopholes in this supposed inevitability. While exploring ancient burial sites across the Mediterranean, archaeologists have unearthed numerous golden tablets, inscribed with guides to the afterlife. These tablets were given to devotees of the mythical figure of Orpheus — who, as mentioned above, famously tried to cheat death — and act as a form of 'golden ticket' to paradise. By being armed in death with crucial passwords required for entry (such as 'I am the son of Earth and Starry Heaven. But my race is heavenly') and being equipped with this engraved GPS of the underworld ('You will find to the left of the house of Hades a spring, and standing by it a white cypress. Do not even approach this spring!'), the wearer may access the most elite spaces in the underworld.

The Eleusinian mystery festival serves as a similarly intriguing example of the ancient attempts to secure immortality. Although breaching the code of secrecy surrounding the festival carried the penalty of death, historians have fortunately extracted several key features of the rites. The festival attracted thousands of attendants each year from across the Mediterranean, and was devoted to celebrating Persephone, the goddess of the underworld. Initiates who participated in these rites did so with the guarantee of a better lot in the afterlife and were promised access to a privileged position in the dreary land of the dead. Participating in the Eleusinian mystery also allowed initiates a form of practice for their own death, as the rituals also involved an enactment of one's moment of death and journey to the afterlife. These significant benefits in the afterlife made the festival so popular across the ancient world that Cicero, the famous Roman politician, considered the Eleusinian mysteries to be the greatest contribution to society that Athens ever produced. Despite the endless list of innovations to emerge from Athens, including the Olympic Games, theatre, and democracy itself, what could be better than eternal life?

Religion

In addition to myth and ritual, religion offers yet another clear method by which humans have attempted to deal with the dread of death across history. This strong focus on allaying death anxiety across centuries of religious texts and ideologies has led some theological theorists to argue that fears of death lie at the heart of most, if not all, of religion. Many of the earliest religious cults, emerging from 4th Century BC, were based on heroes who were said to have cheated death, with the promise of eternal life for their followers. The Abrahamic religions, including Christianity, Islam, and Judaism, emerged alongside such cults and similarly offer literal immortality to devout adherents. Although these three religions' address fears of death through this promise of eternal life, other religions are not always so black and white in their perspectives on death. For instance, Buddhism places a heavy emphasis on accepting one's own impermanence and the inevitability of death. Buddhist scriptures repeatedly encourage adherents to contemplate their transient nature, and even to meditate for long periods on the image of their own corpse, or that of a loved one, decomposing. In fact, some Buddhist practitioners choose to meditate in front of human remains in order to drive home the inevitability of their own death. It is not uncommon for meditation halls to feature human skulls or skeletons.

Despite this clear emphasis on death acceptance in Buddhism, some lesser known practices highlight the universal human striving to conquer death, even in the face of religious scriptures which are emphatically advising the opposite approach. In Japan, the unusual and ambitious practice of 'self-mummification', a deliberate method of dying with the aim of living forever, is one such example of this. Self-mummification involves the monk limiting their diet to berries, twigs, and bark for at least five years, in order to reduce their body fat. For the next thousand days, the individual consumes a tea made from a poisonous substance to protect the body from being defiled by insects after death. Finally, they are buried alive and remain in a seated meditative position until their eventual death. Years later, the tomb is re-opened. Monks whose bodies were successfully preserved after death are honoured as a 'sokushinbutsu', or 'living Buddha'. In the majority of cases, however, the desperate efforts at self-mummification failed, and followers would be greeted with the sight of their leader's decayed corpse. In fact, only around 20 individuals have been able to achieve this difficult feat. Kōbō-Daishi, a famous Japanese monk and poet is one such example of a successfully-mummified *sokush-inbutsu*. Despite being buried alive in a cave in 835, Kōbō-Daishi's followers continue to prepare daily meals for him today, which are brought into his cave by the high priest, in the belief that their leader still resides inside, alive and well.

Ironically, despite the lengthy attempts at self-mummification being a clear denial of death, the remains of individuals who have resisted decay continue to be displayed in temples all around Asia in an effort to remind visitors of their own impermanence. Buddhism is not alone in this regard, with the worship of preserved bodily relics and display of corpses being common in Catholicism. So, although religious texts may attempt to assuage believers' fears of death through the promise of eternal life, or the emphasis on accepting death, the practices observed at religious sites across the world reflect a more complex struggle to embrace our own mortality than that painted for us in the scriptures.

Literature and Art

Across at least 4000 years of human history, fears of death have played a significant role in literature. Most notably, the oldest surviving great work of literature, *The Epic of Gilgamesh*, is centred entirely on one man's struggle to cope with loss. Written in 2100 BC, the Babylonian epic poem tells the story of King Gilgamesh, who is devastated after witnessing the death of his close friend Enkidu. This moment has a powerful effect on Gilgamesh: Not only has he just lost his dearest friend, he has suddenly realised that he too will inevitably suffer the same fate one day. Gilgamesh laments:

> 'My friend, Enkidu, whom I loved, has turned to clay.
> Shall I not be like him, and also lie down,
> never to rise again, through all eternity?
> …Sorrow has entered my heart! I am afraid of death.' (George, p. 77–78).

This prompts him to begin an ambitious quest to find the secret of immortality. Of course, he fails to do so and eventually is forced to accept that mortality is simply his lot in life, as it is for all of us. While the epic story of Gilgamesh is famous for its portrait of humankind's struggle with death, various cultures have similarly dealt with themes in their literature. The plays and poems of the ancient Greeks and Romans were riddled with such themes, and medieval European literature even developed entire genres focused on death, such as the *memento mori* genre of poetry (translated as: 'remember, you will die').

Lived experiences of loss and death have also prompted some of literature's most famous tales. James Barrie, who went on to write the famous children's book *Peter Pan*, was heavily inspired by a family tragedy in his childhood. When James was just 6 years old, his 13-year-old brother died after cracking his skull while ice skating. His mother was devastated at the loss, and James did all that he could to replace the hole that his brother's death had left, even dressing up in his deceased brother's clothes and whistling in the same manner that he used to. James' mother was reportedly comforted by the fact that her favourite son, now dead, would remain a boy forever. It is no coincidence that the full title of Barrie's famous book is: *Peter Pan; or, the Boy Who Wouldn't Grow Up.* English novelist Mary Shelley, who wrote the Gothic novel *Frankenstein*, seems to have been similarly inspired by loss. In 1815, Mary suffered the death of her newborn daughter, whom she had birthed prematurely just two weeks prior. She was haunted by this death, experiencing visions of her baby, and suffering an acute depression. Only one year later, on discussing ghost stories with friends, Mary wondered whether 'Perhaps a corpse would be reanimated'. She immediately began to pen her first novel, *Frankenstein*, which famously tells the story of a young scientist's decision to resurrect a human corpse, after immersing himself in his experiments to deal with the grief of his mother's death. Outside of her work, Mary Shelley's own life tells a similar story of fixation with death. On the first anniversary of Mary's death, her son opened her keepsake box, finding enclosed locks of her dead children's hair, and the remains of her husband's heart, alongside some of his ashes. The bestselling novel *Interview with a Vampire*, which went on to be made into an Academy Award nominated film, has an eerily similar backstory to that of *Frankenstein*. Its author, Anne Rice, wrote the novel in just five weeks, while grieving the death of her 4-year-old daughter. Her daughter went on to inspire the character of Claudia, the 5-year-old immortal vampire girl, who, like Peter Pan, will never grow up.

In a similar vein, art has been used for centuries as a way of grappling with mortality. In addition to two genres of art which specifically depict images of death (the *Danse Macabre* and 'vanitas' artwork, popularised in the 15th and 16th Centuries), almost all of the great artists have depicted death in some form, including Gustav Klimt, Andy Warhol, Frida Kahlo, Vincent van Gogh, Paul Cézanne, M.C. Escher, and Edvard Munch. The motifs of crawling ants that famously typify Salvador Dali's work are intended to represent decay and death, and to remind the viewer of their own impermanence. And, if one wants to see the terror of death immortalised in art, one need only look up Pablo Picasso's final well-known self-portrait before his death, aptly titled *Self Portrait Facing Death.*

The Future of Death: Embrace the Inevitable, or Dream of Immortality?

Today, developments in technology are set to rapidly change our relationship with death. Creative ways of holding onto the physical remains of loved ones are becoming increasingly popular, and include the option of having their cremation ashes mixed with ink to be tattooed onto one's skin, made into a diamond and worn as jewellery, or even pressed into a vinyl record, which can be created to play the favourite song of the deceased, or even a recording of their voice. Further, living in the digital age has led some individuals to design technology which offers a virtual life after death. After the death of a close friend, Eugenia Kuyda developed a program which uses data from a deceased individual's online profiles and message history, so that a user may simulate conversations with their loved ones long after their death. Although the program is not currently available for public use, its development in 2015 shines a light on the direction that modern technology may be leading us when it comes to dealing with death. But do such programs truly help people grieve, or are they one of many ways in which we continue to try to deny mortality?

While the development of such apps offers some sense of, albeit artificial, continuity after death, other technological advancements provide a more literal promise of immortality. One such example is that of cryonics, a procedure involving the preservation of a human corpse at low temperatures in the hope that it may one day be completely revived. Despite the high cost (averaging between $28,000 to $200,000 USD per body) and the absence of any scientific evidence that the procedure will actually work, nearly 2000 people have already signed up for cryonic preservation. These individuals, based primarily in the United States, hope for 'a second chance at life', as the promotional video of one major cryonics organisation optimistically offers, before adding: 'Considering the alternative, which is certain death, cryonics is the rational scientific wager.' But is investing in what may be considered the modern equivalent of mummification, rather than becoming comfortable with the inevitability of death, truly the 'rational' choice?

Fortunately, alongside this technological push to deny death through any means possible, the last decade has also seen an upsurge in the 'death positivity' movement, which hopes to foster societal acceptance of mortality. 'Death cafés' represent one increasingly popular manifestation of this movement. These informal gatherings involve a group of people, often strangers, who meet over coffee and cake to discuss death and dying in a non-judgmental and relaxed setting. At present, nearly 9000 death café meetings have been held across 65 countries, suggesting an encouraging degree of success in the movement's aim of breaking the silence surrounding death, 'to help people make the most of their (finite) lives'. So, although some modern developments may increasingly lure people into denial, the death positivity movement appears to be fighting back, armed with funeral-planning apps, eco-friendly burial options, and death-themed board games and activity books. The increasing popularity of all of these offers some hope that society may strive to accept death and make the most of our precious moments on this earth, instead of fighting off the inevitable.

The Psychology of Death Anxiety

Terror Management Theory

One leading theory in psychology, Terror Management Theory (TMT), offers a comprehensive account of how our fears of death impact a large number of our behaviours. TMT is largely based on the book *The Denial of Death* by the cultural anthropologist Ernest Becker, for which the author won the Pulitzer Prize in 1974. In his groundbreaking book, Becker proposed that the human motivation to survive, coupled with our awareness that death is inescapable, has the power to produce crippling fear. Emerging from this idea came TMT, a theory which argues that humans have developed two buffers to help us manage this paralysing fear. The first of these two buffers are 'cultural worldviews', such as identifying with particular cultural values, supporting a particular political party or sporting team, believing in an afterlife, or pursuing financial or academic success.

According to TMT, by endorsing a cultural worldview, such as advocating for a preferred political party, one gains a sense of meaning and permanence, in the belief that by doing so one will 'live on' symbolically after one's own death. The second buffer proposed by TMT is self-esteem, which we obtain by living up to the various values and expectations of our cultural worldview. For example, if my culture promotes materialism and attaining status via financial achievements, then purchasing a new designer handbag or Lamborghini will increase my self-esteem, give me a sense of permanence and meaning, and protect me from anxiety about death.

Hundreds of studies have been conducted over the last four decades which support the central ideas of TMT. By reminding participants of death in various ways in the laboratory, 'mortality salience' studies have shown the broad range of ways in which death anxiety may drive human behaviour. For example, one fascinating early study examined the impact of thoughts of death on decision making among a sample of municipal court judges (Rosenblatt, Greenberg, Solomon, Pyszcynski, & Lyon, 1989). The judges were assigned to one of two conditions: In one condition, they were asked to write about their own death and the emotions that arise surrounding this, while those in the control condition were not. All participants were then given a brief description of a woman who had been arrested for prostitution (that is, an individual who was arguably deemed to have violated cultural worldviews regarding society norms around morality), and asked to assign her bond. The experiment revealed that the judges who had been reminded of death assigned an average bond of $455, relative to the $50 average bond assigned by judges in the control condition. That is, merely thinking of death for a few moments was sufficient to lead these municipal court judges, arguably pillars of reason and justice in our society, to assign a bond that was more than nine times greater than that considered fair and appropriate by their peers. Importantly, this all happened outside of their conscious awareness, suggesting that all of us are vulnerable to the effects of death anxiety without us even necessarily realising it.

Of course, the effects of death anxiety are not limited only to municipal decision making. Rather, hundreds of studies have shown that reminders of death drive a large array of human behaviours. These include spending behaviour, interracial conflict, aggression towards outgroup members (e.g., those with a different religious faith, or differing political views), driving behaviour, religious practice, and even sun tanning. A vast number of everyday behaviours appear to be driven by fears of death, building increasing support for Becker's suggestion almost half a century ago that death anxiety lies at the heart of much of human action, including procreation, the creation of art, music, and literature, the pursuit of meaningful relationships, and striving for success in our workplaces and day to day lives.

The Dread of Death in Mental Health

While decades of TMT research have taught us much about the role of death anxiety in normal human behaviour, far less is known about the role of death fears in abnormal behaviour. Despite this, there is mounting evidence that death anxiety may, in fact, underlie many manifestations of mental health difficulties. The frequent appearance of the dread of death across the spectrum of mental health conditions and diagnostic categories has led researchers to argue that death anxiety should be considered a transdiagnostic construct, underpinning numerous disorders (Iverach, Menzies, & Menzies, 2014). Although some coping strategies to manage death anxiety may be adaptive, such as pursuing meaningful achievements or building relationships with others, fears of death may also drive unhelpful coping mechanisms, such as avoidance and other maladaptive behaviours. These behaviours, which are intended to protect the individual from their fears of death, may, in fact, play a central role in the development and maintenance of a variety of mental health conditions.

As a result, death anxiety has been implicated in a number of mental illnesses. For example, individuals with panic disorder commonly fear that they are suffering a heart attack, and may seek out medical expertise and appointments with cardiologists in an attempt to keep such worries at bay. Similarly, within illness anxiety, individuals will frequently check their body for signs of disease (including checking their own stools, urine, breasts, heartrate, and anything else that could forewarn death), interpret benign symptoms as threatening, and make repeated requests for medical tests. When turning our attention to the specific phobias, it becomes clear that most, if not all, of the most common phobias (e.g., spiders, heights, flying, water, snakes) centre on feared objects or situations that could directly result in death. Within agoraphobia and post-traumatic stress disorder, an experience of a life-threatening event, such as exposure to a physically threatening event or the loss of a loved one, often precedes the onset of either disorder. In obsessive compulsive disorder (OCD), patients will commonly report that their compulsive washing is done in a desperate effort to protect themselves from germs, and the resulting life-threatening illness that could occur. In a similar vein, those who engage in compulsive checking of locks, stovetops, and electric powerpoints likewise ascribe their efforts to attempts to prevent death via household invasion, fires, or electrocution. Death anxiety, alongside other existential concerns such as meaninglessness, has additionally been argued to play a role in depression.

Among all of the aforementioned disorders, scores on measures assessing fears of death have been shown to predict psychopathology, such that higher death anxiety has been proven to predict greater severity of symptoms. Similar results have also been found for conditions as diverse as alcohol use disorder, eating disorders, generalised anxiety disorder, body dysmorphic disorder, and separation anxiety disorder. However, while these proven correlations build support for the idea that death anxiety contributes to these disorders, experimental research is needed to show that the dread of death does indeed cause these conditions, rather than merely being associated with them.

To this end, although only a handful of TMT studies have explored the impact of death anxiety on abnormal or clinically-relevant behaviours, the results are promising. In support of the theorised role of death anxiety in phobias, one study found that mortality salience (in the form of asking participants to reflect on their own death) increased avoidance and perceived threat (e.g., the estimated likelihood that a given spider is dangerous) among spider phobics (Strachan et al., 2007). Interestingly, the same researchers found similar findings regarding social anxiety, a condition with less obvious connections to mortality. Thoughts of death led to participants high in social anxiety spending more time avoiding a subsequent group discussion. This added weight to the argument that death anxiety drives unhelpful avoidance behaviours which maintain anxiety. In a different study, reminders of death led women to restrict their consumption of fattening foods in a subsequent 'tasting task', and to perceive themselves as being further from their ideal thinness, suggesting the possible role of death anxiety in eating disorders (Goldenberg, Arndt, Hart & Brown, 2005).

Similarly, one recent study used the mortality salience design among a large sample of participants with OCD (Menzies & Dar-Nimrod, 2017). Reminders of death were found to lead participants to spend twice as long washing their hands, relative to those in the control condition, suggesting the central role of death anxiety in driving compulsive washing in OCD. Again, like the municipal court judges described above, these participants were completely unaware that the reminders of death they experienced earlier in the experiment had any effect on their washing behaviour.

Conclusion

Death anxiety is a central part of the human experience, and can be traced throughout 4000 years of human history. While our awareness of our own mortality is something that we must all grapple with, perhaps through bolstering buffers such as adherence to cultural worldviews and heightened self-esteem, this issue appears to plague some individuals more than others. In fact, increasing scientific evidence suggests that fears of death lie at the heart of a multitude of mental health conditions, and may drive numerous clinically-relevant behaviours. If this is indeed the case, what can we learn about confronting mortality from the tales of individuals who have been gripped by mental illness and the dread of death? Part Two of our book explores the fascinating journeys of ten individuals in facing their existential fears.

Part 2

Case Stories

Ross G. Menzies

An introductory note

There are many schools of psychotherapy from short-term, solutions-focussed methods to long-term, insight-oriented approaches. The clinical work of both authors is heavily based on the cognitive-behavioural tradition which emerged from experimental psychology in the laboratory in the middle of the last century. Compared to most approaches, cognitive behavioral therapy (CBT) is generally a brief process since it directly targets the unhelpful thoughts, beliefs and behaviours that are interfering with the individual's functioning. It is not uncommon for a complete course of CBT to involve less than 20 sessions and occur over less than 6 months. However, in intractable and complex cases treatment may be ongoing for many years. As the reader shall discover, the stories that follow generally involve such individuals.

Chapter 2

Eating in emergency

Mary first came to see me in the spring of 2015 when she was 25 years of age. She was an imposing figure — broad framed and tall, striding into my rooms with apparent ease and confidence. Mary was not one to suffer fools gladly, if at all. She had experienced the worst of mental health services and had developed a healthy scepticism for psychologists and psychiatrists. But under this external strength and doubtful gaze, there was a palpable fragility. Mary was an odd mix of cutting wit and a soft interior — an iron fist with a marshmallow centre.

Within the opening minute of our first meeting she was talking about death or, more particularly, her death. It was clear that her life had been dominated by a genuine terror of her own passing. All she could think about were the many ways that she could die. 'We're so fragile, Ross' she told me. 'Haven't you realised that it can happen at any time?'. She imagined death from panic attacks, collapsing in elevators or on public transport, allergic reactions, choking, poisoning, infection from germs and a variety of obscure illnesses. She had fears of cars, planes and other modes of transport. She was even terrified that she might inadvertently take her own life by suddenly driving into oncoming traffic. Mary told me that she couldn't listen to certain songs and artists that she associated with death, and she had magical mantras and rituals that she had to perform to eliminate the chance of death when dark thoughts or images arose in her mind. She was particularly scared of being alone when death finally came to call on her. 'I can't face the possibility of fading into death's arms with no one there — no one to offer me support, no one to comfort me'.

Diagnostically, Mary was a complex woman. She met the standard criteria for Obsessive-Compulsive Disorder (OCD), Panic Disorder, Agoraphobia, Illness Anxiety Disorder and, at various points, Major Depressive Disorder. She had extremely high scores on virtually all the psychological questionnaires and surveys that I administered. Her depression and anxiety scores placed her in the most severe one per cent of the community. When I tested her fear of death on commonly used questionnaires, her profile of scores was extraordinary. Some people fear oblivion — not being, not existing, missing out on events to come (that is, the *death* of self). Others dread the actual process of dying, whether it's the slow decay of the human body from tumours or a more specific terror of the actual moment of death (the *dying* of self). Mary's test scores showed that both issues were extremely prominent in her mind. She had the highest *death of self* and *dying of self* scores that I had ever seen. Surprisingly, despite all these difficulties, her self-esteem test scores were very positive. Again, strength and weakness in the one package.

Of all of Mary's difficulties, her most disabling symptoms related to eating behaviours. She reported extreme terror around the possibility of dying by choking or through anaphylaxis. She worried that she might suddenly develop allergies to foods that she had previously no problems with. She had not eaten peanuts, or any legumes, for many years, and her diet was extremely restricted. She was essentially limited to bananas, watermelon, onions, tomato and bread. Moreover, if she found a 'safe' food or fluid, she would restrict her exposure to a single brand of the product. For example, when I met her, she could drink vodka, but only Absolut vodka. 'How do I know what goes on in the other factories? How do I know it's safe?' she told me. This protective behaviour even extended to bottled water — Mount Franklin was not just preferred; it was the only brand of water she could drink. And she always drank with her jaws closed tight. She would suck fluid through her teeth to protect herself against foreign objects. 'What if there is glass in the bottle? Even a tiny shard could kill me. Why would anyone take the risk?'.

Right from our first meeting I was struck by how limited and difficult her life had become. How can one comfortably eat anything with the constant threat of allergic reactions, choking, poisoning and consuming glass and plastics? 'Well', she told me in a whisper, 'when I'm out, I eat most of my meals at the hospital'. I remember how stunned I was when Mary revealed this to me. Initially, I didn't even understand what she meant — I was just deeply and profoundly shocked. She explained that she would buy food and drive to the nearest hospital emergency department and sit outside to eat. 'Ross, you just never know when it'll save you' she declared. 'I just want to know that doctors are there if something goes wrong'. In situations where this wasn't possible, she would comfort herself by at least knowing how close the nearest medical aid was. She refused to visit any part of Sydney that was more than a few minutes from an accident and emergency department, even if she wasn't eating.

In so many ways Mary was among the most disabled women that I had ever met. In addition to her fears, her mood could rapidly change. She went through regular periods when she was too sad to leave the house. During the early part of our work together we would often talk on Skype because of her immobility. At the best of times, given her agoraphobia, she could only attend my rooms in the company of her partner. However, when her mood deteriorated even this wasn't possible.

I knew from our first session that Mary's treatment was going to be slow and long. She'd been weakened by years of chronic disability, and I feared that her chequered history with mental health services would also hold her back. But as time went on, she grew stronger and stronger in therapy. Step by step she slowly advanced. I taught her that the treatment of anxiety was like trench warfare: 'Just move the trench forward ten paces, bunker down, and don't let the enemy break through your defences. Small gains are all we need between sessions, Mary — that's the way we'll win the war'.

As weeks turned into months, the gains grew larger. I could see Mary becoming empowered in her recovery. She became more positive, optimistic and animated in sessions. She was increasingly engaged and attentive — an ideal patient who was eager to learn and even more eager to recover.

At the time of this interview, Mary had seen me 54 times over three years and she had dramatically improved. Through daily exposure to feared foods and fluid she had slowly mastered meal times. Her first steps were small — merely changing the brand of her bottled water was a cause for significant celebration in the opening weeks of treatment. Slowly she added more foods, and gradually she eliminated all her safety behaviours and magical rituals. She stopped eating near hospitals and slowly reclaimed her life.

Mary is now eating freely, coming to sessions on her own, and travelling with much greater ease. Her mood has been stable for many months and she is completing a course in Fine Arts. She recently married and is enthusiastically building a life with her new husband. To say that she is free of anxiety would be an overstatement, but she is an entirely different person to the woman I first met.

Our interview with Mary

Ross: Thank you so much for talking to me today, Mary. Could you begin by telling me about your family and life at home as you grew up?

Mary: I didn't have a very normal childhood, I guess. My father left when I was about two. My mother left when I was about three. So I grew up with my grandparents until I was five or six. My mum came in and out of the picture at various points in time. I don't blame them really. They were both quite young. I think my dad was 19 and mum was 25. So initially I grew up without them.

Ross: But your mum would re-appear. Tell me about your relationship with her in those early years.

Mary: Very co-dependent, I think. My mother made the world around me a very unsafe place. She frequently told me, from a very young age, how dangerous the world was. So I clung to her whenever she was around. This created its own problems because she suffered with psychotic episodes, even back then. She would see things and hear things and have outbursts of paranoia when I was young. I distinctly remember them. They were like small traumatic episodes in which I came to see danger in things that were quite safe.

Ross: I see. And your father? Did he also re-appear?

Mary: When I was very young, he wasn't there at all, and then he came back when I was five. He's been a figure in my life ever since.

Ross: And what's been your experience of the man? How would you describe this relationship?

Mary: He's not on my birth certificate, which I always find really amusing. I think it's because my mum is indigenous and my dad is white. I think she was too scared to put him on the birth certificate because there was some irrational thought that maybe I'd get taken away. The shadows of the stolen generation were never far from her mind.

Ross: That must have been very difficult for her. Can I ask, when your mum and dad returned to you, what role did your grandparents continue to play in your life?

Mary: Not too much for many years, because my mum took me away. I was around five years of age. I remember the day distinctly. We were at the train station in our country town. I kept looking at my grandmother — I was terribly scared that she was going to die. I'm not sure why I believed this — perhaps because she was old in my mind. We got on the train, and as it pulled away, I saw her fading in the distance. We didn't return to the town for another three or four years. So I went a few years without seeing either of my grandparents. I missed them.

Ross: I see. I was going to ask you about any early losses that you experienced in your life, and you've already mentioned one — the loss of grandparents — of being pulled away from your grandparents. What, if any, was the impact of this event? And of any other losses in your early life?

Mary: I didn't have a lot of losses, but death was talked about a lot in my family. Right across my childhood, death was a regular topic within my home and within the circles of my extended family. Tales were told of the people who had died. Sometimes I even thought, (and at times I still do), that they were imaginary people that my family made up because they were always such traumatic stories. They talked about an uncle that got tragically and mysteriously hit by a car, and an aunt who got killed by the hospital because they wanted her organs. These are the kind of stories I grew up with from a really young age. I started to fear any symbols of death or loss or departures.

Ross: Can you give me an example?

Mary: Sure. I remember the hit song *Leaving on a Jet Plane*. It always triggered fear in me. I'd cry and cry when it came on the radio because I came to believe that it either meant my grandmother was going to die or my mum was going to leave me again.

Ross: I see.

Mary: Yes, so I always had that fear, even after I left my grandparents. Since that day on the train station when they faded into the distance, I've always been waiting for them to die. It's now 23 years later, and they're still not dead. (Mary smiled quietly to herself and shook her head).

Ross: Mary, I was going to ask you about losses or traumas in your parents' lives, perhaps occurring before you were born. You've mentioned that they talked about uncles. They talked about other people that had died. If I'm understanding you, they talked about these happenings a lot. As time went on, did that continue? Was it clear that these events had had a big impact on them; the people in their lives that weren't with them anymore?

Mary: (Mary hesitated). It's a weird thing. They talk about death a lot — death has clearly haunted them. I don't think they've ever really processed the big losses in their lives. My mum was Indigenous, and so her trauma has always been there. My grandmother was part of the stolen generation. She lost a sister who was taken away. And she lost others to early death. All her other brothers and sisters died, except for one that's still alive. She was one of nine, but she lost them all, one way or another. Death was such a big part of her life, and the world has always been a very unsafe place for her.

And the trauma was passed down — it infected my mum. She lost her favourite uncle and her favourite aunt, and a few other important people. My mum also had several other distinct traumas. I've always believed that she was molested when she was younger too. She's very fixated on molestation and rape, something that she's never talked about. She was there when her sister's son got badly burned in a fire and lost his leg. So she's had all these incidents — such a traumatic life. And then there's the imaginary traumas of her world of psychosis. Her life has been so very difficult.

My dad's life was similarly painful — his existence has been pretty brutal. He was one of three boys. His father was a Vietnam veteran. His mum was an extremely severe alcoholic who died in her thirties of liver failure. When she died, his father deteriorated into a type of shutdown. My father had been born with fetal alcohol syndrome. His oldest brother was severely handicapped. So their mum died, and their father wasn't coping. They got a stepmother who was violently abusive towards them — she used to beat my father regularly. And then they threw my father out of home at 14. Two years after his mother died, he got kicked out of home. He grew up on the streets in Parramatta in men's shelters and churches and youth hostels.

Ross: That's just awful Mary, … so much suffering. This has obviously affected you greatly. (We sat in silence for 10 seconds or more, Mary looking downcast). Can I say, for a young woman, you have a lot of detail in your mind about all of these things. You can recount with tremendous accuracy the lives of your mother and father, but also your grandmother's life, including the number of siblings that she lost, and being part of the stolen generation. Is that because you've heard the stories a lot, or because you had a deep interest in your family history or some combination of those factors? Why do you think you can so readily recount all of these histories so very thoroughly?

Mary: I think it's both. I think I have a very vivid mental life, and I had a very vivid imagination as a child, and so all of these people that I'd never met became real human beings to me. Although I've never seen photos of them, I have an image of what they look like and the world in which they lived. But they were talked about a lot. My family rehashes their stories a lot. They're big on storytelling, I think. And as I've said, some of the stories don't even make sense. There's a story about one of my grandmother's brothers joining the mafia and getting shot at, that is just absurd. It's these tales that I know can't be true, which came to influence my view on reality.

Ross: I'd like to ask you more about your family history. I'm particularly interested in your grandmother and the stolen generation, and its effect on her, your mother and then yourself. How much do you think that history — the history of the stolen generation in Australia — has had an impact on you all?

Mary: Oh, massively. I think my family wander around believing they are in an unsafe world where they don't fit in. I remember from a very young age that if I took a day off school, my mum would look out the windows at every car that drove by. If any of them slowed down she'd panic, believing that it was child welfare coming to investigate my absence and take me away.

And I remember so many other odd moments that showed her fear of me being taken. One of the strangest, weird experiences of my youth occurred when I was five or six years of age. It was a period in which dad was fighting to see me more. I remember the scene very well. Mum and dad were fighting, and he called the sheriff. It was this massive emergency situation for my grandmother because she was convinced that the police were coming to get me. I remember her grabbing my mum and I and sneaking us out the back of the house. She took us next door and put us in the neighbour's cupboard. We hid there for an hour because of the terror of them taking me away. It was absurd. It makes no sense. But I distinctly remember that image and my mum holding me in the cupboard and being terrified.

Ross: You being terrified?

Mary: I think so. Now I'm not sure. When I look back at my memory I'm amused and I keep thinking that my family were all crazy. But I think that's because of how I see it now. I remember my mum being distinctly terrified, and me looking up at her face and watching her.

Ross: That's awful. Your mother was obviously a very anxious woman, which is understandable given her experiences and her psychotic illness. Is there any other history of mental illness in your family that you haven't mentioned?

Mary: Oh yeah, a lot. Perhaps most importantly, I had a cousin with the same problems that I later developed. It was my earliest experience with someone truly like me. She had agoraphobia, OCD and severe anxiety and was in and out of mental hospitals her whole life. It terrified my mother because she was always scared of the system — of going into the system because the system is where you just go to die. Hospitals are where you go to die. Mental hospitals. But my cousin Suzanne didn't quite have that fear. She saw hospitals as safe places I think. She eventually died quite young too. She died in her forties. How it happened was never discussed.

That was one of my first experiences of true traumatic death of someone close. I was only 17. Because I'd always linked myself to her, her dying was fairly significant to me. She suffered the fear of death so prevalently, and then she died Ross! (Mary stared straight at me with an expression of disbelief). I never found out if she killed herself or not.

Ross: I see.

Mary: A few of my aunts have attempted suicide. There's also a lot of addiction in my family — from alcohol to ice. Several cousins have bipolar, and phobias seem very common in the family.

Ross: So there's really a very broad range of fears, phobias, anxiety, substance issues, and significant mental health disorders — bipolar and psychosis.

Mary: Yes. My family is riddled with mental health problems.

Ross: I want to turn away from your family now, if that's okay, and move the focus to you. What are your earliest memories of your own anxiety? The earliest memories you have of being fearful, worried, or afraid?

Mary: I think they start in Darwin. When I was four or five, it was after my mum took me. We went to Darwin to find my dad because he'd gone there with some idea of joining the army. I also had an aunt who lived in Darwin. As I've said, I was already rattled about leaving my nan. I was scared that she was going to die when we first left home. But in Darwin, traumatic things kept occurring that still come into my mind.

I remember a terrible incident when we were driving in Darwin. We came upon a dead man — he was just lying there on the side of the road. We slowed down and I could see him clearly. It was terrifying. Then a man came and knocked on the window of our car. He wanted my mum to call for an ambulance. My mum freaked out and got really scared. She wouldn't do it, 'No, no, no, I have my little girl in the car'. She just drove off. She didn't want to be part of the situation. I remember being torn — I wanted to get away as well, but I was overwhelmingly sad at the same time.

Dramas seemed to follow us in Darwin. We were broken into while we were inside the house. I remember being scared, but my mum was terrified. Her mental health was always delicate. She could have short psychotic episodes when things were too stressful. I remember her breaking down after an indigenous man, speaking a native language, was screaming at a shop owner. I don't remember the scene being extreme, but my mum got me and stuffed me in the footwell of the car.

Ross: Oh dear. Each of these events would have been quite traumatic. I'm not surprised you remember being very anxious and fearful. But what about the first things you came to fear in an ongoing way? What were the earliest stimuli that had you afraid on a regular basis? The first fear objects or fear situations in your life?

Mary: I remember being terrified of the toilet at around this time. I was afraid of being pulled into the toilet and of falling into the toilet. But mainly it was a fear of an arm rising up from the toilet and pulling me in. I wouldn't go to the toilet by myself. I'd always ask my mum to take me to the toilet.

Ross: At home as well as out?

Mary: Everywhere.

Ross: I see.

Mary: I just wouldn't go by myself. The toilet scared me a lot. I wouldn't sleep by myself either. I remember being afraid of something getting me from under the bed or from the cupboards. And I was afraid of water. I was scared of something, like a shark, coming from the bottom of the pool and dragging me down. And at around the same time, I developed a fear of being kidnapped or taken away. These were the earliest fears.

Ross: How did those early fears progress over time? Did they fade one by one? Did one of them become dominant? Did they all die out? What happened over the early years with those specific fears?

Mary: I think they changed, but some are still with me in an altered way.

Ross: Okay.

Mary: The toilet one, for example, later became a focus for my OCD. I had very strong obsessions and compulsions about the toilet.

Ross: Tell me about that?

Mary: I couldn't lift the lid, flush the toilet, wash my hands, and wipe. If I did all four of those things, I would die. I had to skip at least one step. And I couldn't sit on the toilet on an angle. I had to be perfectly straight. If I sat sideways I would die. I also had to go to the toilet a lot. I was scared that my bladder would explode and that I would die, so I had to go to the toilet a lot.

Ross: When did this all stop?

Mary: Occasionally I still worry about these things.

Ross: Right.

Mary: Just every now and then. Sometimes, if it's really late at night, I'm still cautious about going to the bathroom.

Ross: The other fears — like sleeping on your own — when did they pass?

Mary: Sleeping on my own wasn't possible until about 13. Checking under the bed? Well, I'm still working on that. (Mary smiled).

Ross: You still worry about something getting you in the night?

Mary: Sometimes, I'll deliberately kick my foot under the bed for a few minutes. Same with checking the cupboard.

Ross: So some of the remnants of your first fears are still here.

Mary: Yes. They just change. They adapt to my logic and my reasoning. They try to find a way to survive despite my thinking maturing.

Ross: Okay. If I'm hearing you right, you might still fear being alone in bed, but it won't be so magical? It mightn't be due to monsters in the cupboard, but fear of an intruder or something like that?

Mary: Yes. It could be that. Or it could be due to a health fear. What if I have a stroke or aneurysm in the night and I'm alone? I still have some sensible caution in deep water, although I'm not expecting sharks in pools! But there are still magical aspects to some of the fears, like checking for things under the bed.

Ross: So the fear stimulus has remained, but the outcome you fear may have changed?

Mary: It does fluctuate, yeah.

Ross: That's very interesting. Tell me, what other things have you feared? What have been the dominant fears in your life? The worst things from your point of view that have caused you problems?

Mary: A lot of food-related fear about anaphylaxis and choking and contamination and poisoning.

Ross: Certainly, when I met you, these fears were far and away the most significant part of your suffering. Do you think they've been the most disabling set of fears you've ever had?

Mary: Perhaps, although the fears of things I had no control over may have been worse. Of course, they're just different aspects of the same thing — a fear of sudden death. But the ones that I had no control over — so the aneurysms, the strokes, not being able to breathe — were so disabling. In the end, I just said to myself that if I didn't leave the house it wouldn't happen. I also remember thinking that if I did have an aneurysm I'd rather it be at home. On the other hand, I could do something about the food things. I could only eat completely safe foods, and only eat in completely safe places, like accident and emergency departments at hospitals.

Ross: Right. So it was the fear of sudden medical mishaps that led to the agoraphobic avoidance.

Mary: Yes. But you know what's weird? I had a period in my life, from about 13 to 15 years of age, where I'd say I had no fear at all — where it all completely went away. I don't remember suffering any fear during that period of time. I caught a plane by myself. I walked everywhere by myself. I slept in my own bed. I was totally self-sufficient and functioning very well.

Ross: Was there anything about that period that you can put it down to? Was there anything in your life at that time that was fundamentally different to the period before it or after it?

Mary: I think for the first time in my life, I had a purpose. I had a job at 13 and felt real purpose. School had never given me purpose. I always hated school. It made me anxious — I had a lot of panic attacks and fears at school. I remember one of my earliest fears, which I still have now and again, was of meningococcal meningitis. There was an outbreak when I was about 12. I remember I had a diary that I used to write in because I was so terrified of getting it. My parents gave me a phone when I was about eight years old because I'd have anxiety attacks and I'd just call them from the school bathrooms.

Ross: So at 13, you got a job.

Mary: Yes, at Domino's. And I felt a purpose for the first time.

Ross: Suddenly you were doing something that felt meaningful, and your fears left for several years.

Mary: That's right.

Ross: You were working in that job across that whole period?

Mary: Yes.

Ross: And then your fears returned. When and how?

Mary: I don't know exactly, although I have some ideas. Things had been going so well. I was working and I'd discovered boys. I was dating, and at 15 I had a boyfriend and was staying at his house a lot. He would go to work and I'd be by myself a lot. But I was very relaxed. I was not afraid at all. But then … I don't know … I had a situation where I was coerced into sexual activity with a man who was much older than I was. It was straight after that my fears returned, although I've never believed that it was the sexual encounter itself that caused it. I think it had more to do with feeling let down by people around me. You see, I told everyone what had happened and they made it sound like I just wanted attention and that I'd wanted to have sex with this older man. Everyone I'd trusted turned against me. So maybe that was it. Soon after that, I remember getting the thought 'I have a brain tumour.'

Ross: I see. So suddenly you had a brain tumour thought and …

Mary: It just overtook everything.

Ross: … the anxiety's back.

Mary: Everything came back. Yes.

Ross: I see. In the midst of everyone letting you down.

Mary: That's right.

Ross: People that you trusted and believed in. And you would've been quite surprised, I imagine, that these people that had been in your trust network suddenly abandoned you. So perhaps, again, you came to believe that the world was a more dangerous place than you had realised. People that were meant to be relied on weren't there for you. Have there been any other happenings in your life that you think intensified your fears? It could include bullying or actual illness or accidents. Is there anything else you haven't mentioned that happened to you that clearly occasioned an increase in the intensity of the fears? Anything else?

Mary: I suffered severe bullying all through school because I was a weirdo. I am a weirdo. I remember I had an argument with my teacher when I was 12 years old because I said that there were no differences between girls and boys and that little boys were allowed to play with Barbie dolls. Everyone just thought I was odd. I liked poetry, and I liked witchcraft, and I liked exploring things, and so kids didn't like me. I didn't fit in.

Ross: Okay. So bullying may have played a role?

Mary: Maybe. But I don't think it did. It was fairly traumatic though. I was always excluded and sometimes it got fairly violent and volatile. It got exceedingly worse as I got older. During puberty, when I was around 13 or 14, the violence increased because a lot of the older girls saw me as a threat to their boyfriend. But that never seemed to phase me — I always thought there were more important things like purpose and death, so everything else was kind of irrelevant.

Ross: Okay. Mary, I'd like to change topics again. How did you first come to treatment? Tell me about your first experience of treatment?

Mary: Well, I can tell you when I first got properly diagnosed. I was about 15 and I had the thought that I had a brain tumour. I flew to Melbourne to see a specialist. I flew down by myself and was feeling okay. But when I got there I swallowed a fingernail and it terrified me. You see, when I was six years old I ate some popcorn and nearly choked on it. It got lodged in my throat and my throat swelled up. I lived on fluid for a week because of my swollen throat. It hurt when I ate and I was scared I'd choke on solid food. So here I was at 15 and I swallowed a fingernail and I was scared that the same thing would happen. I was terrified that my throat would swell, so I wouldn't eat solids for weeks. I was terrified that I'd choke and die.

Ross: Sorry to cut across you, Mary, but that happening with the popcorn at six is very interesting because so many of the fears in later life have been around choking.

Mary: My family's fixated on choking.

Ross: I see.

Mary: Like you don't eat that, don't run with that. You'll choke. Sit down. Choking is a big thing in my family.

Ross: You heard a lot of that talk as you grew up.

Mary: Oh, yes. Constantly. Everything was a choking hazard.

Ross: I see. Let's get back to Melbourne. You swallowed a fingernail and became terrified about choking. Did that bring you into treatment with a psychologist or a psychiatrist?

Mary: No, but it was how I first got diagnosed. You see, I wouldn't eat at all. I ended up quite disoriented and had a massive panic attack — one of the biggest attacks I've ever had. The ambulance came. I went into hospital. I was quite weak because I hadn't eaten in weeks. The only thing I'd had was fluids like Sustagen. The doctor in emergency diagnosed me with panic disorder and told me I needed to see someone.

But my family don't like dealing with psychologists and psychiatrists, and so they didn't really encourage me to see one. So I went back home and I stayed in Dubbo, moving back in with my dad and my mum. We all lived together again. My boyfriend at the time came and lived with us as well.

It's at this time that I became agoraphobic. All my friends were still at school. I wasn't because I'd dropped out. I was painting. And I was smoking a lot. I was smoking and painting, and I wouldn't leave the house. At times I tried, but things seemed to go badly. I tried to get my driver's license. I thought that would help. I got my learner's permit and started to drive in my street. I knew I had to go further, so one day I tried to drive to the local shops to get a chocolate milk. But on the way there a car crashed into the back of us.

Ross: How old were you?

Mary: I was 16. It was just after I came back from Melbourne. It was like a three-car pile-up, and we were at the front. I got out and I had a massive panic attack. The ambulance came and they suggested I follow up with the GP immediately. I really couldn't calm down. When I got to the GP, I was freaking out. He was really kind and very caring. He became my primary source of help. He was at the Indigenous Medical Centre. He was the one who put me on the path to seeing a psychologist.

Ross: I see.

Mary: The first psychologist was awful — just awful. She kept calling me Emily. She wasn't helpful. She gave me her mobile number and she told me to use paper bags for hyperventilating because I was hyperventilating a lot at that point. I didn't really know how to stop the sensations. I left her after three months.

Ross: Did you move on to another psychologist?

Mary: I saw many over the years because I moved around so much. We didn't stay in Dubbo for very long. My life was very unstable. I moved from Dubbo to Brisbane, Darwin, Port Brisbane, Melbourne, back to Dubbo, and Sydney.

Ross: A lot of movement. And did you engage with different therapists in each of those places?

Mary: Yes, I've seen a lot of psychologists. I would say ... six or so that I can distinctly think of, but there would be more. There were many that I saw for just a few sessions because they weren't helpful. Some of them caused me harm! I remember one psychologist told me that 'There's people who think that they're having a heart attack so much that it actually happens.'

Ross: Right. He actually heightened your fears! Is it fair to say that you found psychological and psychiatric care over the years to be inconsistent in quality?

Mary: Because I was so poor — my family had no money — I couldn't afford to see private practitioners when I was young. And once the agoraphobia began I couldn't get to a lot of services anyway. I relied on the GP at the Aboriginal Medical Service — he helped me a little bit. He tried to get me involved in online programs which was a good thing.

Also, we moved to Brisbane, and then my anxiety improved a little. I went on medication at that point, and I think that did help me.

Ross: Medication has played a useful role?

Mary: I felt like it helped me function in short-term bursts, but that was it. I don't think it necessarily helped with therapy. On medication I could do stuff, but it wasn't actually progressing anywhere if that makes sense.

Ross: Yes, I see what you mean. In all the therapy that you've had, and you've had a lot with various people, what do you think have been the most effective components? What procedures or tasks have most moved you forward?

Mary: To be honest, for me, the very first thing was talking to someone who wasn't an idiot.

Ross: Right.

Mary: It was so important to talk to someone who understood what they were talking about. Mostly I've felt that mental health professionals didn't actually understand what was going on with me at all. And then they'd fumble around and try to get me to do exposure and it was all too extreme. It was all too traumatising.

Ross: I see.

Mary: I did learn about breathing from some early psychologists. And about not fearing sensations — learning the difference between sensations and symptoms. I think all of this was really helpful for my panic disorder because it meant that when I had a panic attack I could control my symptoms. One psychologist got me to deliberately hyperventilate through a straw and spin around so that I got used to bodily sensations. That was helpful.

Ross: Getting exposed to the interoceptive cues — the body cues — and realising that nothing bad happened when you had those sensations.

Mary: Yes. Yes. I did find that useful. But none of that really helped my OCD, which I have always seen as the biggest problem. Before you, no one really helped with the OCD or understood it even, I think. They didn't seem to understand how to use exposure to get me to confront my fears. I remember one psychologist saying 'your fear is death, and I can't expose you to death, so I can't use behaviour therapy'. I was shocked. Too few professionals seem to understand OCD.

Ross: That's really interesting. You met with a lot of people who didn't seem to understand the problems you had and were, in your view, fumbling around a little.

Mary: You know what? I also think that a lot of professionals that I worked with had their own death fears. I think this is a big issue — I think it's another reason people avoid working directly on the death fears of their patients. I realised that I was dealing with fearful human beings trying to tell me not to be fearful. I thought, 'How is that helpful?'

Ross: I understand why that would make it hard to listen, and perhaps to trust. Yes, that makes a lot of sense. Mary, I'd like to change topics again and ask you about your feelings toward death. When you think about death, what emotions arise in you? What emotions arise in you at the thought of your own death?

Mary: Sadness. Just sadness. No (Mary paused), maybe angry as well. (Mary paused again). I don't know. All of the negative emotions. (Mary paused again). I think about the experience of death and the realisation that I'm dying and leaving people I love. And then I think about death on a spiritual level — of the universality of it all and what might happen afterwards, which makes me angry.

Ross: In what way?

Mary: Like, why the fuck? Like, for what point did any of this happen? Like, if we are some kind of spiritual being in the universe, why do we exist? Like, what? I just want some kind of answer, I guess. I feel like maybe that's in death, but I don't want to die.

Ross: What do you think will happen to you as you physically die, and once you're physically dead?

Mary: I don't know. I think death itself … It's interesting because the way I picture it is absurd and isn't how it's going to happen, which is like the realisation of death, like the thoughts of knowing you're dying. But that's not how shit happens. It just fucking happens and then you're dead. I often think about it in slow motion. I see myself from the outside — closing my eyes and seeing my partner Michael for the last time or realising that it's all done. And then I believe that you probably wake up and do it all over again. I don't know. I think I don't tend to believe that this is it. So I do have some kind of sense of continuity.

Ross: Expecting something beyond this?

Mary: Not necessarily in consciousness. Maybe I mean a sense of the connectivity of the world — an experience of your consciousness dissipating and you no longer feel like you're an individual, you feel peace with everything and everything that exists. Maybe that sense of oneness.

Ross: I think I understand. Do you expect some ongoing sensory experience? Some ongoing awareness?

Mary: I think so. But I also have a fear of that change of awareness, rather than there just being nothing.

Ross: Can I ask you what relationship you see between fears of death across your life and your experience of everyday living? Is it an extremely tight relationship? Has fear of death been the ultimate driver of most of your 25 years of living? Or has it been a smaller part of your life?

Mary: I think my relationship with fear of death has changed in the last few years — since beginning treatment with you, Ross, and also in finding more of a purpose. But before that, it was my world. Everything was about distracting myself from death, staying safe from death, and avoiding it, avoiding even saying the word 'death'. Everything was about closing the blinkers and not focusing on it, or alternatively, obsessively thinking about it. I spent years obsessively thinking about death and exploring it thoroughly and then trying to avoid it altogether in any way that I possibly could.

Ross: So once it was your world, but these days it's not as dominant. You said that since entering an effective therapeutic relationship, things have changed. But you said that finding more purpose has helped you. That's very interesting because you mentioned feeling purposeful in the teenage years in which you were free of anxiety. Can you tell me more about what makes life purposeful or meaningful right now?

Mary: Multiple things. I have an increased sense of the possibility of leaving a legacy, I think. The idea of working towards something for life to be meaningful resonates with me right now. But I also get meaning and purpose by genuinely enjoying what I'm doing — enjoying life and the experiences around me.

These days I also believe that even negative experiences are worthwhile — they are still experiences. I'm caring less about survival. I'm less insular and less protective of myself — I'm caring more about others. I'm trying to focus on others and that definitely helps. The more I think of others; the less death seems to worry me. I have always thought that I would find the answer to life in other people. That has been a recurring thought of mine, and something that I tried to seek out at various points in my life. I have always sought out people who I could respect or admire or look up to — people I could learn from. Now that I'm doing so much more in my life, I feel like I'm surrounded by a lot of people with unique perspectives. I feel that I have a lot more people to get answers from.

Ross: You have only a few remaining fears. You've beaten most of your specific fears in recent years. The fears that remain — fears of planes, elevators, restricted egress, not being able to get out of some places — do you see them as an echo of your dread of death? They seem to still relate to the possibility of harm. Is that how you see them?

Mary: In part, but it has a lot to do with just being uncomfortable in those situations.

Ross: Okay.

Mary: I feel like I don't want to be in a situation where I'll feel discomfort for any length of time. I feel like my fear of death is somewhat separate from these current fears.

Ross: So do you feel then that you're finally winning your battle with your fear of death? Do you think you're finally conquering it?

Mary: Yes and no. Before, I was running away from it, and now I feel like I'm sitting at the dinner table with death. And I can look at him and I'm suspicious, but I'm also curious and somewhat comfortable. Every now and again, I get the impulse to run away. I don't feel like death and I are best friends. But I'm not terrified of him anymore. I'm cautious of him, but I'm moving toward acceptance.

Ross: That's a great place to finish, I think. Thank you very much Mary.

Chapter 3

The caveman

For more than a decade, Berat rarely left the apartment that he shared with his mother. During the worst of it, a period that lasted for over three years, he would not permit any light to be switched on, day or night. His insisted that the refrigerator was permanently turned off, along with the washing machine and dryer. No cooking of any sort was allowed. He didn't sleep in a bed, preferring a thin mat on the floor. He lived in primitive conditions and almost complete darkness, like a caveman.

Ten years ago, Berat's desperate mother appeared in my rooms. Through tears, Elif described her son's worsening condition. Berat had been losing weight and was becoming weaker by the day. Elif would bring him takeaway meals so that he could have hot food, but he rarely kept anything down. Typically, fears of poisoning would overcome him and he would regurgitate the meals. Elif was shaken by his decline and ruminated about where it would all end. 'You've got to help my son' she pleaded. 'He's going to die'. I moved him to the top of my wait-list and managed to see him for an assessment within the week.

Berat was a wild, wiry figure with long hair and a pale complexion resulting, no doubt, from an appalling lack of sunlight. He resembled

Rasputin — and seemed similarly indestructible. Despite vomiting up his food on a daily basis, and living in prehistoric conditions, he was sprightly and somewhat animated in our first session. I wondered whether his mother had exaggerated the way he was living, but Berat told the same story. No lights, stove, washing, or refrigerated food. 'I can't have any of that, doctor — I get too agitated,' he said.

By Berat's account, his mental health had declined over a long period following a near-drowning at the age of eight, an event that continued to affect him. 'Being near water is very difficult, doctor, and I try not to drink it if I can' he told me. To avoid anxiety and the sensations of impending suffocation that he associated with that early trauma, Berat slowly developed a complex set of magical routines. And, as in so many other individuals that I've seen, the rituals had become increasingly complex over time and had to be perfectly performed to prevent harm. Every object in his apartment had its place and had to be returned correctly, or Berat would become unstable. He would only leave his home for appointments with his specialists, and then as infrequently as possible.

Elif faced tremendous difficulty getting her son to my office and successfully home again. Everything had to be done in patterns and reversed and done over if there was an error. On one occasion, near the beginning of our work together, it took Berat more than an hour just to walk down the five sandstone steps between my front door and the gate of my clinic. I watched in shock from the window of my consulting room. It was like looking at an acrobat performing a deft routine at the circus. He would leap down two or three stairs at a time only to spring back up in reverse and repeat the action. This happened at the end of many of our early sessions. If I came to the front door and insisted that it was time for him to leave Berat would do so. But, left to his own devices, he would be there for many hours, bouncing back and forth with the stamina of an elite gymnast.

Berat's most dangerous behaviours related to this habit of retracing his steps and repeating behaviours to get them right. On the face of it, such compulsions are not unusual. In fact, the need to walk back through doorways, or repeatedly open and close locks and light switches, are quite common in Obsessive Compulsive Disorder. But Berat took reversing rituals to a whole new level. Firstly, he would literally walk backwards down the street, rather than turn around to retrace his steps. He would do the same on stairs and, most dangerously, even in cars. 'In the past — not now, doctor — I've done it on the road' he said sheepishly. 'I've put the car in reverse and gone backwards down a street, doctor. I just had to start the street again', he said searching for understanding, if not approval.

Berat had other odd beliefs and behaviours on the road. He strongly maintained that one should only drive to a place if you could return by the same route. This superstitious belief is much harder to implement than one might first imagine. Though it's possible to do it at times, what happens with one-ways streets, no right turn intersections and single direction tunnels and bridges? You simply can't go back the way you came in those circumstances, or so I thought. 'I even did it in the Sydney Harbour Tunnel' he declared. I sat speechless as Berat described riding on a bike in the wrong direction, dodging the oncoming traffic, just to ensure that he could travel to the north side of the city on the same road that he had travelled south. 'I could have died that night, doctor, on my little bike with its lawn mower motor' he said with a grin, reminiscing on an event that was clearly a triumph for him.

When I first met Berat, he had no belief in himself. His confidence in his ability to recover was almost non-existent. He had suffered from extreme levels of anxiety for more than 20 years and he couldn't see the way out. Maybe others could recover, but not him — more than anything he needed to believe. I knew he could face his fear, but he didn't. This concerned me greatly because, in my experience, no-one achieves more in therapy than they think they can.

Berat and I quickly established excellent rapport, something that is generally easy to achieve with patients who are engaged and transparent in sessions. Honesty is a powerful bonding agent, melting away the masks that humans so often hide behind. Berat had a delightful simplicity in his manner, and I always enjoyed seeing his name in my appointment book. As our therapeutic relationship grew, so did his confidence. 'Little by little' he would say with a grin. 'I'll get there little by little' he would tell me as we set his homework at the end of each session.

Over our 49 meetings during the 10 years that I have known him, I have watched a transformation in this man. His diet began to improve as he allowed his mother to cook again. He stopped regurgitating food, and he started to gain weight. He reconnected with old friends, had his teeth mended and capped, cut his hair, and started dating. I watched a lonely, isolated young man re-enter the world. It was my great privilege and joy to witness Berat's rebirth over this decade.

Sometimes in therapy the things that impact people the most are not what we'd expect. Was it the complex formulation that I'd provided? The specifics of the homework tasks? My feedback for the thought challenging exercises? 'No, doctor,' he said, smiling at me recently. 'Doctor, it was when you told me that I looked like George Harrison. And you told me that together we would sculpt me out of hard rock — bit by bit we'd chip away to reveal all my potential. Do you know how many times I've told that story, doctor?' he announced, beaming with joy.

I don't remember saying this at all. But Berat does, and that's what matters.

Our interview with Berat

Ross: Berat, thank you very much for your openness about being interviewed. Can you firstly tell me about your family and life at home as you grew up?

Berat: Sure, I was born in Bulgaria. We moved to Turkey when I was two years old, and from Turkey, we came to Australia to live when I was four years old. Since the age of four, I've been living in Australia, and I have no brothers or sisters. I'm an only child, and it's been an up and down situation in my life.

Ross: In that early period, what was life at home like?

Berat: Life was good, life was good, yeah, life was pretty good actually, everything was okay. Nothing was strange — everything was normal.

Ross: How would you describe your relationship with your mother as a child?

Berat: My mother, my relationship with my mother, was very good. With my father, it was okay, but it was a bit more better with my mother. I don't know if it's because ladies will love more? Fathers will love — it's not that fathers don't love — but I used to be a bit more closer to my mum I think than my father.

Ross: I see. And did that continue? How would you describe the relation-
        ships now?

Berat: Very much the same. I'm still very close to my mother.

Ross: Did you experience any losses in your early life? And if there were
        any, what impact do you think those losses might have had on you?

Berat: Well, I've had a few losses. I've lost my grandparents, but they were
        elderly, and it was expected. When I was older, I had two other losses
        that really affected me. One was a cousin in Bulgaria — my mum's
        sister's son. They had a lot of animals and they used to move the
        animals from one place to the other place and to migrate the animals
        so they can settle down in certain places. While they were moving
        the animals, my cousin who was in front of the herd crossing the
        road got hit by a truck and he passed away at the age of 12.

Ross: Right.

Berat: Yeah, that affected me a little bit, because in the sense that it was
        very unexpected.

Ross: I see.

Berat: It was sudden, and that was the last thing we pictured for him, I
        guess, going to his funeral.

Ross: How old were you?

Berat: I was 24 or 25 years old maybe.

Ross: That had an impact on you.

Berat: Yes, it did.

Ross: Any other losses that you think had an impact on your life?

Berat: I've had one more cousin as well; he's my age, we're exactly the
        same age, the difference is he was married with one child. He was a
        bit of a naughty boy at times, doctor, but we all get naughty, but he
        was a bit extra naughty, and he disappeared one day and we
        thought, all right, because he was naughty, we didn't think nothing
        of it. We thought oh, maybe he's driving around and causing a bit
        of havoc or causing trouble, but then we found out that he was …
        he actually … he was murdered.

Ross: Oh, I see.

Berat: Yeah, he was murdered, and my auntie, she found out by getting private detectives for the case and asking around, and then they found out the person, they caught the person that done it. The way that my cousin died was a bit horrific, because they stabbed him in the neck, where his life vein is, and after they stabbed him, they chopped him up in pieces, and after they chopped him up in pieces, they burnt him.

Ross: Right.

Berat: Yeah, and they just found my cousins bones. How they know what happened was that they got a man to confess. That played with my mind a little bit, doctor, because I should have thought positive about him, not negative, no matter what, because he's my cousin, and after I found out that he's dead, I regret thinking not good things about him.

Ross: I see. When did this happen, Berat?

Berat: Maybe when I was 30 years old, doctor.

Ross: So a little older than the death of your first cousin. What a very horrific death.

Berat: Yeah.

Ross: What about in your parents' lives, perhaps even before you were born. Are you aware of any losses or traumas that might have affected them?

Berat: I have no knowledge of that, doctor.

Ross: Okay. Were either of your parents anxious? Would you call them anxious people?

Berat: I'd say my dad's a bit anxious, compared to my mum. My mum's not anxious, but my dad's anxious. He's a perfectionist; he likes to do everything spotless.

Ross: Yes.

Berat: If he does something, it has to be good. I don't know; I thought that maybe when I was growing up, he used to do a few things that made me think, 'Why does he do these things?' He might have the same problems as I do.

Ross: I see.

Berat: The doctors … we went to one in hospital when I was 14 years old and the doctors asked him the question, 'Do you suffer from the same situation or the same problem or do you experience the same things?' He said, 'No.' But I think he does. I have two examples. One, where if you washed the piece of fruit for him and you gave it to him, he'd still wipe it.

Ross: I see.

Berat: Then one day when he was driving, he actually drove home the same way he'd come even returning the wrong way down a one-way street.

Ross: Right.

Berat: 'Dad,' we said, 'What are you doing?' He said, 'Oh, I didn't see it; I got confused.' It didn't just happen once, doctor, it happened about two or three times.

Ross: Two or three times he drove back, is that what you're saying, Berat? He drove back the way he'd come, even returning the wrong way down one-way streets, just as you later did as a part of your com-pulsions. How old were you when you saw that?

Berat: Maybe 16 or 17.

Ross: Okay, so you were quite young, you mightn't have begun to drive yourself when you first saw it.

Berat: I was just starting to drive myself, beginning to drive. I got me L's at that time.

Ross: Okay, and you saw your father need to go back in the same direc-tion, that's very interesting. I'll come back to that later Berat. Is there any other history of mental illness in the family at all? Other than what you've said so far?

Berat: Not from my dad's side, but from my grandfather's sister's side, I know she's a bit autistic I think, doctor, and she's got a bit of problems where … they didn't let her get married because of her problems, and she wanted to get married, she wanted to do a lot of things, but because of her situation, they didn't think that she was capable of managing it.

Ross: I see.

Berat: Yeah, so when I go there, I try to see her, doctor, and she's not young now. She's about 45 or 50 years old maybe.

Ross: That's nice of you Berat. Let's move from your family to you. What are your earliest memories of being anxious yourself? Of being fearful, worried or afraid?

Berat: My earliest memory of being afraid was when I was first going back to Bulgaria. I was nine years old. To go to Bulgaria, the plane lands in Yugoslavia and then from Yugoslavia it goes to Bulgaria. When the plane landed, there was a lot of fog. All the planes got cancelled after we landed.

The airport was full of people, doctor. There was certain people there — a group of men, about four or five people — a bit dark-skinned and I thought they were always looking at us, me and mum, me and mum, me and mum, they were walking around looking at me and mum, me and mum.

Ross: This was in the airport?

Berat: Yeah, and I said to my mum, I said, 'Mum,' I said — when it came to the point where I couldn't keep it inside — I said, 'Mum, let's get out of here, let's get out, we have to get out and we have to go.' She said, 'Why?' I said, 'These men,' I said, 'They're following us; they want to hurt us.' She said, 'Why would they want to hurt us?' The thing is, they're not going to want to hurt me, they're going to want to hurt my mum, that's what I'm thinking in my mind, doctor.

Ross: I see.

Berat: Yeah, I'm scared for myself, I'm scared for my mum more than myself, that they're going to hurt my mum, going to hurt my mum and take my mum, and …

Ross: You were worried that these men in the airport might take your mum away.

Berat: Assault my mum. So I ran away, doctor, I ran away. I'm trying to distance myself from these men, and my mum's running after me, she says, 'Where are you going?' She started crying, 'What's wrong with you, son? There's nothing to be scared of; there's nothing to be worried of.' I just couldn't beat that fear, doctor.

Ross: Right.

Berat: I couldn't beat that fear. The men were still there, we were stuck in the airport for God knows how many hours. Them hours felt like days, doctor. The fear factor, I just couldn't control it, I couldn't get rid of it, and I couldn't think anything else different. The only thing that gave comfort to me that day, doctor, was there was a Bulgarian weightlifting team at the airport, and they were going to Bulgaria as well.

Ross: Right.

Berat: The plane that didn't take off, they were catching the same plane, and they said to my mum, 'You can stay with us and we'll help you out.' Because my mum had told them the situation. Once they said that we could stay with them and they will help us out, that's when I relaxed a bit, doctor.

Ross: You felt relieved.

Berat: Yeah, relieved, but the fear factor, I still couldn't get rid of all of it, doctor. We went to the hotel. I waited for them to get us in the hotel and this and that, I still couldn't relax, I was thinking at the time, were the men downstairs, the weightlifting team, doctor. Until I got to Bulgaria and I seen my uncle, that's when everything was all right, doctor.

Ross: That was a very traumatic experience. You were very, very anxious.

Berat: I was very, very scared, doctor, yeah. That's the least to say, very, very scared. I didn't know why I was that scared, and I didn't know why I thought like that. It wasn't about me; it was more about really getting my mum hurt there.

Ross: That fear that something will happen to mum, how did that progress over time? Did it come back to you across your youth at all? Did you worry at other times about mum being taken or something happening to mum?

Berat: The only time, doctor, when I thought of that, was when my parents got divorced.

Ross: Right.

Berat: Yeah, because my mum's by herself, I said, 'This is important, yeah, is she going to be all right, is she going to need help? Am I going to be there for her? What can I do to help her out?' A million and one questions always in my head, doctor, for mum.

Ross: Can I bring you back to your earliest fears. Before the trip to Bulgaria, the year before, I think there was an incident when you nearly drowned at Bronte Beach, is that right?

Berat: That's correct, doctor. I was 8 years old and I was at Bronte Beach with my parents, over at a rock pool there. Well, my parents were probably four or five metres away and I went into an area where the water was. It was chest high, and I was just learning how to doggy paddle then. I took another step and the step that I took, I couldn't feel the floor, and the second step that I took it really put me down in the water. I think I was doggy paddling, because I just stayed bobbing up and down thinking how am I going to get out of this? I started screaming out help in Turkish, 'Imdat, imdat.' Imdat means 'help' in Turkish. I don't know why I screamed in Turkish, doctor. I seen a fat lady and I grabbed on to the lady, but she pushed me away. I started bobbing up and down again. She didn't help me out, God knows why. I couldn't get air, couldn't get my breath. I was terrified that I couldn't get air. Then I saw a gentleman, and I started screaming, 'Help, help,' in English this time, and he came and picked me up. Because if he hadn't come and picked me up, doctor, I was going to drown in a rock pool four or five metres away from my parents.

Ross: That's awful.

Berat: Yeah, and he took me to my parents, and he said, 'Is this your child?' 'Yeah, what happened?' 'Oh, your child nearly drowned.' My parents were very anxious that it nearly happened to me. It scared me, doctor, I thought I was going to die.

Ross: That fear of not being able to breathe, you weren't going to get enough air, you were going to drown, how has that stayed with you over the years?

Berat: Yeah, that's stayed with me, doctor, when I drink water it feels like the water that I drink is going to drown me instead of making good for me, so I can't drink much water. I try drinking little, little, little, just little by little. I can't get full stuff in. Yeah, to this day I still don't drink much water, doctor.

Ross: Right, because of that incident, because of the fear of drowning.

Berat: Yeah.

Ross: You are how old now?

Berat: I am 42 years old, doctor.

Ross: That incident, as an 8-year-old, is still really present with you every day.

Berat: It's present with me, doctor, but not as severe as before. Now when I'm very thirsty, I can drink little by little by little. And now I can take tablets. For years, as you know doctor, I couldn't swallow tablets with water. Now I can.

Ross: Over the years, how have your worries changed? What other things have you feared over time?

Berat: I've always had excessive fears doctor, but it all got worse when my parents separated, and my girlfriend left me. Then I lost a job that I had. After I lost my job I stayed away from my friends, and my anxiety was getting worser and worser and worser. The thing was, doctor, I didn't realise that it was getting worser and worser and worser. I just thought nothing of it. Suddenly I couldn't leave the house. I was at home for 10 years doctor; I didn't leave the house for 10 years.

Ross: Tell me more about that period. When you didn't leave the house for 10 years, what were you afraid of?

Berat: It was all to do with the street lights, doctor. I had a rule to stay safe — that if I left the house with the street lights turned on, I had to be back home with the street lights turned on. Otherwise, I wasn't safe. Everything depended on this pattern. I thought instead of struggling and living and going through all this drama, it's easier for me not to go outside and just stay in the house, doctor.

Ross: Just so I can understand it if you left in the early hours of morning, and the street lights were still on from the night, you would have to stay out all day, to wait for the lights to come back on.

Berat: That's correct, yeah. I would sit in the gutter outside for hours and wait for the lights to come on before I could open the door.

Ross: Life became very, very difficult and you tended to just stay inside.

Berat: That's right.

Ross: Often week after week at a time. You would not leave the house at all.

Berat: Correct.

Ross: That went on for many years.

Berat: 10 years it went on for, doctor.

Ross: In that 10 years how often would you have been out of the house?

Berat: Maybe once every month. It was very hard doctor. I switched the TV on; I didn't switch it off for three years. The lights in the house, we wouldn't switch on, at night time we'd just stay with the TV's light. My mum wouldn't wash clothes because the washing machine affected me. We switched off the refrigerator because it made certain noises when it used to start and turn off. No fridge, no washing, no cooking, the TV on for three years, lights not on.

Ross: You started to form magical patterns and beliefs with everything. You couldn't have the fridge motor kick on and off, so you turned it off. You literally had no refrigerated food for three years.

Berat: That's correct doctor. And I wouldn't let mum cook. So my mum used to bring me takeaways quite a lot. And I had hundreds of other rules. I couldn't get one thing from one room and put in a different place and leave it there. I had to get it and put it in the same spot, the exact spot. I wouldn't stop until I had that perfection feeling.

Ross: Can I ask, with all these obsessions, what did you fear would happen? What were your worried could occur if you broke the rules you had set?

Berat: I just couldn't control the anxiety level, doctor. I couldn't control my thoughts and the feelings that I used to feel. I thought I wouldn't get enough air, doctor, like when I was drowning. I had to do everything right. I wasn't even able to sleep in a bed. My rule was to sleep on a foam mat on the floor.

Ross: They were a very difficult, disabled set of years. You were living without light. You were living without cooking. You were living without a fridge. You were living in the dark and sleeping on the floor, and you rarely went out. They were extraordinary years, Berat. You were living almost like a caveman.

Berat: That's right, correct — I was like a caveman in the dark. But of the 10 years, only 3 or 4 were this bad. Then, with treatment, it started getting a bit more better.

Ross: You started to be able to turn the lights on, and use the fridge again. Step by step with exposure you started to be able to confront your fears.

Berat: Yes, when I met you, doctor. Before that I was just self-medicating with marijuana. I knew what marijuana was at the age of 14, but I didn't touch it until the age of 17 years old, doctor. It was good for me. Some people take medication like tablets, but I couldn't swallow tablets, doctor. I couldn't swallow tablets, I couldn't swallow capsules, so I couldn't take any medication. The smoke, it calmed me and then it gave me a feeling where it's relaxing me, making me think less about what's happening. This stayed with me, and I found for many, many years until I found treatment, the right treatment from the right doctor, that marijuana was good. No, the only thing is I believe in God. Some are going to say, 'Oh, doesn't that conflict one another? It's like you believe in God, but you're smoking drugs.' But for me it's the intention that matters, doctor. Is it a good purpose or a bad purpose? A lot of people will smoke marijuana to get high, to have a good time, but I wasn't like that doctor. My one purpose was just to come back down to earth, have a bit of a breather, where I can relax for a couple of minutes or however long it lasted. That was my only getaway 'cause I didn't have no-one friend-wise, human-wise and all-wise to turn to. I always turned to God. 'God, please help me out… God, please help me out,' and it would work for me. I've seen a lot of doctors, and now I've taken a lot of medications, but my turning point in the whole thing was meeting you, doctor.

Ross: Thank you.

Berat: If it wasn't for you, if I didn't meet you, and I was just going to other doctors, this is my belief, from my mind to my heart, that I'd still be on the same path, and I'm just smoking pot, and I'm still worried about the light, and I'm still worried about the TV, and I'm still worried about the washing machine. I'm still worried about the fridge. I would still be worried. I believe that I would have still been in that condition, doctor.

Ross: I see.

Berat: What got me out of it is the confidence that you gave me, and the way you explained things to me, doctor. You gave me an understanding of what I didn't know, what I didn't understand, what I wasn't capable of … wasn't capable of understanding, doctor. Because with OCD, when you look at the end of the tunnel, it's so small and far away. In my eyes, there was no way to the end because you're just going to suffer for your whole life, in the same process as what you're living now.

Ross: Yes.

Berat: You changed that process by making me think differently, act differently, and wanting things differently, doctor. That helped me out. Am I one hundred per cent cured? No, but I'm seventy per cent better doctor. The 30 per cent I'm controlling with the medication, the proper medication, that the doctor has given me. Being able to swallow medication now has also helped. Without your help, the medication's help, I truly believe that, as much as I believe in God, that I wouldn't be in the good position that I am now, doctor.

Ross: Certainly, when I met you, you were living a very restricted life. Once you started to believe that little by little, you could face one fear and eliminate it, and then the next fear and eliminate it; I think you started to recover.

I want to pick up on something we discussed earlier, which was your compulsive need to drive home the exact way you'd gotten to a place. That's another way in which your fears developed over time, isn't it Berat. You were very concerned about not being able to go back in the same direction. It's very interesting today to hear you say that you actually saw your father do this in your early life when you were just learning to drive. Can you tell me about this problem? I'm particularly interested in how it stayed with you for so long — for over ten years.

Berat: Sure, doctor. As I've said the rule was you had to return the same way you come to a place. I had done that for years before my 10 years at home. Then one day, when I was 21, my friend wanted to see a few girls in Newcastle, and he said, 'Would I be able to drive him down?' I said, 'Look, I'll drive you there. As long as I can go the same way and come back the same way there's not a problem; I can manage it. I will be able to do it for you.' He said, 'Yeah, not a problem, we'll go the same way and come back the same way.'

Doctor, when we got there, we got to see the girls, we talked, we had a good time, whatever. Then when we were coming back, he didn't know the way back. As soon as he said that he didn't know the way back, this automatically created anxiety in me, and it just sparked things, really doctor. It was just like you throw the lighter onto petrol. You've got a burning, and I said, 'Joe, you promised me that you were going to take exactly the same way, and now you're telling me you don't know which way. What am I going to do mate?' I started speeding, and he said, 'Relax ov, relax ov, relax ov, relax ov, relax ov.' Ov means older brother in Turkish.

Ross: He was saying, older brother relax.

Berat: Yeah, relax, relax, because he was so scared that I was going fast and there was another passenger in the front, who was all right, he was a Slav boy who wasn't saying nothing. I turned, I chucked a u-ey [u-turn] on the freeway, and when I was on the freeway, I found a police car, doctor.

Ross: Yes.

Berat: I found a police car, and I got next to the police officer and I said, 'Officer, I'm from Sydney.' I told him what happened, a quick version, I said, 'I'm from Sydney, we went to Newcastle to see a few friends but I'm lost now. I don't know how to get back to Sydney, can you please guide me?' He said, 'Tailgate me.' I tailgated him for many kilometres, doctor, until he got me on to the right pathway that said Sydney. I waved thank you to him; he waved thank you to me.

Ross: I see.

Berat: But then it all went wrong doctor. When I got towards Sydney I had forgot that there were two ways into the city — the Harbour Bridge way and the Harbour Tunnel way. I didn't realise I was in the lane for the tunnel, doctor. It was a disaster doctor. I had to go over the bridge because that's the way we went to Newcastle. But now I was locked into going through the tunnel. You can't change lanes. So I'm going through a tunnel now, that I don't want to go through. I'm having anxiety, where I feel like I'm having to hold my breath and that I can't breathe properly, but I have to breath because I'm going to conk out if I don't. I'm screaming, and I'm saying, 'Look what you've done, you've made me come into the tunnel. I can't get out of the tunnel.' The thing is, doctor, I can't reverse back with the car through the tunnel. I can't reverse back and go back over the Harbour Bridge. Now I'm at a no return point.

Ross: Yes, because you had used reversing before, hadn't you, if you were anxious?

Berat: To get out of certain places, I'd be reversing, reversing, reversing. That's quite correct, doctor, and because I couldn't reverse and get myself out of the situation, that just brought out the anxiety to a new level, doctor.

Ross: I see.

Berat: Some anxiety situations last five minutes, some last five hours, some last five days. This I carried with me, doctor, for 10 years.

Ross: That's amazing.

Berat: Yeah, 10 years I carried it with me, but then I solved it. Do you want me to explain that to you?

Ross: Yes, absolutely. How did you get past it, after 10 years of anxiety and worry. You'd gone to Newcastle in one direction, and gone into the tunnel in the other direction. How did you address it?

Berat: Well, it was very hard. At first, I didn't leave the house and I started making up all those extra rules. I made up all my other rules to stay safe. I was stuck in the house for all those years, doctor. I tried seeing a doctor but he was making it worse. He was making me think of the past — opening up feelings again about things. Instead of making it smaller, it was actually a worse situation here, doctor. I wanted to go to hospital for a treatment program, but he wouldn't let me.

Ross: I see.

Berat: It didn't matter how much marijuana I smoked. I'd smoke and smoke and smoke; I'd smoke a lot, just to get the thought of the tunnel out of my head, doctor. I'd smoke a lot. The turning point for me was when the doctor said, 'No, no, no, no, no, no, you can't, you don't have to go to the hospital.' I got very upset, and he called the police on me. After he called the police on me they took me to hospital and they explained to me that they're going to have to keep me inside here. They had a talk with me about why I was scared, what I was doing, and what made them bring me to the hospital? They wanted to keep me by force. I said, 'Please don't do this to me.' I said, 'Give me a bit of time, and I'll come to the hospital myself if I can't solve it.' I didn't like the hospital, doctor. There's a lot of people where they don't let you out of the hospital, they just keep them in there, doctor. They lock the doors at certain times and cut certain privileges.

So now I'm at home again, there's no-one around. I'm by myself, just like I'm the only person in my mind. 'Please God help me out, I'm on the marijuana again, I'm smoking, and I just can't beat this anxiety feeling. I just can't beat it' I said. Now I couldn't believe it, doctor, but I said, 'I have to go back the same way. If I go back the same way I'm going to be all right, nothing's going to happen.' I bought myself a bike, a normal average bike, but this bike, it had a lawnmower made on it, doctor. It was like a motor bike where you just pressed the pedal and it will take you.

Ross: This was a pushbike with a motor on it.

Berat: That's correct, doctor. I said to my mum, 'Mum, I just can't beat it.' I said, 'After years of smoking and repressing it and leaving it behind me; it's still like I'd experienced it yesterday.' Doctor, I said,

'The feelings, the scary feeling, the obsession feeling, the anxiety feeling, the feeling of not being able to control my mind and sticking to another place', I said, 'I have to do this in reverse and get it out of my system.'

There's cars coming one way, so I'm going to put people at risk, so I put flashlights on the bike — flashlights that turn on and off, on and off, just to make sure, to make them aware.

Ross: Yes.

Berat: When I first came into the tunnel, doctor, there was a lot of cars coming, and there was a bay where you could park the car if you break down. I went there and waited for the cars to go past, and I thought, I'm going to die doing this, but if I don't do this I'm going to die with the anxiety, doctor. I have to do this. I'm going to die either way.

Ross: So you thought you might die doing this, but you would end up dying from the anxiety if you didn't.

Berat: That's right, doctor, for this had come to a level where I can't control my anxiety feelings, I can't control my anxiety thoughts. I haven't left the house for years. I thought, if that little thing gives me a little bit of comfort and a little bit of relief, I'm willing to do it and take it, doctor. I went to the tunnel, I've got a place to put my flashlights on, for I didn't want to hurt no-one, kill no-one, harm no-one in the process, but I had to do it, doctor.

To overcome this situation, I just couldn't suppress it, hold it any more. I went through the tunnel, cars are coming on to me, when I see cars on the left lane I was dodging in the right lane, when I see them on the right lane I was dodging them on the left lane. I was dodging cars, and got out of the tunnel.

Ross: It must have been extremely frightening.

Berat: The thought was in my mind, doctor, I just want to get out of here as quick as possible. I just want to get out of here as quick as possible, I just want to get out of here as quick as possible. As I said, I was just thinking, I have to accomplish this, accomplish this, accomplish this, so I can get rid of these thoughts that have been in here for 10 years, doctor.

I got out the tunnel and up to the Harbour Bridge. But when I was doing a u-turn some police officers busted me and they stopped me. Then he said, 'Mate,' he goes, 'What are you? I think you're just stuffing around.' I said, 'Why officer?' He said, 'Mate, you can't be riding on the Harbour Bridge, riding your bike there.' I said, 'Well it's got a motor.' He didn't care if it's got a motor or not, he said, 'You can't be on here mate, we're going to have to get you out of here.' They were going to put me on the side where there's a walk path, doctor.

The thing is, I'm going to be creating a new problem. I told them, I said, 'I suffer from OCD and if you put me in there then I'm just going to want to come back. Can you please help me out?' They asked me 'What do you want us to do for you?' I said, 'Can you just give me a lift into the city with my bike, and then I'd get out.' They said, 'If the bike fits into the paddy wagon.' They put the bike into the paddy wagon. I got out of the paddy wagon in the city, doctor, and I drove home. After that I didn't use the bike again, yeah.

Ross: Such an extraordinary incident, Berat. You just felt you had to correct that one, it was too hard.

Berat: That's correct, doctor.

Ross: Now I have a few more questions, I want to just change topic, to death itself, to thinking about death. I want to ask you, Berat, what emotions arise in you at the thought of your own death?

Berat: My own death, doctor. This is my own belief, everyone has different beliefs in life, but when we die we don't take nothing with us except for the good things and the bad things we did, doctor. We're not going to take a mountain of gold or a chest of money or a chest of treasure; we're just going to take ourselves.

I'm scared of dying; I'm scared of dying. There's two things I'm scared of, doctor. First, the process of dying, the feeling of dying. Second, after I die I'm scared of where I'm going — how am I going to answer for all the ugly things that I've done, that I have to answer for? There's two things that scare me, doctor.

Ross: That relates to my next question Berat. I wanted to ask you what you think will happen to you as you physically die, and what do you think happens once you're physically dead?

Berat: Well, our religion — I'm a Muslim — says once we've passed beyond our deathbed, that there is nothing, no family, no friends, no relatives that will come and help you out, that can come and help you out, because it's impossible. The only help that you will get is where we're told that we're going to be asked certain questions in the grave, doctor.

In the grave, if you can answer them certain questions good you'll be all right, you'll be in a better place. The place that you're in will feel comfortable, but if I've been a bad person and I've been bad to other people, and I've taken their rights away from them, or I've stolen something from them, I have to answer for that. Death, for me, it's inevitable, and if I'm a bad person I'm going to be in a bad position until the day of judgment, doctor, that's what I believe.

Ross: I see. How often, Berat, do you think about death? Do you think about it often?

Berat: I used to think about it lots, doctor.

Ross: Did you, in the past?

Berat: Yeah, yeah.

Ross: Would you have thought about it most days in the past?

Berat: Yes, when I was doing my OCD, doctor. I'd be walking down the stairs backwards, forwards and backwards, running down the stairs backwards, doctor. Going through one way tunnels the wrong way — I was constantly thinking my rituals would kill me. But I'd suffocate and die if I didn't do it doctor.

Ross: It's interesting. With your rituals, you were desperately trying to stop death coming, and cope with the anxiety, but you were actually increasing the risk of death through everything you were doing.

Berat: That's correct, doctor.

Ross: What relationship do you see between thoughts about death, fears of death, and everyday living or everyday life? Are the two connected do you think?

Berat: I'm not sure, doctor, how much they are connected, but my main key, the main thing for me, was just not being able to control the fear. The fear feeling. Not only the thought of death but the feeling of anxiety. That was my main thing.

Ross: I see.

Berat: Yeah. I've done a lot of dumb things in my life, doctor. I know that one occasion was when they tried sending me to Turkey when I was 14 years old, they found a Turkish family with me, they gave me a bit of money at the airport actually. I didn't want … I told them I didn't want to go, I told them the day I was at the airport, but no you're going to go, you're going to go, you're going to go.

Anyway, doctor, I went, I'm at the airport, I've said my goodbyes to the family and friends, so I went into the airplane and I seen the lady that I was going to spend the next 20 hours or odd hours next to her, in the airplane, just the look of her scared me, doctor. She had … the look of her scared me, she just had these freaky eyes, and I said, 'There's no way I'm going to sit next to someone that's scaring me.' I can't do this, doctor, she just scared me.

I got my bag, and I'm going back out, and the lady said, the hostess said, 'Oh what are you doing?' I said, 'I'm going home.' She started laughing at me. I said, 'Just look.' She goes, 'What are you doing?' I said, 'I told you, I'm going home.' Then she quickly goes after me, doctor, she's pretty well chasing me through the airport, and they're screaming, 'Stop, stop, we don't want to hurt you, we don't want to hurt you. We just want to talk to you; we just want to talk to you.'

I'm not stopping, doctor, with the bag, I'm just full blast, and it came to a point where I couldn't run any more. I stopped and actually tourists were passing by, 'Where are you running?' I told them the situation, I said, 'Look, they want to send me to Turkey, I'm scared of this and that, and when I went into the airplane I got more scared.' I said, 'I just don't want to go. They said, 'Oh, a lot of people want to be in your position, to go for a holiday. Because you're going to have a good time, yeah, there's nothing to be scared of.'

They tried to give me positive thoughts, doctor. I just couldn't get the positive, turn the negative into a positive, and I said, 'I just can't do this, I won't do this.' They said, every half an hour that the airplane doesn't leave, it costs the airplane $30,000 in fuel money, doctor. I said, 'I'm sorry to disappoint you all, but I can't go.' I thought, when I get home now, they announced to my parents through the microphone, and they weren't gone yet, because the airplane was still there. I thought my dad was going to kill me; there's no return, I'm going to really, really cop it for this one.

Well, when I got home he just asked me, he said, 'What happened?' When I told him, he didn't even raise his voice at me, doctor.

Ross: That's very nice.

Berat: Yeah, and so the way they got me out of that situation was, a couple of months later they sent me with my mum.

Ross: That was much better.

Berat: Yeah.

Ross: The close relationship to your mother has been very important in your life. One final question Berat, what makes your life meaningful? What is it that you think gives meaning to your life?

Berat: Just being able to function normally. Eat, sleep, rest, go out, interact with other people, being able to talk, being able to watch TV, or being able to talk with people, being able to socialise. It's just being able to function that's given me a lot of joy, doctor. A lot of happiness. Before if I wanted to, I wouldn't cook because it would take me a couple of goes to cook things, doctor. If I was going to cook scrambled eggs, instead of breaking two or three eggs, I'd break the whole box, just to cook one egg, doctor.

I wasn't going to go through a whole box here every day just to cook one egg; I wouldn't cook, doctor, I would leave that process. Now, that I have that ability, to still overcome my fears and my thoughts, and enjoy it, and to actually do these and feel good about it, I'm at a different level, doctor.

Ross: It gives you meaning and purpose.

Berat: Meaning in life, doctor? Yes, just to function normally.

Ross: That's fantastic, Berat.

Berat: With all this that I've been through, experienced, I sometimes thought I'd never make it. When I didn't see any light at the end of the tunnel, everything was dark for me, you and God were my shining points, doctor. You said, 'There's a light at the end of the tunnel. There's a light there. It might not be a big one, but there's light there.'

You told me this, and you explained this to me, and I like the way you said, 'It's not going to happen overnight where there's a bang and it's all gone, but it is going to happen'. I took that on board with you, doctor, and I truly believe that if I didn't see you, or come across you, I wouldn't be seeing that light in the tunnel. I just wanted to say to the people that there is a way out of anxiety, sadness and repressed feelings. There is light at the end of the tunnel. There is light at the end of the tunnel. You just need the right doctor, the right medication, and the right understanding.

Ross: Well that's a lovely way to finish, thank you very much.

Berat: Thank you, doctor, and saying thank you is enough for me.

Chapter 4

My father's son

The family systems that we emerge from have a huge impact on our later psychological wellbeing. Loving, caring and supportive parents can do a lot to correct neurotic vulnerabilities. Unfortunately, in equal measure, hostile, aggressive and vindictive parenting can create trauma in a young child that will continue for decades. For John, the fates had placed him on this latter path.

John grew up in a remote area of Austria with a thoughtful and considerate mother. But his father was a tyrant, an aggressive man with a vicious streak who enjoyed taunting his children. From all that John told me, his father was physically and emotionally abusive over many years. He would delight in scaring his children and would pit them against each other in various aggressive activities. 'He'd make us fight each other' John said, 'and he'd get pleasure from watching us. Whoever won the fights would be his favourite'. There was disgust in John's eyes whenever he talked about the man. On some level, he knew the terrible impact that his father had had on him.

John's father had a military background, and he kept rifles in the house. Death was never far away from John as his father loved to hunt. He would go high into the mountains, returning with the dead carcass of an Alpine Chamois or Ibex over his shoulder. 'He'd be covered in blood, draining down all over his body. It was quite a sight, Ross. Then we'd have to watch him skin the animal and cut it up. He'd hang the skulls, after bleaching them, on our walls. I was no more than six or seven years of age when I first saw all this'.

Unsurprisingly, as John grew, he developed a multitude of anxiety-related problems. Most of his specific fears centred on death. 'Will I have a heart attack when I'm lifting weights at the gym?' he would wonder. 'Will asbestos kill me?' The topics of his worries varied considerably over the years — his mind seizing on new and inventive ways that he could die. But of all his fears, it was his concern about aggressively attacking others, or himself, that would cause the most problems for him. John experienced a range of intrusive, violent images. They involved pictures in his mind of stabbing people, pushing people in front of traffic, throwing them off bridges, and the like. Equally, many of the images were directed at the self. 'I was terrified I'd throw myself into a tree mincer. I even feared I'd open the door in a plane and jump out' he told me.

Such aggressive obsessional images and ideas are not uncommon. It's estimated that around one per cent of the population suffer from the problem. However, John feared that his genetics and his early traumatic life might mean that the images were a reflection of who he'd become as a man. John had been bullied relentlessly across an extensive period at school and, in his youth, would dream of revenge against the perpetrators. 'They were dark dreams' he told me. 'Revenge with explosive violence' he said softly.

'Maybe I've become a psychopath?' he pondered in fear. His father had constantly said he was mentally unwell, calling John a 'retard' and a range of names implying he wasn't normal. What if there was something deeply, darkly wrong with him? The combination of his father's aggression, the early experience of bullying and his desire for revenge set the scene for con-sciousness to slowly wind him up. In addition, there was his own military training. John had volunteered for the army, and he knew how to kill. He was a tall, muscular man who had worked on strengthening his body in the gym. In fact, he admitted that he had trained himself to become an invin-cible force so that no-one would taunt him again.

John had watched violent movies in his youth, and enjoyed heavy metal music. 'I can get angry, you know' he told me in an early session, watching my reaction closely, looking for any sign that I thought he was a risk to the community. And then there were all the images that dominated his mind. Why did he have them? 'Don't psychopaths have similar thoughts?' he would ask. 'And why can't I control them?' The more he tried, the worse they got. 'Maybe this is who I am deep down — a mad man that will cut loose one day and cause havoc. After all, I am my father's son!'

Individuals with aggressive obsessions often have these 'snap theories' of human behaviour — that one day, a man just snaps and suddenly kills, almost against his will. The fear of the images leads the sufferer to try to supress them, a practice which has been shown to increase the frequency of the thoughts. This, of course, causes more concern and strengthens the belief that the sufferer is getting close to breaking.

Inevitably, at some point, individuals with such fears end up in the consulting room of a health professional for reassurance. Unfortunately, like so many others before him, the initial response that John received only worsened things. He told a counsellor about the images and thoughts that he had when he was around knives, about plunging them into his partner's stomach. 'If you think it, you want to do it' she had told him. I don't know why I was staggered when he told me this. I'd heard of similar scenes in therapy before. In fact, I'd seen many patients that have been given this poor advice. In every case, it led to a significant increase in anxiety and distress. If a health professional seemed concerned or afraid, how could the sufferer be expected to normalize and trivialize their thoughts? But, intriguingly, John didn't falter. Intuitively, he told me, he knew something wasn't right with what he'd been told, and so he sought other help. He saw several clinicians before he found his way to my rooms. Some helped him to an extent. Some didn't move him forward at all. Psychiatrists had trialled medication, but it hadn't agreed with him, and he was craving a solution to the problem, not a means of covering it up. 'It was time to stop mucking around' he told me.

Across our sessions John came to understand that he had never been a danger to himself or others. 'Look at your reactions to your thoughts, John,' I put to him. 'They fill you with fear and disgust because they're not consistent with who you are as a person. The psychopath would enjoy these thoughts and images — but you've been terrified by them'. Slowly John came to understand that the thoughts were normal and commonplace in the community. His only mistake had been to give the thoughts significance — to listen to the chattering voice of his mind. This had amplified the thoughts and, along with his habit of trying to suppress them, increased their frequency. He had been repeating this error with each and every new idea that consciousness had thrown at him.

John was a determined man, and extremely compliant with all the homework I set him. For the next three years, he would keep a large kitchen knife beside him when sitting with his wife. He spent hundreds of hours confronting his fears, proving that they were wrong. He would hold his wife and hug her with a knife in hand. He would put on aggressive movies and music with knives nearby, all to prove to himself that the first counsellor's comments were wrong. Bit by bit, his fears left him, as he confronted them in every situation we could imagine.

John provides a striking example of the harm that can be done to someone in their early life. At the same time, he shows us what hard work in behaviour therapy can do for fear and anxiety. At the time of the interview, I had seen him 36 times over 4 years. Sessions were now spaced well apart and were designed to simply review and maintain his gains. He no longer met diagnostic criteria for any mental health disorder.

Our interview with John

Ross: Thank you very much, John, for coming in. Can I begin by asking you about your family and life at home as you grew up?

John: I was born in Austria. My mum was from England but married an Austrian guy. He was actually very controlling. He didn't like it if she back chatted, I guess. He would get aggressive and angry if that happened. He could snap very easily. I remember an incident when my dad threw vegetables at my mother because he found a caterpillar in them, and he couldn't cope with that. That's the sort of thing he would snap about. Very simple things.

I think he was a bit of a 'mummy's boy', as well. You could see that he adored her, but everything had to be his way. That's the thing. Everything had to be what he wanted, and being in an Austrian alpine village, as well, the man was the boss, that sort of thing. He had an incredibly bad temper. A lot of people in the village were actually scared of him because he'd get so furious. They were scared of the guy and wouldn't help my mum I suppose, or take my mother's side because they knew if he got to hear about that, he would get nasty towards those people.

Ross: Tell me about your relationship with your mother in those early years.

John: I had always got on with my mum very well. She looked after me very well, as best as she could I suppose in the circumstances. I had two brothers come along, as well. But I was the one who used to cop it from my dad, being the first child. And I would irritate him. I used to wiggle my arms when I was young. When I was excited, I'd wiggle my arms, so he decided that I was nuts because I expressed myself physically when I was three or four years old, and he tried to put me in a backward school for that reason — because I wiggled my arms.

My mum didn't want me to go there, but as I said earlier because what he said goes, he ended up putting me in this backward school. I had a bad start I suppose at the beginning because of that, and there were people who were disabled. I certainly wasn't disabled. My mom did everything she could to try and stop me going there, but that happened because I used to wiggle my arms.

Ross: You had a really positive relationship with your mother. But it sounds like it was a much more difficult relationship with your father.

John: That's right. He liked to make you do feats, huge feats. He'd take you for walks up the mountainside when you were a young kid. That's probably why I don't like heights because he used to take me there as it was very high up. We went for a walk along a very narrow walkway to the top of the waterfall in one instance. You look down and realise you're 150 foot up. You're on a narrow pathway, and there's no fence. It's a thin pathway to get across the top of the cliff.

Ross: How old would you have been?

John: That would have been about probably six, something like that. Yep.

Ross: Do you remember being scared on the walks?

John: That's something I've even dreamed about. It's something I absolutely hated. I didn't want to do it, but he pushed me into it. 'Come
on, you got to do this,' and grab you, and pulls you along, makes
you walk. I didn't want to do it. I just didn't want to do it. He
actually took pleasure I think in the fear. He'd laugh when you
looked over, and I think that's a bit sadistic — thinking that things
like that were funny.

That's just one instance. Another, was later on when I was a bit
older where he took me across a large dam which is on a pass. I
didn't particularly like that because one side is filled with water, and
the other side is obviously a sheer drop. I remember back then I
tried to face it by looking over one of the turrets straight down. I
hated that, too. I think that the reason I don't like heights and
maybe why I got some anxiety from it was because he made me do
something like that. It just gave me an impression. It just felt unsafe.

Ross: Were there other things that he did in your early life that distressed
you — other things you witnessed?

John: There were lots of things. When my first brother came along, the
second eldest, I remember him beating him, grabbing him by the
legs like that and punching him.

Ross: I see.

John: He used to make my brothers fight. He used to enjoy that. I
remember him fighting my brother after me. Peter was made to
fight Steve, and dad relished it. Steve was his favourite because he
was born prematurely, but he was a bit of a fighter. He became my
father's favourite because he used to beat Peter.

Ross: That's terrible.

John: When you'd go along walkways, and they'd have these pull-up bars,
he'd try and make you do pull-ups. He'd want you to do so many
pull-ups. It was a competition. He made you compete physically.

Ross: He was a hunter, as well, wasn't he?

John: He was. He used to go hunting. In the military, you keep your own
rifle upstairs. You'd keep it at home, which is not a good thing.
There would be a hunting season. He used to take that rifle and just

go away for a couple of days. I remember him walking down the mountain with a dead Chamois on his shoulders, covered in blood, dripping all down him, and then he'd string it up in the garage and skin it in front of us. Show us how it's done, pull the skin off, and then cut the stomach, and the intestines fall out all over the floor, and then just chop it up.

Ross: How old would you have been?

John: That again would have been about six or seven. I remember the first time I saw it.

Ross: Very young.

John: Very young. Another thing he used to like to make me do, and this is when I got a bit older — I think around eight. He would make me make these bee frames because he had bees. I'd sit all afternoon on a Saturday having to make these bloody bee frames, and he wouldn't let me out. My friends were all outside, but he wouldn't let me out. I made all the bee frames for him. He used to get these electrodes and touch the wires on the edge of the frame, and it would melt the wax into the frame, and they would be put in a hive, and obviously the bees would fill it up with honey.

He was violent towards my mum. I used to see him beat my mum. He threw her down the stairs on one occasion.

Ross: A very aggressive man.

John: And then stuck a gun in her face. The gun was pointed in her face once. It had nothing in it. Honestly, he was a very nasty piece of work.

Ross: Yes, indeed — it all sounds horrific.

Can I ask you about any deaths or losses that you experienced in your early life? What early losses, if any, did you experience and what impact did they have?

John: The loss of a normal childhood. Calling me a 'retard', and all that sort of stuff, and watching your mother having to put up with being beaten. She took to drink because of that to try and alleviate the pain. Eventually, we ended up leaving Austria because she divorced him. It took years to get a divorce. Escaping from him was difficult.

After the separation we had to still see him, but we'd try to escape. One day I was seeing him at my uncle and aunts. They were chatting to my father, so I climbed out the bathroom window and ran up the hill. My aunt and cousin chased after me on a moped.

It's chasing me up the hill. I'm running up the mountain; this bloody moped is chasing. There were many moments like that. I remember my brothers hiding in bins so he couldn't find them. He went to pick them up at school. He was allowed to see them, but they didn't want to see him, and so they'd hide.

Ross: I see. This is after the separation.

John: This is after. The separation had taken place, and the divorce was going through. Very difficult to get a divorce up there because they're very religious. I used to hate going to see him. I remember locking him in a room once, and I've got my cousin pinning me on the floor yelling, 'Where's the key?' I wouldn't tell him where the key was, and he's going mental in the room.

Ross: It's understandable how you all felt about him given the way you were treated.

John: My mum claims that a friend of my dad tried to run her over, and didn't stop when she was screaming. She thinks that my father put him up to that when he was chucked out of the house and stuff.

Ross: Did she think he was trying to kill her?

John: That's what she says. That is exactly what she says. She could hear a car behind her, and she turned and he wasn't stopping. I remember that incident quite well, too.

Ross: How old would you have been?

John: At that time, probably about nine.

Ross: Very young to be hearing these things.

John: There's another time that my brother Steve got stung by my father's bees, and he had a reaction to it. His eyes were swelling, and all my dad did was laugh. My mum was panicked, and she eventually got him to a doctor, and he had to get some injections to ease that. Things like that.

Ross: He was clearly a very cruel man.

John: He was. I try to laugh about it now because it was all so traumatic.

Ross: Are you aware of any losses in your father's life or your mother's life, perhaps before you were born, that may have shaped who they became?

John: Not that I'm aware of.

Ross: Were either of your parents anxious at all? We know your father was cruel and angry. Your mother, perhaps?

John: My mum? I think she was, in a family way. I think she was brought up in a strict English family. I think my grandmother liked to tell my mum what to do, and that obviously annoyed my mum. My grandmother was a great lady, don't get me wrong. My granddad was in the Navy, so he had a very powerful, booming voice, and he expected things to be done when he said so. He wasn't a nasty man, but he was just a strict bloke because in the Navy, when you tell a guy to do something, he's got to do it without question. That's the sort of guy he was. That was my mum's upbringing.

You can always see even now that she longs for acceptance from the family and stuff like that, although my gran is dead now. I think that did have an impact on mum — that tough upbringing.

Ross: Yes, I'm sure. Is there any other history of mental health issues in the family that you're aware of?

John: I'm just trying to think. I think there might have been some addictions, to be honest. Gambling and stuff like that. That's one thing I do know about.

Ross: Was that on your mother's or father's side?

John: That would be on my mum's side. And I think my gran's mother was anxious as well. That's about it I think.

Ross: Can I turn to you now, John. What are your earliest memories of being fearful, worried, or afraid? Was it the walks up the mountains, the hikes, the dam, the waterfall? Were they your earliest memories of being afraid?

John: They would be the earliest ones, but I also have early memories of panic attacks. I can understand them because I thought I was going to die, basically. I couldn't understand. I was trying to run away, and they wouldn't stop. There's acceleration. That abated when we moved eventually to the UK. I had it once or twice because of the bullying in school, and then it reduced and went for a few years until I was about 25.

Ross: Those early, sudden, panics where you thought you were going to die, how old were you then?

John: The first one would have been, again, about eight, something like that.

Ross: That's very early, John.

John: Very early. Then a second set with the bullying when I went to the UK, maybe 12, 13, around that age.

Ross: Can I ask about the development of the fear of heights. When you experienced fears as you were walking up to the waterfall, and near the dam, those fears of toppling over — you would have already been somewhat afraid of dad at that point?

John: Oh yes. I did stick up for my mom. I had to because that's all you could do, and do what you can. Yeah, definitely afraid of him by then because he was nasty. He was violent. You would get a beating, and he could just lose it. You can't reason with that, I guess.

Ross: It was a terrible time in your life, John. Something that no-one should have to experience. Tell me, those early fears — the fears of heights — they've stayed with you in one way or another, haven't they?

John: That's the one that's really stuck in me. The height one. I hate heights. I do things to face it now, but I don't like it. I just do not like it.

Ross: Standing near barriers, standing near…

John: Cliff edges.

Ross: Bridges, cliff edges, looking over the edge is still difficult?

John: I don't like it. It's easier now because I'm doing exposure, so I would definitely say it's making me stronger, but I wouldn't say I like it because of those early memories of really skinny roads. He didn't fear heights. He's the sort of guy that will walk to the edge, and climb down, and not worry about it. He had friends that used to look after the cable cars, and the cable car used to stop and break down, and then they would just climb up with their arms. It's 300, 400 foot swinging, and they're getting up there with no ropes, and fiddling around, and getting back down again.

Ross: Wow. Amazing!

John: Watching that was also probably a contributor because I used to look at them and think, 'How the hell can they do that?' No ropes, nothing. Just climb up. It wouldn't be allowed now, but back in the day, that's what they did.

Ross: Those fears have remained, although as you say with your exposure work, they have lessened.

John: Yep.

Ross: Over the years, how have your anxieties changed? What other things have you feared? What got added to the list over time?

John: There's certainly a little bit, I suppose, of doom, of having got a disease, I guess? That can sometimes pop up. Have I got a deadly disease? That can sometimes come in. I try and ignore it. Not ignore, but try and just go with it, and build a flow. What's that lump? What is this? Those sorts of things. That's another thing that's developed, I think.

Ross: Yes. Illness fears.

John: Illness fears, and then, of course, the OCD that I was diagnosed with.

Ross: Yes. Tell me about your obsessive fears.

John: The violent force.

Ross: Yes.

John: Got some sexual ones, as well.

Ross: Yes.

John: Anything that's not allowed. Anything that's dangerous or inappropriate will come in. I remember the first time I had those thoughts, I think I was about 25. I was walking with my wife, and it was saying I was going to attack her. I couldn't understand why. Why am I thinking this? This is ridiculous. You're not allowed to. I was trying to push it out of my head. This was before I knew what it was. I suppose it could have begun in England — I used to like all my CDs in order back then.

That was something that I had back then, and I remember there was once in England, a cop's daughter got murdered, and then my mind started thinking about that. I had thoughts because I used to go to my friend's house, his dad was a cop, and I feared that I was going to smash the video recorder in front of him or break his antique furniture, vases and stuff like that.

Ross: That's interesting.

John: That was the very first time I would say I had the aggressive thoughts.

Ross: You were how old roughly then?

John: That would be about 15, probably.

Ross: At 15, you had your first aggressive, intrusive thoughts that just pop into consciousness.

John: They just came in. They didn't stay that long at the time. They evolved later on, but I did think, 'What's this? Why isn't it going away?' Paul's dad, this is my friend's father, you know he would be very upset if something happened, and it's going, 'You're going to knock that vase over, or you're going to damage his video recorder or something.' Then you try and brush it out, and it becomes more and more, not out of control, but panicky because you think you're going to do it.

Ross: Then later, the fears, these aggressive fears became about hurting people that you'd pass in the street.

John: I'd say my gran's doorstop, that was one of the worst ones. It was a metal doorstop, and my mind was saying you're going to whack her over the head with that. That was really, really scary. You didn't know who you should approach, whether they're going to lock you up because you're going, 'That's not me. I don't want to think that.' You couldn't get it out of your head, and you couldn't get that warning sign, I guess, that panicky feeling out of you to try and switch it off.

Ross: You would try in those early days to block it.

John: Try and push it out of my head.

Ross: Which probably increased the fears and the aggressive thoughts.

John: Absolutely, yeah, but I didn't know that back then. There was nobody there to help and say, 'What you have to do is face it.' You're just going, 'This is not normal.' That's the first thing. 'You shouldn't think this'. That was the first thing that comes in. It was just trying to look for issues, people you care about, stuff just to make it worse.

Ross: Have they been the worst examples of the problem when it's been your partner or someone else you care about?

John: I think they've all been pretty bad, to be honest with you, even when they're about the self, that you're going to do something to yourself or you're going to crash your car into a truck. There's some really funny ones. You should laugh really because they sound funny when you say them out loud. You could have them in a comedy, I guess.

Ross: These are ones to do with yourself, hurting yourself?

John: Yeah, that's right. Exactly.

Ross: Tell me about them.

John: You got the one where I was going to throw myself into a tree mincer, a tree grinder. I couldn't look at the grinding machine because I somehow was going to launch myself in there and throw my head in, get ground up. On another occasion, I feared I was going to jump into the lava pool or a volcano which was 1,000 degrees in heat. I think, 'That's nuts. It's weird to think that'. The plane one is something that I used to hate because I used to think I was going to open the plane door and literally jump out of the plane while it's flying. Yeah.

Ross: Can I ask which type of fear has been more common for you — the fears about hurting others or hurting yourself?

John: I would say both. That's what was so weird, and I couldn't understand. It was just going over every aspect of it, every single aspect you can think about, whether it's self-harm or harming someone else, or whatever. Anything that's inappropriate, basically.

Ross: Yes, I see. The chattering voice attacked you on anything and everything. Have there been happenings in your life, that we haven't heard about so far that you think made your fears more intense? It could be bullying or loss or accidents, illness. Is there anything that you think is relevant?

John: Bullying, I would say.

Ross: Bullying?

John: Definitely. There was a lot of bullying when I went to the UK. Being beaten up and stuff because you had a foreign accent and stuff like that. Also, I could say in some ways my granddad used to have a go at me quite a bit, because I wanted just to sit down and take it from them, I guess. He disagreed and was always picking on me. I think that was part of it.

Ross: How do you think these incidents of being bullied, for example, intensified your fear when the thoughts came? What's the relationship you see?

John: I think maybe I had the predisposition to it, obviously, and I think maybe that was a catalyst because it's too much stress. It's just an overbearing ... maybe it's a survival mechanism. I don't know.

Ross: Yeah. In your own view, the bullying was a contributor. It set the scene.

John: Just too much of it. My dad did it. It just didn't stop and calling you 'mental' and all this sort of stuff. I think all that, because it's not really what you call a calm upbringing, is it?

Ross: No, it's not. Do you think it made it harder, John, that when you had thoughts of hurting people, do you think it made it harder for you to dismiss them? Do you think there was a part of you thinking, 'Well, I am angry about the way I've been treated?'

John: I was angry, and I used to have dreams about revenge.

Ross: I see. Revenge on the people that had bullied you?

John: Yeah.

Ross: On your father, as well?

John: My dad. I remember because he used to say I was mental and stuff. I would go back and exact revenge. That is what I used to think about and dream about. I ended up going in the Army and doing martial arts and weights to become invincible. That's how I started. I used to like the Rambo movies and stuff like that because this guy is kicking these people's butts, and they're not going to harm him again, so there was a lot of that.

Ross: Yes. Do you think that contributed? Because here you were learning martial arts, learning self-defence, joined the Army, and then you start having these aggressive obsessions.

John: Yes, it did. My mind told me that I was an aggressive person. I think part of it was that I liked heavy metal music, too. I used to like watching horror flicks, and then I started questioning, is that normal? Is it normal to watch Friday the 13th with Jason going around lopping people's heads off?

Ross: I see.

John: I used to enjoy those movies, and my mind started to question whether it was normal. You have to remember that I'd been told I wasn't normal, so I started questioning it myself. 'Is this something people should be even thinking about?' I would ask. Obviously, I now realise it's nothing. It's just entertainment, but back then I was worried.

Ross: How did you first come to treatment?

John: It wasn't easy. I went to … what do you call them? One of those counsellors and I went to try and broach the subject, and she just simply told me, 'If you think it, it means you want to do it.' That was one of the worst things. I thought, 'What are you on?' I just walked out. I just said, 'This is not for me' and I walked out. I knew somewhere deep down that this couldn't be true.

Ross: It didn't scare you, what the counsellor said?

John: It did, but I questioned it. I did question it. I didn't just accept it. I didn't believe, deep down, that it could be right. I told myself that what she said had to be crap.

Ross: It can't be right.

John: It can't be right. Even though I'm fearing it, it can't be right. Then I went to an Indian doctor and said, 'Can you please give me a referral to a psychiatrist?' Because I just needed to get to the bottom of it. When I told him what it was thinking, he quickly wrote out a referral in panic. I didn't want to tell him because I was concerned that he would call the cops or something. It's very difficult to broach. You feel you can't talk to anyone, because they might decide you're dangerous, and the cops will listen to them and not me.

John: It's very difficult, but at least I said, 'I want to see a psychiatrist.' I saw one quickly, and he diagnosed me with OCD. He said he could treat me, but he wasn't talking about therapies that you could do. He was talking about taking medication.

I thought, 'There must be more,' but I thought I'd give it a go. It didn't do it for me. I just got a bad reaction to it. Just didn't like it — didn't feel awake, didn't feel myself, so I came off it. I went searching for therapies. I went to see some guy who wanted to hypnotise me. I didn't like that, so I said, 'No, you're not hypnotising me'. It was a bad time. It was really hard to find someone who could actually treat this. Then I started reading research on the internet. Everything recommended exposure therapy, but finding someone to do it properly — to guide me — wasn't easy. I went to a guy in the city, but that didn't work out. I went to another doctor who did a bit, but it wasn't intense enough. Eventually, I looked you up on the internet. That's when I decided it's time to stop mucking around.

Ross: Yes. It's been quite a tour of mental health services.

John: Because they don't understand it.

Ross: Yeah, you saw a lot of people.

John: They don't understand it. They just look at you strangely. I think there are some people out there that are actually very harmful towards people who have got a condition like me.

Ross: I understand how you feel, John. Tell me, what do you think has been the most important thing in treatment that has reduced your fears?

John: I'd say definitely exposure therapy. Other things are helpful - keeping busy, like going to the gym, that sort of thing, doing something physical, and just approaching it as it comes. Just deal with it as it happens.

Ross: With your exposure therapy, you've been very diligent — very hard working. What are some of the things you've done that you think have really reduced your anxiety?

John: The main thing was the knife exposure, which I did with a kitchen knife. I used to sit with it next to me, and I'd cuddle my wife with it in my hand. Hold it to the back of the neck, stuff like that, and just did that every day. Then I moved on to watching movies that involved knives while sitting with my wife and the knife. That's really done a lot of good.

Ross: Yes. You no longer fear the knife in the kitchen.

John: That hardly ever comes up these days. I've beaten those fears.

Ross: It's fantastic John. You did that work consistently for …

John: At least three years.

Ross: Amazing!

John: Non-stop. Yep. Some others are a bit harder because there are bridges and driving. You can't drive on a highway all the time. When I do go to Canberra, anywhere like that, then I do exposure. That's the only time I can do it because you can't be driving up to highway back and forth for a whole year just to make sure. Yeah.

Ross: I want to turn now to a very different topic. Death itself and thinking about death. What emotions arise in you at the thought of your own death?

John: I don't particularly like it, to be honest with you. I always look at ways of extending life - keeping fit and strong and stuff. I have also looked at things about extending life, just doing research, and recently there was something about a pill that might be doing it in a Sydney Morning Herald. It's not for sale yet, but they reckon it'll make people live to 150.

Ross: Those sorts of things interest you.

John: They do, yes. They do because I suppose for whatever reason, I don't like the idea of being nothing. That's just me. I have seen some death, to be honest. I saw my partner's mum die. She got pancreatic cancer, and that wasn't particularly nice. You got to see someone pass away, so it's not nice at all. That was harrowing. It was harrowing for Mary, as well.

Ross: How long ago was that?

John: That was 1997. She was only 62. Young, as well.

Ross: Do you think that intensified your fears?

John: I do think it did, yep. That definitely increased my fears for myself, and also for Mary. I don't want Mary to get sick like her mum got sick. Sometimes I think about that. And I try and think that maybe I'll be alive long enough till the next thing comes along that will extend it, and maybe reverse things. There's a lot of genetic stuff happening out there. You never know in the future. Like a car part, they might be able to replace or get cells to regenerate something or other. I don't know. That's what I think about. I'm curious about the future, as well, I guess. What's going to be in a thousand years' time? I'd like to see that.

Ross: What are your thoughts about what happens to you as you physically die, and once you're physically dead?

John: I don't really know.

Ross: What do you think happens when a person dies?

John: I was born a Catholic, and they had their own view. That's not what I believe in. I've got a belief where there might be another dimension. Maybe you float into that other dimension. That's been scientifically proven. Even Steve Hawking talks about it. Well, probably not proven, but probable, because Stephen Hawkings talks about it. Maybe we just shed this body and go to another parallel universe. That's how I look at it. I don't believe in a guy with a beard on a throne, but I believe that there might be another plane.

Ross: Is that idea comforting?

John: Yeah. It is comforting, but it's also, something to think about, it may even be possible. We don't know. We don't know for sure yet.

It might be the end, but it might not be. I just think that's what I tend to try to believe in. There might be another plane. Some people claim to have seen it. Even some of the people who were in the place where Mary's mum died talked about experiences where it makes them believe that there's another plane.

Ross: How often do you think about death, John?

John: Not overly often. I try not to because I want to live my life. I can get stuck in that. I might have a disease or something. Just stupid. That's a mind playing the same trick as it does with you jumping in front of a truck. 'I'm going to now talk about you and disease' it says. 'You might have this, or you should do that, you might get this' and so on. The asbestos one is the perfect example. I know I've been near the stuff, and I've even broken a shed up and stuff, and that starts my mind up saying, 'When I'm 70, will I get sick?'

Ross: I see. How often would you have thoughts like that?

John: That's irritating. Look, maybe twice a week, something like that. But I can get stuck in it.

Ross: What relationship do you see between your fears of death and your experience of everyday living? How important do you think it's been in your life?

John: A close relationship. I've survived so much, and death now seems terrible. It's the survival instinct gone into overdrive. Your brain has to do something to survive when so many bad things are happening around you. So I react to every danger around me and became the strongest person I could, so nobody will ever hurt me again.

Ross: Like your fears of death have sprung from a desperate desire to survive?

John: Yes, that's how I'd put it. Not to become nothing, because you survived this much. You just want to keep on surviving.

Ross: I see. Do you see your earlier avoidance of the tree mincer or high bridges or standing near railings as simple attempts to cheat death — just doing anything you could to keep yourself safe?

John: Definitely, because the fear was I would lose control and do it. If I didn't go there, then I don't die.

Ross: Yes, I see. Within therapy or outside of it, what have you found most helpful in dealing with the dread of death? What is most helpful in defeating your fear of death?

John: I guess the plane thing that I was talking about before. I think if I allow myself to believe that there might be another plane, another universe so that I don't just decay and be nothing. That's probably the most helpful belief I have.

Ross: This form of spiritual belief is the thing that's given you most comfort.

John: I guess the way I look at it is, I'm trying to put it together. What sci- entifically could be possible? They say there could be other planes. If there's another plane — I know it sounds very strange — but that's what they talk about, that it could be a possibility through mathematics. If that's possible, maybe we're just in one plane. Maybe that's how we transcend into the next one because you might not physically be able to go there, so you might go another way. I also think to myself, I try to think to myself, 'Surely, I'm not just a piece of meat in here.'

I think when I look at Mary, there's more there than just a liver or whatever, or a piece of meat. That's how I try to think. There's something more there. We can't explain it. We're not meant to explain it. People can try and explain it till the cows come home. We can't explain the big bang. How did that happen?

Ross: I see.

John: I guess there are things we're not meant to know, and you can only try and look at what you see.

Ross: Finally, John, I want to ask you about what makes your life mean- ingful. What, if anything, do you think gives you meaning and purpose?

John: I keep myself quite busy doing different things. Helping people, I enjoy my car; I enjoy my sports. I don't get bored. I've got things I actually enjoy doing. I like my electronics. I like going to electronics shops, and I like going on holidays. I like doing physical activity. I class myself as someone who doesn't get bored, and that's one thing that's good. Even though I've got this condition, I don't actually get bored. I don't go, 'Oh, it's boring.' It's all doom, if you will, for some people.

Ross: So, what gives you a meaningful life is being busy and actively engaging in life, engaging in pleasurable activities.

John: Living it, trying not to waste it. That's why I want to tackle this, because I don't want to be someone stuck in a room that's paralyzed and won't drive here, and won't swim there, because then you're not living, are you?

Ross: No, you're not. That I think is a very, very nice place to finish the interview. Thank you very much for your time.

John: No problem.

Chapter 5

Dinosaurs are hiding

D eath anxiety has no favourites. It cripples the rich and the poor, the wise and the foolish, the old and the young.

Rose was a strikingly bright 13-year old girl with an analytical mind. She was sharp and incisive, and always economical with her words. Not one to simply enjoy the sound of her own voice, she only spoke when she really had something to say. This, of course, made her all the more worth listening to. She was the sort of girl that everyone wants on their group project team at school. With Rose on the job you could rest easy — every part of the assignment was going to get covered. Unsurprisingly, her grades had been consistently excellent at the two private schools that she had attended in Sydney.

Rose was tall and slender, with an athletic physique from years of dancing. She moved lightly, with balletic ease, and was always impeccably groomed. In the three years I'd known her, I couldn't recall a single hair out of place. Like Mary Poppins, she was, at least on the surface, practically perfect in every way. But below this flawless exterior, she was a deeply troubled girl.

Rose had been crippled by the anticipation of danger since her pre-school years. Her fears were imaginative and outrageous, often impossible rather than improbable, but always wonderfully creative. For a time, she believed there were rotting corpses in her mattress supporting her body as she slept. She lived in terror of entering an alternate universe, far from her family's protection, by opening the wrong door or cupboard at home. She feared random gunshots that could strike her down through the glass-frosted front door of her home, and the red glow of car tail-lights augured monsters on the streets. She believed her fears with a rare intensity, despite how strange and unlikely they seemed to her family, therapists and any fair-minded listener.

Perhaps the oddest of all her early fears involved dinosaurs. At five years of age she'd seen a television documentary about these reptiles that included images of various species standing next to humans to allow easy comparison of height and weight. One dinosaur had particularly grabbed her attention. Though smaller than a person, its shape, size and appearance would haunt her for the next five years. 'I thought they could be anywhere, Ross,' she told me, 'but mostly I feared the older section of our house — this is where they'd hide'. Her need for certainty, a common characteristic of the anxious mindset, was her undoing with this, and many other fears. How can one prove, with absolute certainty, that nothing is lurking in the dark? As you leave one area perhaps the creature had moved, always managing to avoid your gaze? Like the wonderful weeping angels from *Dr Who*, perhaps their movement was too fast for you to catch a glimpse of?

Why such a bright, articulate person can believe so strongly in the out-rageous imaginings of her mind remains a mystery in modern psychology. Further, as it was for Rose, it's typically a mystery to the sufferer herself. 'I don't know why I believe the chatter of the inner voice, ' she told me. 'I just always have.' Rose treated the proclamations of her mind with the respect that a cult member gives their leader. Consciousness was her guru — it could say no wrong. If it told her there were dinosaurs in the house, she would be watchful. If it told her that the red glow of car break-lights was really the eye of a terrible monster she would duck and hide. If it suggested that steel blades could impale a moving body in her bed, she would lie perfectly still until she slept.

Each fear would come and go, soon to be replaced by another, and despite none of the long list of terrors ever coming true, Rose remained a devotee of the chattering voice of her mind. Perhaps she'd just been lucky so far, she wondered, as she considered the fact that all previous proclamations had ended up deceits. 'Your mind is playing with you, Rose,' I told her. 'You treat consciousness as a friendly ally, but it's a wolf in sheep's clothing — an enemy in disguise. Why aren't you angry with a voice that's lied to you about monsters and dinosaurs and corpses in the bed?'

In therapy, I have used the image of a stalking wolf under the cover of a sheep skin for many years. I regard it as a most effective representation of the inner voice of the human mind. 'You listen to your mind as if it's helping you by keeping you alert, Rose. But all this time it's been a predator, stalking you and looking for weaknesses to attack. All these years its been the cause of your agitation. There's never been anything to really fear — it's all been lies,' I told her.

Why had Rose come to see the world as such a threatening place? In my formulation of her case, the autism of her brother played an important role. I've seen this pattern many times, an older brother on the spectrum who is somewhat unpredictable, feeding the anxious temperament of the younger child. What will he do next? The younger sister grows alongside watchfully, never quite sure how the brother might act. 'Will he throw something at me? Will he poke me? Will he run out of the house?' Unpredictability spells danger in so many contexts for so many animals, and it does so for humans as well. Many studies have shown that mammals want controllable, predictable events in their lives. Humans, perhaps more than any other species, try to control the outcomes around them. It is well-established that when we're placed in situations beyond our control, where unpredictability reigns supreme, anxiety quickly rises. In my view, Rose's fears had risen in this context, in a world that she couldn't control, a world in which her brother might do anything at any moment.

Equally uncontrollable were the movements of her parents, both working on planes, both in the sky day after day. 'Will something happen today? Will they return? Will they get caught up in transit? Will weather delay their flights?' Worst of all, of course, always lurking in the dark recesses of Rose's mind was the ultimate fear, 'Will the plane go down? Will they actually be outside when I walk out from school today, or will this be the day that the bad news comes?' These are the questions that the wolf would pose to Rose as she tried to get through her school-day.

My work with Rose began by getting her to list all of her previous fears. I wanted her to see just how many lies the chattering voice had got away with in the past. 'After all this pain and all these deceits, how can you befriend consciousness, Rose? Get angry with it! You'd be angry with another person if they'd told you all this rubbish and crippled you with fear'. The goal of this work was to slowly change her relationship with consciousness — for Rose to become a sceptic rather than a disciple.

At the time I met Rose, the focus of her fears was contamination, particularly from public transport. Touching most things outside of the house was difficult. For example, she couldn't play volleyball at school. 'The ball is touched by other people, Ross, and some of those girls will have been on buses and trains today. They'll pass the germs from the bus to the ball to me' she told me. The social implications of having to sit out of sport and similar activities at school are significant. Rose was isolated, lonely at times, and feeling like progress was unlikely. In fact, even attending school had become exceptionally difficult, and she had had several long periods of school refusal. Further, her fears were proving intractable. When I met her, she had already had extensive psychiatric and psychological treatment and was on significant doses of various psychotropic medications with little effect.

Initially, despite good therapeutic rapport, progress was very slow. In fact, for a time confronting her fears was simply too difficult for Rose. Her mood was low, and her cleaning behaviours were spiralling out of control. Soap and antibacterial wipes were no longer sufficient. She increasingly sought stronger household cleaners for her skin. Over the opening months of treatment she needed two hospital admissions as her level of agitation was too high for her to cope with. Her parents and everyone involved in her care were understandably deeply worried.

Working with young people often involves patience and long periods of waiting. Anxious, obsessional adolescents have to achieve a very high level of 'readiness-for-change' to be able to move forward with their lives. When that moment comes, they need to know that the therapist will still be with them — still ready to guide them out of the woods in which they've been so hopelessly lost. I was always confident that Rose's time would come and, after a year of cajoling, coaxing and encouraging, she seemed to decide that it was finally time for recovery. Almost overnight Rose began to truly confront her anxiety for the first time in my work with her. One by one, Rose faced her fears, slowly dropping each of the safety behaviours that she'd developed to defend against imagined threats. And with the safety behaviours dropped, and each fear proved untrue, her confidence grew. She was finally breaking the guru's hold on her. It was as if she was leaving the cult.

At the time of this interview, Rose was still only 16. I had seen her 58 times over two and a half years. She is happier than I have ever known her, having shed all but a few of her contamination concerns. She no longer misses classes, and engages in all activities at school. She travels on public transport, admittedly only when needed, and has stopped carrying anti-bacterial handwash wherever she goes. No longer isolated, Rose is building stronger relationships with her peers.

It would be untrue to say that Rose has completely recovered. Her treatment is ongoing. But this young woman is determined to get there.

Our interview with Rose

Ross: Can I begin by asking you about your family, Rose — life at home in the early years of growing up.

Rose: I live with both my parents and I have an older brother. It was a pretty standard upbringing, or at least from what I can tell in the early years. There were some issues with my brother, who was diagnosed with autism, so he had issues at school sometimes. I didn't know what those issues really were or why they happened, but I was always aware of that. I feel like that impacted me. I always kind of wanted to be different in a way, which is sort of weird. You don't really want to wish mental health upon yourself, but I always wanted to be different.

Ross: Right. And you attribute that to your brother being identified as different?

Rose: Yeah, and it might have also have been that he got attention in the sense of, 'Oh, we're going to an appointment for Peter.'

Ross: I see.

Rose: 'Oh, we're doing this with Peter,' and I would feel sort of left out. As a little kid you don't really understand what's going on and that it's not really a good thing obviously.

Ross: Yes, that's very interesting. Can you tell me about your relationship with your mother in the early years of your life?

Rose: I've always had a really good relationship with my mum. I haven't really had any issues, and I don't think there were any big things that really happened in terms of a relationship or what might have changed that.

Ross: And the relationship is still very positive. I mean, the two of you are very close, really. You get on well and there's not a lot of tension.

Rose: That's right.

Ross: Do you think there's less tension than for most girls your age? In terms of your girlfriends at school, do you think they seem to have more problems with their mums or not?

Rose: I guess it varies depending on the person. For the most part, I think my relationship with my mum is better than most people's. I think that maybe partly because of the time she spends away from home with her job. She's not always there and so it's never too suffocating I guess.

Ross: I understand. Can you tell me about your relationship with your dad?

Rose: It's also been good except there have been times when he gets mad at my brother. When I was younger Peter might be doing autistic things and dad would get mad. I didn't really understand what was happening, but it made me sad because I didn't want our family to fight.

Ross: I see. With your brother being on the autistic spectrum, his behaviours could be unpredictable. Do you think any unpredictability about your brother contributed to you becoming anxious? To developing anxiety?

Rose: I think it was definitely a part of it. If he didn't have autism, I still probably would've been anxious but in a different way. I guess it was always the unknown and that still is sort of something that gets to me today — not knowing what's going to happen, and with Peter he was very unpredictable at times. He would often do things that he knew made me stressed or anxious just because he wanted a rise out of me, or he just did something dumb because he thought it was funny. For example, he might get into my bed and then into his own because he thought it was funny, but it would really stress me out.

Ross: I see.

Rose: Sometimes he wanted to make me mad and other times I think he just thought it was fun and games. I never really knew what he'd do next.

Ross: Did you have any losses in your early life that you think had an impact on you in any way?

Rose: I haven't really had any really major losses. When I was one year old, my grandpa died, so obviously it wasn't fresh but I guess I've always sort of grown-up wondering what was he like and just not knowing what he was like makes me sad because I never got to know him. But I didn't really experience the loss because I never met him in the first place. We did have a budgie for 12 years and when she died, that was hard. Obviously, that was my first sort of close death, but it wasn't of someone or something, I guess, that I knew well. I mean, there had probably been family members overseas. Like second cousins or things like that, but never anyone I really knew. So I guess that was probably the first loss that was close to home.

Ross: And then recently you had another grandparent die, and that did have an impact. I remember you saying that you felt your washing had gone up after that.

Rose: Yes, I think my washing went up because I was distracted and stopped trying to keep my washing down. I think that happens a lot, that when I'm stressed, or my mind is preoccupied with something else, I will find myself washing more because I'm not focusing on improving.

Ross: Okay. In terms of losses, perhaps before you were born, do you know of losses or traumas in your parents' lives that may have had an impact on them?

Rose: Well, probably the main one would just be my grandfather's death. So, when I was one. I don't really remember her grieving, but every once in a while we'll talk about him and it'll make mum sad, but I don't think it's anything unhealthy. He wasn't super old or super young. I think he was in his 70s, so it wasn't an early death. Obviously he could've lived longer, but, I mean, they knew it was coming as well. It wasn't a shock which I think can add to stress and feelings of loss. But besides that, I don't think there have been any major things that were necessarily bad.

My dad did move to Australia when he was 16 and I think that was hard on him leaving everything he had known to a new country, a new language and things like that, but he never really talks about that so I'm not too sure.

Ross: Would you say that either of your parents are anxious people?

Rose: I think they both are to an extent. My dad probably more than my mum. I guess they get anxious about the regular sort of things, but my dad also gets anxious about things that aren't really … not that they're invalid things to be anxious about, but they're not standard worries, and he's very hardworking, so I think that's a way that he deals with his anxiety, is by just working all the time. He doesn't know how to relax. If he's stressed about something, he'll just keep working and, for example, when his father died, my grandfather recently, he was doing stuff constantly. He was never resting. I think that's because he wanted to occupy himself and stay away from his thoughts.

Ross: What sort of things has he worried about over the years?

Rose: Well, he worries about getting things done and he gets upset quite quickly when something changes or plans change. So if I call him up and say, 'Oh, can you pick me up an hour earlier,' that'll make him really anxious because he hasn't planned his day to be like that.

Ross: I see. Rose, are there any other family members with any mental health issues. You've mentioned your brother being on the spectrum and your own anxiety-related conditions, but is there anyone else that you know of with a history of mental health disorders?

Rose: I have a cousin with depression and OCD, and another one with OCD and I'm not sure about any other diagnosed illnesses, but it is quite apparent in some of them that they do have anxiety or depression. I have a second cousin who we are quite sure has autism. My mum says that he acts in a lot of the same ways that Peter did, or my brother, when he was younger. Nothing really has been that visible to us because we're the only ones besides my grandma living in Australia, so we don't see them very much and it's all through talking to people that we've sort of found out about what it's like. We haven't really seen it first-hand.

Ross: The two first cousins with OCD, are they on the same side of the family?

Rose: Yes, yes. Mother's side and that's the same as the second cousin who I think has autism. On my dad's side, my aunt, she has a very strong fear of flying and of some other things, and my grandma's also a very anxious person. I guess you could say a worrywart. She always worries about things that she doesn't have to worry about. One time I accidentally took the wrong train and I had to wait for another one to come in the other direction. She called my phone maybe 10 times. When I walked in the door at the end of it, she was like, 'Oh, where were you? I was calling you. I was so worried.' Even though I called her and said I was going to be late, she still kept calling to see where I was and what was happening.

Ross: So you have many anxious relatives. If I can turn now to you, to your own anxiety, what are your earliest memories of being fearful, worried or afraid?

Rose: I guess I was worried about some general things like the dark and being away from parents, but there were also, I guess, social worries. I wasn't super aware of it but I was always a bit … not on edge, but wary in social situations and how I presented myself. I was quite shy when I was younger. I didn't like talking to people very much unless I was really close with them, and then I had a bunch of irrational fears and imaginations that sort of came from TV shows and movies and stories I'd heard from other people.

Ross: Tell me about some of those.

Rose: Probably the weirdest one … well, they're all weird … but I watched a documentary when I was younger about what dinosaurs would look like if they were still alive today and I can still remember what it looked like. It was just a bit smaller than a human. It was sort of brown and looked almost sticky, had a weird head and skinny, bony arms. After I watched that, I was convinced that they lived in my house and that they were hiding and that if I went into a room by myself, they would come and get me if I didn't protect myself, so I would walk really loudly, or I would just hurry really quickly through rooms. Especially since the house we live in is renovated and the front section is still older, that's where I felt that they lived — in the older section of the house.

Ross: That lasted quite some time. From my notes, you had that fear for about five years between the ages of 5 and 10.

Rose: That's true. It started as an intense fear. I think as I got older, closer to 10, I knew it wasn't quite so rational. But I would still sort of play along with the fear and run quickly through that part of the house and would turn the lights on until I had to leave. I would only turn them off at the last second because when it got dark, they would come out.

Ross: I see. What other fears in that period of childhood did you have?

Rose: I worried a lot about dead people. I don't really know where this came from because I hadn't been to any funerals for anyone that I had a close relationship with. Still, at one point I was convinced that there were bodies used as filler in my mattress, which was quite stressful, being as your bed is supposed to be where you relax and sleep, so trying to fall asleep thinking that there were dead people right underneath me was quite a stressful thing. Also, I didn't like going past funeral homes and things like that. I also had lots of issues with driving past and seeing, say, a butchery getting a delivery and you could see the pigs hanging up in the truck. I hated that, and it would make me really scared.

Ross: Right. With the bodies in the mattress, you believed that these corpses were just slowly dissolving in there?

Rose: Well, I was too young to really think about it.

Ross: How old were you, do you think?

Rose: Maybe seven. Six or seven. So I was too young to think about the bodies decomposing and things like that, so obviously now if I had that fear, it'd be the scientific side of my brain saying I would smell them obviously. The mattress would get mushier and things like that, but because I didn't really know about what happened to bodies, I would just imagine they were solid in there and dead. And I'm lying on them.

Ross: Which would have been terrifying — like really terrifying. I would have imagined that to be very distressing. I also remember you mentioning that at one point you feared spikes would impale you in the bed, Indiana Jones style.

Rose: Yeah. We watched an Indiana Jones movie. I think *Raiders of the Lost Ark* was the one it was from. In the movie he was going through into the tunnels and there were these spikes that pop out if you walk into the light, and his partner got impaled and it showed an image of him with the spikes through his body, and that night I was laying on my side and making myself as narrow as possible so that I had a lower chance of getting impaled by spikes that might come out of my bed.

Ross: That was short-lived, that fear?

Rose: Yeah. Just a few nights. I think we were probably too young to be watching that movie and I think my parents forgot that it was graphic in that sense.

Ross: You had another film-related fear after seeing the movie *Coraline*. Can you tell me about your fear relating to that?

Rose: Yeah, that movie horrified me. I haven't watched it since then. I'm kind of curious to see what it would be like watching it now from a different perspective, but it was very creepy. In the movie, she opens up a small trap door that leads to an alternate universe. I became scared of finding the portal to the alternate dimension, so I would be cautious of opening small doors and things like that.

Ross: All of these examples show that you were very suggestible. You could take an idea from a film and believe that that could now occur to you.

Rose: Yeah. There's another one, in fact, that I'm remembering now. We watched this movie. I think it was just called *Nine* or *I Am Number Nine*. It was about a post-apocalyptic world where the scientist had split his soul up into nine parts and put each of those parts into a doll, and they were fighting robots that had taken over the planet who were, in fact, made by the same scientist who was trying to save the world in the end. This robot had a massive eye that was bright red, and so having a frosted glass front door I would get scared in the night if the glow of a car's tail light came through the glass. I would always run through the hallway quickly and up the stairs.

I obviously didn't have much knowledge of cars, and even if my family told me it was a car that didn't help. Because knowing a car was out there also told me there were people around. I was old enough to know that cars didn't have any lights on when they were turned off. So whenever I saw a red light shining outside, it was like, 'Oh, there's someone there. What are they doing?'

Ross: I see, I see. The door, the glass door you mentioned — I know it caused other problems over time because you had thoughts that a bullet could come through that door.

Rose: That's right, and I worried that people could see where I was going and when I was heading to the stairs. That was another reason I raced past that door.

Ross: So you had a very broad range of fears across the first decade of life, between the ages of five and 10. A very large number of fears, with the dinosaur fear being the most stable.

Rose: Yeah, I think that was my longest fear.

Ross: Those fears appeared at various points and left you over time. But they'd be replaced by other fears. Now you're in the second decade of your life — how has it all developed?

Rose: Well, my earliest rational fear was of planes. It's because both my parents work on planes and were constantly away on flights to different places. I would always worry about something happening. This was before I had a mobile phone, so I had no means to communicate with them. So at the end of the school day when I had known my parents had been away in the morning, I would worry, what if their plane crashed and they won't come and pick me up? That was a big fear for me. I didn't have any means to prove it untrue so I would just believe it until the car showed up and then I'd be like, 'Oh, it didn't happen today.'

Ross: So you feared their death regularly.

Rose: Yes, absolutely.

Ross: And they were traveling all the time. Many times a week, you might have had the thought, 'They could be dead and I don't know yet — I'm going to find out when they're not here.' Again, that would have been very difficult.

Rose: Yes, it was — it still is.

Ross: Just experiencing relief every time that they're there.

Rose: Yeah. I think a big part of that stemmed from a time — I can't remember what year it was — but both of my parents were overseas or on the other side of the country and a volcano erupted somewhere in Indonesia or somewhere else, and there was so much ash that no planes were flying, so they couldn't come back. I was staying with a friend. It had all been arranged. It wasn't super last minute. They had thought that it might be a possibility so they had prepared in advance, except I didn't know when they would come back and obviously not knowing what volcanic ash in the air meant in terms of flying, I worried. What if they're flying back and the wind carried it and they can't see and the plane crashes? Especially seeing all those things in the news of the people that had died from the volcano and the repercussions that it had, it just intensified my fears I think.

Ross: So that was the first of the fears that you see as being reasonable. What about most recently? What are the things you currently are anxious about?

Rose: I think my biggest fear now would probably be the ocean. I really don't like the ocean. I just don't like the fact that I don't know what's there, and that something could be lurking underneath, but I don't know what it is. I'm not necessarily afraid of sharks per se, but I just don't like the fact that it's a vast unknown and that it's so deep and you can't see it. So, if someone said, 'Oh, we're taking a boat out into Sydney Harbour and we're going to go swimming,' I would not want to do that by any means.

Ross: In some ways, it's a little similar to your dinosaur fear. It's a fear there's something there that you're unaware of and you don't know what will happen.

Rose: Yeah, and the majority of the ocean is unexplored, so my fear hasn't really been disproven. I hate not knowing.

Ross: You also, of course, have been really troubled by contamination-related fears. Tell me about those. They have been the dominant daily struggle for you in the most recent period of your life. When did that begin?

Rose: I think that began around seventh grade, so that would be about three years ago. It started off with small things like using hand sanitizer more frequently. Ever since I was little, my parents had always said, 'Use hand sanitizer after touching public transport rails. You don't know who's touched them.' It was never something that was unhealthy at the beginning, and I would just use the hand sanitizer after touching it, but eventually it started to become more obsessive, and after taking public transport, I would need to clean myself more and more vigorously. If I had touched a seat or things like that, the window, I would wash that area specifically because I was afraid of the germs that might be there.

Ross: It's interesting the way you describe it, Rose. Your parents had raised the idea of never knowing who had touched things. That has become so entrenched in your thinking, hasn't it? Sitting in a chair here in this room is easier than sitting on a train or bus seat because you tell me fewer people have touched my office chairs. You've managed to cut back on things like hand sanitizer. How have you done that?

Rose: I think the main thing that's gotten me through it is me realising that there was no way these fears were going away unless I just stop listening to them. So I guess at one point I just realised that I had to change my mindset, and I couldn't be thinking, 'Oh, the medication will eventually make it go away,' and I knew I didn't want to keep living my life washing my hands over 100 times because I felt dirty, like I had germs on my hands. I knew that wasn't a way to live my life. So I guess over a few days I just decided I couldn't keep doing that.

With contamination, I've always had rules. Like, 'Oh, if you touch this, five washes — touch that, 10 washes,' and so on. So say someone took the train and they held a rail and then they touched the tissue box and then someone else touched the tissue box and then they gave me a high five, I would think, 'How many times have the germs transferred,' and then I'll wash according to that. So I guess I just took all of my rules and reduced them and I would just keep reducing them, so in the beginning I would take washing many, many times, like into the hundreds or so on, down to 10, and that was my solid number, that after 10 washes, you are completely clean no matter what you've touched.

Ross: Treatment, psychological treatment for these conditions involves changing the way you're thinking about things and also the determination to change the behaviours and push through the anxiety. You said before, 'I didn't want to keep living like this. I knew I had to change my thinking about things.' Did you mean that changing your thinking, in your view, was more important? Which is more important in your view? Realising that your thoughts aren't to be trusted, or attacking the behaviours and saying, 'I just have to cut this habit and put up with the pain'? What do you think has led to the most change in you?

Rose: Well, it's hard because I never really believed that washing my hands 200 times was rational, except it's what I felt like I needed to do, and if I didn't do it, I would feel horrible. It was mainly the way it made me feel. So, I guess when it came to changing my behaviours, I already had the mindset that it's all a lie, but I still have to keep doing it because that's what's 'right' or makes me feel okay.

Ross: So changing the behaviours was the really critical thing — committing to the idea that 'I refuse to keep living this way.'

Rose: Yeah, I think that was the bigger thing.

Ross: The ritual prevention has been important. Have other things in your life, other than treatment activities, lightened your condition or improved your condition or fears? New friendships, improved mood? Are there other things that you think have helped you reduce fear?

Rose: I think the main thing was me wanting to find purpose. So, I knew I wouldn't get anywhere in life if I lived in my house without going outside ever. Just washing my hands all the time would mean that I wouldn't ever contribute to society and my life would be a waste. I think that's still a bit of a fear, because that's something that I try to live my life by — purpose. I need to have purpose in my life.

Ross: And realising that your fears would stop you achieving a purposeful life...

Rose: Yeah, it motivated me.

Ross: What about the opposite? Have there been any happenings or events in your life that led to a worsening in your condition? You've mentioned one event already. You told me that the recent loss of your grandfather led to a period of more washing. Has there been anything else that you think happened across life that led to a deterioration in your condition? That could be bullying, illness, accidents. Anything else you can think of?

Rose: I think over recent years the stress I put myself under at school has hurt me. I felt an intense need to do well in school and achieve everything, I guess, to the best of my ability. I think that sort of worsened my mental health because I was so focused on my grades that I wasn't focused on myself and how I was mentally.

Ross: That's very interesting, Rose. So your desire to achieve and lead a purposeful life was a positive and a negative.

I want to turn to our last topic, which is death itself. I mean, in various ways we've talked about death along the way, but I want to specifically get some thoughts from you about death. What emotions arise in you at the thought of your own death? What do you feel about that?

Rose: I think the main thing I think about dying is that I must die after I've made a contribution to the world. I don't really fear dying, but I have to make my contribution first. I think I would actually be more afraid if I was immortal because I would hate to see the end of the world. That would be awful, I guess. If your life was unlimited, it would be harder to find meaning in doing things because it would seem pointless and superficial because all life would just continue and continue.

Ross: So you're calm about death on the assumption that you've led a meaningful life and you've contributed something. That's very interesting. Do you think the reason why your youth has been dominated by fears, then, could be that those contributions are yet to come and that if something happened now, it seems more tragic to you?

Rose: Yes, I think so, but it's very complicated. At times I've thought 'I'm never going to do something meaningful with my life. What's the point of even trying?' So that was my mindset at one point, but I managed to get over that. I think if I had a date that I was told I would die on, things would be different in terms of how I acted. If it was closer, I'd work a lot harder and things like that, but I think I'm trying to — I know it sounds like a cliché — but live life in the moment.

Ross: What do you think will happen to you as you physically die and once you're physically dead? What are your current thoughts about what death is? What happens to us?

Rose: Well, even though I am technically Catholic, I don't really believe in life after death. I don't really believe in souls or the idea that when you die, a part of you goes somewhere else or into a different body or things like that. I think death is just the end. It's just empty and nothing.

Ross: So a biological, scientific view of it?

Rose: Yes.

Ross: How often do you think about death? I mean, you used to think about it a lot. Well, particularly the death of your parents in planes. Will they pick me up today?

Rose: I don't think I think about death that much in terms of death specifically, but I do think about other things that are sort of surrounding the idea of death. So going to a religious school, obviously, we are told about Jesus and him dying. The resurrection, heaven, things like that. While it isn't specifically about death, it's things relating to death. That'll happen at least once a week, and also having friends that are quite political or quite invested in politics and the way our world is … sometimes we'll talk about current issues like the newest American mass shooting or things like that. So, at times like that, I'll think about death, and that something could just happen instantly and it could all be over and you wouldn't even know what had happened.

Ross: So, is it fair to say, Rose, that the younger you, say the girl between five and 10, thought about death a lot more often? You thought about bodies in the mattress and you thought about the dinosaurs and whether your mum and dad would live through the day. There were lots of specific death thoughts then, far more than now by the sound of it.

Rose: Yeah, I think so too. Yeah, a lot more.

Ross: What relationship do you see between your thoughts and attitudes to death and everyday living? You've said that death motivates you to excel. That's one relationship. Could you expand on that or on any other relationship you see between thoughts about death and attitudes to death and what happens to you every day in life and how you experience life?

Rose: I think the main thing with that is me thinking about other people and not necessarily helping them but allowing them to live a meaningful life and I occasionally think about people living in poverty who, if they were given the same life as me, could do amazing things, and they will just die being unknown and unnoticed, living a life where they don't really make a big change in the world. I guess I think about that more than I think about my own death.

Ross: I see. In terms of fear of death, what do you think has most helped you? What do you think is the thing that's been most responsible for fears of death, sudden death, just drifting away?

Rose: I think the main thing would probably be just education. So, learning about things in the world and how the world works has helped me to see how those fears are irrational and obviously couldn't happen. But in terms of just death itself and thinking about death, I think it has been me just accepting the fact that death is inevitable. I guess coming to terms with it and knowing that it'll happen regardless, so there's not a big reason to be fearful of it because it's going to happen to everyone eventually.

Ross: That's interesting, Rose. Stoic acceptance of death's inevitability has been important to you.

        This is sort of my last question. You have already covered this in various ways, but I'll ask it directly. What, if anything, do you think makes your life meaningful?

Rose: I volunteer at a vet clinic and while I'm not saving animals' lives or anything that extreme, I think seeing animals is just a nice thing not just because they're cute or cuddly or soft or whatever, but that they live their life without thinking about fears or worries. They're just innocent little beings that just go through their life not thinking about death or worrying about things that might happen. They're just really innocent little things, and that makes me happy. And I feel I'm making a difference. Recently I helped someone in our area with their cat who was quite old. The owners were also an elderly couple, and they weren't really caring for him in the best way. Seeing him prompted me to help him and make a difference in his life. He was such a helpless being; he couldn't change his circumstances. He needed someone else to help him, so I guess that was something that really showed me that you can make a difference, and the opportunity to make a difference will arise naturally at times and sometimes it will require you making the first step. So, I guess the first step for me helping this cat was bringing it into the vet. We didn't know if it had been hit by a car because it was quite distressed one night and after that, we developed a connection with him and we met the owners, and after that we helped him and made his life, I guess, better.

Rose: The owners told me he was about 20 years old, so I got to know him at the end of his life. He has now passed away, but knowing that I made a difference, albeit a small one for a very small portion of his life, makes me feel good. I think, even though he's just a cat, he has fulfilled a life that he needed to fulfil.

Ross: I understand. Thank you very much for your time, Rose. It's been fascinating.

Chapter 6

Bring me back

A cross decades as a therapist I've met many who deny the reality of death. They struggle to accept that one day, like all before them, they will be gone and may not be coming back. For many years, refuting this truth would dominate most of the daily activities of Michael. He simply had to find a way to survive forever.

I first met Michael as 19-year-old suffering from panic attacks and obsessional fears. He was a quietly spoken, intelligent man, more widely read than most people his age, and he listened intently to all the advice that I offered. Right from the beginning, he was particularly interested in my formulation of his problems. He wanted to deeply understand what was happening to him. No superficial account would satisfy Michael. He wanted evidence to support any direction we took in treatment and any explanation that I provided for his cluster of symptoms.

Michael was plagued with intrusive thoughts and images that would enter his mind, disturbing and upsetting him. At times the images suggested that he was gay, while at other moments he wondered if he was becoming psychotic. But above all else, his mind was dominated by thoughts of dying. He had a pervasive and desperate fear that at any minute, he could be gone. He could drop dead and nobody might be able to do anything about it — no-one might be able to bring him back. This realisation terrified him and became the genesis of the panic disorder that had developed.

Michael's panic attacks were clearly ferocious. He would become overwhelmed by the sensations in his chest and found it impossible, at least in the early period of treatment, to avoid a fast dash to hospital. In one period of fewer than six months, Michael visited emergency services on more than 100 occasions. 'I have to be with people who could bring me back, Ross. It would be tragic for my heart to stop in the wrong place' he said. Naturally enough, he started to doubt that emergency doctors were taking him seriously. So, to check their assessments of him, he would leave one hospital only to drive to another. He had multiple recordings of his cardiac function with 24-hour Holter monitors. He sought the advice of many specialist cardiologists and would send his ECGs to international experts for opinions. Despite their reassuring words, Michael continued to seek more and more professional opinions regarding his health. He simply couldn't live with the prospect that at any minute he could die, and saw it as a personal responsibility to take every action possible to prevent it.

Michael wasn't selfish in his desire to live. He felt no-one should have to face death — that it was inhumane. He saw his destiny and purpose to find a solution to the problem for all mankind. He explored a range of career options that involved working to undermine death. He considered a career in IT, intrigued by the idea that one day humans would be able to digitally record the self. 'What if consciousness, and all of my memories, could be downloaded on a daily basis' he proposed. 'That way, if I drop dead, I can return. Someone could start up the last download, and I'd only have missed a few hours. They could bring us back, Ross' he said, looking at me hopefully. At other times he considered working as a medical researcher, getting involved in the fight against cancer. But even this wasn't enough for Michael — it wouldn't stop him from dying. Still, maybe medicine could offer more. 'Couldn't we solve all the diseases and disabilities of man?' he questioned.

Our sessions were, at times, frustrating for Michael as I tried to push back on his thoughts. There were moments where I'm sure he found me dismissive of his ideas, invalidating his search for a solution to death. As I gently encouraged him to accept the fate that awaits us all, Michael continued to read and seek solace in alternative and novel ways of thinking about the universe. He developed an interest in eternalism, the idea that all points in history are still with us; that time is a construct that humans have arbitrarily determined involving a past and a future. He was very drawn to the idea that all the happenings of his life were still here, and that the clock is simply measuring the distance between two existing points in time, just as a ruler measures the distance between two existing points in space. Of course, quite transparently, his enthusiasm for this worldview was born out of his fear of the impermanence of the self.

At other times, like many who struggle to accept death, he became obsessed with religion. But this offered little ongoing comfort, serving instead to further complicate his anxiety. 'How can I know which religion is correct, Ross? If I commit to one and it's a mistake, I suffer eternally' he pondered. He spent endless hours reading and re-reading forum posts on the belief systems of the various faiths around the globe, digging an ever-deeper hole of confusion and doubt. The more he read, the worse he got, but he found stopping his research too difficult to face.

At various points in his treatment, Michael would enter periods of death acceptance. Some of these moments would come from trawling through the tomes of the great thinkers of the past. He immersed himself in the philosophy of the stoics and existentialists, looking for solutions in such intellectual giants as Marcus Aurelius, Seneca, Epictetus, Sartre, and Simone de Beauvoir. At other times, he would make breakthroughs himself that seemed to lead him out of his troubles. On one occasion, he wrote to me with great enthusiasm:

'Ross, I have managed to produce an amazing thought experiment. Suppose I had conversed with God and God revealed that there is no reason for my existence, then what would I do? The answer is, I would leave and be free. I'm free to make my own satisfying outcome to life. I feel a lot better regardless of whether there is purpose or not. I feel completed in knowing that it doesn't hurt to not have a purpose, even if I had to hear it from God before I understood the concept. I do still somewhat fear the impermanence, but this makes a world of difference in tolerating it. I'll discuss this more next week. Thank you, Ross for being a compassionate and understanding therapist. Cheers, Michael'.

I was obviously happy when I received this email and wrote quickly back: 'This is fantastic, Michael. Well done — a wonderful thought experiment. You may have found your way to peace. Each of us must find our way. This is great news indeed. Let's talk soon. All the best, Ross.'

Inevitably, however, these moments of acceptance would slip through his fingers, and he would become overwhelmed by the pain of death once again. Less than a month after this message, he wrote to me again:

'Sorry Ross that I need to say this. Now that I'm facing my death anxiety again, my thoughts have become depressing, and I've been crying since I woke. Picture a prisoner about to be executed by electric chair. Upon arrival of his last meal, no matter how good the food, the fear of death has besieged the man. The only possible scenario I could see a person to be at peace in the face of the electric chair is if he was religious. I can see parallels between the prisoner and myself. No matter the joys offered, death is approaching, be it tomorrow or 60 years from now. The fear is consuming me, but it feels more like despair. That is not my main fear though. It is that I have knowledge that the execution will take everything I love away in time just as it will to me. Ross, how can I enjoy the meal if my fear of death is consuming me? You can see the dilemma, right? The knowledge of death is something I can't face, and no matter which way I turn, it continues to face me. How am I supposed to kid myself into believing it's okay that everything has to decay, just because it's a matter of fact? This is all a bit much for me. I know everyone has to face it, but just because everyone's doing it doesn't justify it. What on earth should I do?'

Over many years, our sessions meandered through positive and negative times where his mood would rise up, only to re-enter darkness in the weeks or months that followed. There were long periods of relative wellness, where Michael rarely sought my services. But, like the changing of the seasons, inevitably his anxiety and existential angst would return. For a decade Michael found it extremely difficult to completely confront his fears, stop the avoidance, reassurance-seeking, reading health and religious forums on the internet, and doing the many other things that maintained his anxiety disorders.

It's now 13 years since I first met Michael as a teenager and I continue to see him at sporadic intervals. At 31, he's focusing more on relationships, on building attachments and getting on with living. He's travelled and spent time in interesting places with interesting people and is living a much larger life than he did as a younger man. Whether it's due to accomplishing these things, or whether it's because his fears of sudden death have been disproved by the passage of time, Michael is much less wedded to his thoughts of threats these days. In our most recent meetings, he has consistently reported that he has stopped ruminating about religion, and has significantly reduced reassurance-seeking through websites and internet forums. His current estimate of sudden death is one in ten-thousand, a far more realistic appraisal than the one in ten figure that he gave me for many years. Michael is functioning positively and thoughtfully as he tries to build his life. Whether he's defeated his existential issues, time will only tell. But this lovely young man is in the best mental health that I've ever seen him.

Our interview with Michael

Ross: Hey. Well, thank you, Michael, for coming in.

Michael: Yeah, no problem.

Ross: I'd like to start if I can, with your early life. Can you tell me about your family and life at home as you grew up?

Michael: Where do I begin? My family and I, we moved around a lot. As I was growing, I remember never having a place at all in the world. There was my grandmother's, where we kind of kept shifting back-and-forth between there and everywhere else, but I don't recall ever having really a permanent area to stay.

Ross: It felt quite disjointed? Your early life?

Michael: It was interesting. I mean, it was interesting that I got to see so many places. At the same time, I missed out on things. A lot of people I've spoken to have told me, 'I've got marks in the wall of my height — I can see my changes from when I was a kid to an adult from the marks on the wall.' And I've never been able to do that.

Ross: Oh, I see. You envy people that were in the one house?

Michael: Yeah.

Ross: ... and there they were growing in that house, whereas you moved around from house to house a lot. Within the same city?

Michael: Sometimes, it would be out of Sydney, but still in the same region.

Ross: Okay. Can you describe your relationship with your mother in those early years?

Michael: Mum's always been really caring. She cares about me a lot, and she's always tried to look out for me. You know?

Ross: So a positive relationship.

Michael: Yeah. Yeah. It's always been great.

Ross: And it was from those early years. You were very close to mum.

Michael: Yeah.

Ross: And your father?

Michael: Same kind of thing. Dad's always been a bit stern, but we've had a close relationship. I mean, growing up, I kind of had my moments, where I was a rebellious teenager and all that, but I always cared about him at the end. And they always get me. It was always this kind of mutual relationship.

Ross: Positive.

Michael: Yeah.

Ross: What, if any, early losses did you have in life? Were there any deaths in your early life at all? To anyone of note or significance? Relatives? Friends?

Michael: People would die. Never anyone that I was very close with.

Ross: Can you remember any particular loss that had an impact on you?

Michael: I recall, at somewhere between 8 and 12, I had a cousin who suddenly died of a heart attack, when he was walking.

Ross: Right.

Michael: Yeah. I don't remember understanding it much, but I'd see my mum really distressed.

Ross: Are you aware of any losses and traumas, other than the one you just mentioned, in your parents' lives? Perhaps before you were even born, are there any great events that you think had an impact on them?

Michael: Yes. My mother had a baby sibling that passed away suddenly. My mum was really young too, and she'd been taking care of this baby all the time, and all of a sudden it's just dead.

Ross: Right. So your mum was only a young girl looking after her baby sibling?

Michael: Yeah.

Ross: Did she talk about that much?

Michael: I'd hear it from time to time. Yeah. She was really kind of distressed about it, but she'd accepted it in a way, but it was always kind of this looming fear in the background.

Ross: Would you say either of your parents were anxious? Anxious people?

Michael: I know that my father had a history of anxiety growing up. My mum, if she was anxious, it was only ever about us.

Ross: What sort of things worried her?

Michael: She seemed to be kind of anxious about anything happening to us.

Ross: Okay.

Michael: She was concerned about our welfare overall.

Ross: Okay. And you said your father suffered with anxiety in his earlier life.

Michael: Yeah. I recall something had happened with his head. He was in a car accident, and he had a pretty bad hit, smacked his head really hard against the front chair. The thing was like a steel chair. I don't know what was going on. The frame or what have you. They found a scar on his brain when they did a scan, and it triggered this fear that he would die.

Ross: Right.

Michael: Yeah. And he became very sick as a result. And anxiety wasn't a very common diagnosis back then, so they were just saying, 'We don't know what's going on with you.' The doctors were confused because I mean, I don't know how frequent anxiety disorders presented themselves.

Ross: How old was he when this happened?

Michael: I think he was in his 20s?

Ross: Okay. So if I understood you, it wasn't even necessarily the accident itself, but the result of the scan …

Michael: Yeah.

Ross: … that really convinced him that something's wrong here. 'I'm damaged.'

Michael: Yeah. So it was the scan in conjunction with sensations that he would have.

Ross: Okay. And he started to fear that he might die?

Michael: Yeah.

Ross: And did that continue for him?

Michael: For a long time.

Ross: Right. He worried about sudden death?

Michael: Yeah. Or getting very ill. He ended up losing a lot of weight, I think. Because he was so anxious. He wouldn't eat.

Ross: Is there any other history of mental illness in the family?

Michael: Yeah. Anxiety runs throughout a lot of my family — cousins, aunties, uncles, my grandmother. Yeah. A lot of family members have anxiety disorders and obsessive-compulsive disorder. They've both been fairly common throughout my extended family and my immediate family. Both of my siblings have had, or do have, anxiety disorders. Yeah. At least one member of each family — there was about five families.

Ross: Okay. At least one member has had an anxiety state or obses-sive-compulsive problem.

Michael: Yeah. Sometimes all of them do.

Ross: Wow, that's very interesting. If I can turn now to you and your own life more directly, what are your earliest memories of you being anxious, worried or afraid?

Michael: There's one that really stands out in my head. I wasn't a very fearful kid up until one point, and I think this is when it really started for me. I remember I was sitting, and I was starting to think about if doctors could bring me back if I was to die, and that thought horrified me. I came to the realisation that they couldn't, and that eventually, I would have to die. All of a sudden, it's this kind of doom just came over me. I ran to my mother screaming and crying and saying, 'Are they gonna bring me back? Are they gonna bring me back?'

Michael: And she said, 'What do you mean?' And I said, 'When I die, can they bring me back?'

Ross: How old would you have been?

Michael: I would have been about seven or eight.

Ross: So it was just an out of the blue meandering of your mind about dying, and then puzzling over could you be brought back if that occurred?

Michael: Yeah.

Ross: And becoming terrified of the idea that they can't.

Michael: Yeah. I remember vividly having this image in my head of being on a kind of table with doctors around me, and them being unable to bring me back, and I was old. It's incredible because I actually ended up seeing something very visually similar to that when a family member passed away.

Ross: Of seeing the body on the table?

Michael: Yeah. And the doctors around, and the lights, the way they were, and kind of these faded colours around … it was very surreal to see what I was scared of in front of me. That it was this ancient terror, and it was here in reality.

Ross: This particular theme of desperately wanting to be brought back, how did that develop over time? Because you've had variations on that, haven't you?

Michael: Yeah. I mean, firstly, there was just this kind of reassurance thinking that I would do for months after that realisation happened. I'd go to my parents, and I'd kind of ask them constantly if there's anything that one could do. Then, as time went on, I delved very heavily into religious belief.

Ross: Yes.

Michael: And not just that. Another thing that had happened was … I had a firearm pulled on me, and I was robbed at gunpoint very young.

Ross: Yes. How old were you?

Michael: I would have been 13.

Ross: Yeah.

Michael: I recall doing a lot of checking, so looking out the window to see if this person or someone similar would come. I would surround myself with people who were tough or criminal types. I hung around with them a lot because I felt like they could protect me.

Ross: I see. That's very much about trying not to be killed in the first place.

Michael: Right.

Ross: But can we go back to the deep desire to be brought back. You mentioned religion …

Michael: Yeah.

Ross: … and you spent a lot of time, didn't you, years really …

Michael: Yeah.

Ross: … ruminating about religious belief and trying to sort it out.

Michael: Yes. Trying to sort out if one religion was right or another religion; wanting to gain clarity because I had to get it right. If it exists, I've got to get it right to be brought back? Yeah. This started early on. Would've been as soon as I understood kind of religion at all really, 'cause I went into communion and did all of the things that you would do normally growing up in a Catholic family. As I kind of started to realise there are other belief systems, my uncertainty about that started to grow, and I had a lot of questions. This kind of progressively became this issue of having to solve what's true.

Ross: Yes.

Michael: How can I get the truth because if I'm going to come back, I don't want to be thrown in a pit of fire. I don't want to have some eternally recurring issue or fear or some horrible situation

that could happen from a daily event or a circumstance. Hell —
that was a big one. Coming back to torture was a really horrifying prospect to me, so I felt like I had to solve that.

Ross: How long do you think you spent, and over how long a period
           did you try to sort out the search for truth on religious belief?

Michael: Well, it's waxed and waned over my life. My teens, my early
           teens, it started, and then it went away, and then it came back. It
           kept coming and going through my teens, and then eventually in
           my 20s, it became extremely prominent, when I had kind of
           been reintroduced to some Islamic beliefs. Then there was a
           clear dichotomy between two religions that I didn't know how to
           solve, and I would spend hours, days, months thinking about it.
           It went for about four years straight.

Ross: I see. It sounds very derivative of that early fear of 'will I be
           brought back?'.

Michael: Yeah. I was thinking at the time, if I get this wrong, I might not
           be brought back. Or worse, I might be brought back to hellfire.

Ross: Yeah. You also explored other ways of 'being brought back',
           didn't you? There was a period, where you thought a lot about
           cryogenics and the resurrection of consciousness. Can you tell
           me more about those periods, and what your thoughts were?

Michael: With cryogenics, I had a brief kind of idea that I could be frozen,
           or somehow some part of me could be preserved so that I could
           be brought back. And I hoped that science would advance until
           we could download consciousness. That way, if I died, I could
           just be rebooted as a machine.

Ross: Yes. That was another one.

Michael: I didn't really understand what consciousness was, I don't think.
           No one really does.

Ross: Yes.

Michael: But I became really … I would obsess a lot about it. In general, I
           would obsess about ways to overcome my own mortality.
           There's one that's recent that comes to mind that I'd like to
           explain.

Ross: Yes.

Michael: It's the idea of machine consciousness and super computing —
           where machines have genuine artificial intelligence.

Ross: Yes.

Michael: They gain intelligence far greater than humans. A machine is
           developed with a god complex and brings everyone back in this
           kind of Christian judgment.

Ross: Right.

Michael: Yeah. It could happen. At the moment it's kind of some science-
           fiction bent to an early apocalyptic belief that I had.

Ross: So the idea is that some super learning machines that we're
           developing now, like AlphaZero, find a way to resurrect con-
           sciousness of those who have already been here over time.

Michael: Yep, then that could lead to bringing people back.

Ross: I see.

Michael: There was another theory that I was really interested in by a
           physicist. Goodness, I forget his name, but he had this idea there
           was an Omega Point and that ... I might not be entirely correct
           on the specifics ... that the artificial intelligence that we're
           building now will eventually want to simulate everything that's
           happened in the past, and that'll expand outwards, processing
           this information outward to eternity. I don't know. It's pretty
           far-fetched, but at the same time, it's got some people who agree
           with the idea. I think Max Tegmark, from memory, was really
           interested in it. I've been looking, especially in science, about
           ways of overcoming death.

Ross: Even time travel as I remember it.

Michael: Time travel. Yeah. I was interested in the possibility. I've often
           thought that the reason *Doctor Who* is such a popular show is
           the immortality idea. Time travel still interests me. It's always in
           the back of my mind. You could go back and see yourself earlier.

           I might mention this. I had this belief from when I was younger
           that God himself had given me some kind of a purpose, and that
           purpose was to figure out a way to make people live indefinitely.

Ross: Yes. Yes.

Michael: And as I waxed and waned throughout my religious beliefs, I still held onto this idea that this had to be my purpose.

Ross: Yes.

Michael: And that if I didn't do it, that my life would've failed because I would've let down everyone around me, and they would all succumb to death. And I still hold that, even though maybe I'm a bit more sceptical about my initial inclinations. I still hold onto this idea that if I don't figure it out, or if someone around me doesn't figure it out, I would've failed.

Ross: I see. Yes. You mentioned many times over the years various possible professional areas for your future, and they've often involved things like extending life.

Michael: Yeah.

Ross: You wanted to identify ways to defeat death, and that's interesting to hear that you saw that very early on as a goal. Very early on. And maybe even a destiny.

Michael: Yeah.

Ross: So there's been many, many things you've explored over time on this 'bring me back' theme. I need to pick the right religion for eternal life, or be cryogenically frozen, or be brought back by mega AI developments leading to the replaying of all human happenings, or be brought back because of software developments that allow downloads of my consciousness. They've all been various solutions to this problem that you first were struck with as a very young boy.

Michael: Yeah.

Ross: Can I return you to this image of you on a slab, and doctors struggling to bring you back, and perhaps failing. Is it still overwhelming?

Michael: It's still very distressing. This idea. It's still very vivid in my head. Whenever I think about it, it's a very strong and old feeling — this dread.

Ross: This dread that something will happen, and you won't be able to be brought back?

Michael: Yeah.

Ross: Could I ask you to comment on another of your beliefs because I think it links nicely to the 'bring me back' theme. I'm talking about your belief, that you've had for a long time, that there's something fundamentally physically wrong with you — that this flaw could take you out of the game and could take you out very quickly. This led to the development of panic attacks and panic disorder and a lot of concern about your heart and a lot of check-ups. Tell me about all of these medical fears.

Michael: It began when I started to get fit in my late teens or early 20s. I remember an incident when I'd been riding. I went up to this shop on my bicycle to get some food to go and cook. Now, I'd exercised fairly rigorously to get there and I remember stopping suddenly — I wasn't aware that you're supposed to cool down 'cause your blood pressure drops or what have you.

I exerted myself very hard, and then stopped suddenly, got off my bike, and then was talking to the lady at the counter after I had grabbed some stuff. And all of a sudden, I felt like I was about to pass out, and I had to drop to the floor. I made out like I was doing my shoe up or something. At the time, I was embarrassed. And then my heart was racing, and I thought that this is it. I'm a goner.

I panicked. I called the ambulance and called my parents, and I got taken to the hospital. They did some blood tests, and it came back that there was nothing wrong. But I recall the doctor telling me that, 'Sometimes people your age die of a heart attack, and it's good that you came …'

Ross: Right.

Michael: '… cause you don't know' he said. And I burnt that idea into my head that, 'Oh, this could happen to me.' So whenever I had these twinges or sensations, it progressively got worse, I would have these fast heart rates and what have you. Eventually, I would be going to the doctor, or to the hospital more likely, to the emergency department, once every two days. I lost so much time and money. I would spend a lot of money because I didn't have a university library access at this point. I spent a lot of money on journals, on scientific journals, about sudden death in people with a variation of normal physiology. A variation on it. It's early repolarisation. So they recently discovered that some of the people that have it might be more at risk of sudden death. But a very small portion.

Ross: Yes.

Michael: Just a statistically significant small proportion. I think that's right. Enough for them to be concerned, I think.

I started to panic about that because I have a really weird form of this variation. I spent hours and days thinking I was going to drop dead suddenly. I contacted almost every cardiologist researching in the field, and they all got back to me.

Ross: Yes, it was remarkable. I remember that at one point you thought you had Brugada Syndrome and you wrote to its discoverer, Dr Brugada, with a copy of a recent ECG.

Michael: Yeah, and he got back to me. He said, 'Just trust your cardiologist. It doesn't look like you have it to me'.

Ross: You would send cardiologists ECG images and ask them to comment.

Michael: Yeah, I did. Eventually I got an event monitor, and it came back that I might have had a heart condition, and that really kind of solidified my fear that what I was doing was justified.

Ross: Yes.

Michael: We went in, and they did a study. They weren't able to trigger it. They told me it's probably SVT, but it's not dangerous. Don't worry about it. But I continued for a very long time to constantly scan my body. Even though I had an answer as to why I was feeling the way I was with the fast heart rates, it still wasn't enough. I still thought, 'I can never tell the next moment, and because I can never understand what is next, and there's no amount of inductive reasoning I can do to get to the future because there's always some small probability ...'

Ross: Yes.

Michael: ... 'that I'm gonna die.' I had to go be in a place where I thought they could bring me back.

Ross: As you said, at your worst, you were in emergency every two days.

Michael: Yeah.

Ross: I think, correct me if I'm wrong, that you on occasion would even go from one emergency department to another emergency department at another hospital. You'd leave one hospital if you were dubious ...

Michael: Yeah.

Ross: ... about the way they were handling you.

Michael: That happened. Yeah.

Ross: Hundreds of visits to hospitals over the years.

Michael: Yeah. I've got a very large file.

Ross: Yes, indeed. And again, it's interesting to hear you describe it in terms of the need to be brought back. Earlier on, I had conceived of your hospital visits as the simple result of believing that you had a fragile cardiovascular system. But it fits in more neatly with the 'bring me back' theme. You wanted to be in a place where, if something did happen, they could bring back. If suddenly you had a massive cardiac event and dropped dead, you needed to be in emergency at the time.

Michael: Absolutely.

Ross: It so clearly relates to that young boy's fear. The fear that had been dominating your mind for so many years. Tell me, how did you manage to pull away from the regularity of being in the hospital? How did you manage to get on top of this behaviour?

Michael: I believe that in some ways, it was a very unfortunate circumstance that led me to stop going. It was watching my uncle die in front me in hospital.

Ross: Right.

Michael: When I realised that they can't save you sometimes.

Ross: I see.

Michael: I stopped.

Ross: So seeing him die brought home the universality of death to you. Death will come and there is nothing to do about it?

Michael: Yeah. He had everyone there, and they could do anything they wanted. But they didn't. And I watched him die. Yeah. I think that stopped me racing to the hospital all the time. Acceptance.

Ross: Accepting that it's real, it's true. There's nothing to be done about it. Death occurs.

Michael: Yeah. And it doesn't matter where you are. It doesn't matter if you're in the best hospital care in the world. Sometimes they just can't save you.

Ross: So, in your case, a traumatic event actually reduced your fear. It led to some acceptance. Have there been any happenings that made your fears more intense? Now, you've mentioned one — the original incident on the bike — where you first had a physical reaction that led to a sudden growth in your fears. But have there been other things along the way that intensified your fears? It could be anything from bullying, loss, illness, accidents. Could be anything at all.

Michael: Yeah, there's plenty of things that ramp it up. Thinking about losing the people around me is always a trigger. So some of the things that worsen my fears happen in my head.

Ross: Right.

Michael: With the religious fear, I had a friend that I would talk to about religion, and her beliefs scared me. So when she spoke about it, I was scared of her conviction.

Ross: I see.

Michael: Because it was a competing narrative that was staring me in the face, and I could be wrong. I could be wrong, and that wouldn't be great. I remember the first time we had that conversation in which she showed the strength of her belief. I said, 'What have you done?' because I was so horrified at the prospect that I could be wrong.

Ross: So that different worldview was very threatening?

Michael: Yeah.

Ross: So some events have intensified things over time, and other events can do the opposite.

Michael: Yeah.

Ross: Can I ask you about treatment? How did you first come to treatment for anxiety?

Michael: It was getting out of hand — the intensity of it. I knew I needed help.

Ross: Okay.

Michael: My parents were opposed to the idea because they didn't want me to be labelled. They were worried it would carry on throughout my life. But I said, 'Look, I think it's time I go in.' The first person I saw never said I had OCD, but then I went to a psychiatrist who said I most definitely did.

Ross: Can I ask who recommended you see a psychiatrist? Did you ask for this or did your GP or a psychologist or someone else recommend it?

Michael: I think it was a GP.

Ross: Okay.

Michael: And then he sent me to a set of counsellors. I don't know why I started seeing counsellors a lot more. Some of 'em had what I would consider fairly unethical techniques. They did things that were really … they weren't great. But because of that, because of their not very good way of practicing …

Ross: Yes.

Michael: … my father, he went and looked for someone that was very qualified, and that's what led me to you.

Ross: Okay. And in treatment, what do you think has been the most useful thing? What do you think it is about cognitive-behaviour therapy, when it's helping, that's helpful? What do you find useful in reducing fear?

Michael: Holding out, I think, is the most important part of it because the initial part never feels like it's going to work. But if you hold on for long enough, and we don't know how long that time will be, but when you do, it works.

Ross: When you say holding out, you mean not going to the hospital, not getting the check-up, not engaging in the reassurance seeking or safety behaviours, not going back to the computer to read another article about religion or AI and so on?

Michael: Yeah, because everything in me would tell me to do it. And not doing it seems ridiculous.

Ross: Yes.

Michael: It almost seems illogical. Why wouldn't you go check? You need to know if you're gonna die. How can you stop yourself from checking? But there's that part of me that through CBT made me realise that holding on past all of the noise in the head if I can get to the end, it'll work.

Ross: That's fantastic, Michael. You've achieved so much through exposure. I want to turn to our last topic, which is very much focusing in on death itself very directly. Can I ask you what emotions arise in you at the thought of your own death? What do you feel when you think about your own death?

Michael: It's a mixture of feelings, and it depends. Sometimes I feel different things than other times. Now, I have the belief that might sound a bit weird. I don't know. But I don't think that there's anything special about this idea of the self or that I exist objectively. I think it's this trick that my friend's playing on me. It's hard to talk without using these descriptions, me and myself and I. I don't really think I'm here. So when I feel as though I might die, I look at that and say, 'Well, what's the big deal?'

I think I told you the other week that I had this feeling that I was gonna pass out when I was walking. And I had this idea that nature is constantly churning life and death.

Ross: Yes.

Michael: And I felt small and didn't really matter in the big scheme of things, so I was okay with it. But there will be times where I don't like the idea.

Ross: Yes. It depends on the state you're in.

Michael: Yeah.

Ross: Sometimes you're very at ease with it, and other times, the small voice of terror of not being brought back is still there.

Michael: Yeah, definitely.

Ross: What do you think will happen to you as you physically die, and once you're physically dead? What's your current belief about what actually happens to a person as they physically die, and once they're dead?

Michael: I don't think that anything happens to me. My set of experiences, I believe, are always somewhere in the past for eternity. Once I'm here, I'm here forever. So when I die, it'll be meaningless to me because I'll be dead. And everything that I've lived will always be.

Ross: Okay.

Michael: But the process of dying, I guess, scares me. Just the pain that I'll experience. Maybe I won't experience but …

Ross: You worry about that sometimes?

Michael: Yeah, I watched my grandfather slowly wither away from peripheral vascular disease. I don't want to end up like that. Yeah. Other than the pain, I'm okay these days.

Ross: How often do you think about death?

Michael: Every day.

Ross: Many times across the day?

Michael: Yeah. Almost constantly.

Ross: So it's a concept that's never far from you.

Michael: Absolutely.

Ross: And what relationship do you see between your thoughts about death and fears about death and your experience of everyday living? Is it a very close relationship?

Michael: Yeah, definitely. It affects every part of my life. It's almost as if death is someone standing in the background, constantly. It's smiling at me. 'I'm still here', it's saying.

Ross: I see.

Michael: Even in my happiness. Even in the best moments of my life. It's just standing there.

Ross: Standing and watching? Death is?

Michael: Yeah.

Ross: So casting a shadow over …

Michael: Everything. I remember even some of the best moments of my life. I remember seeing it in my head. Like I was on a beach once, and there was just this immense scene. No one was there. It was a huge beach. And there was mist in the air, and it was incredible. I remember looking at the sun and saying to my partner at the time, 'the sun's about to set.' And it came to my head straight away. I'm not here forever.

Ross: Yes.

Michael: Even in this beautiful moment. Yeah. It's always there.

Ross: Within therapy, or outside of therapy, what have you found most helpful in dealing with your dread of death? What's the most helpful thing you've found to assuage your fears of death?

Michael: Not being in my head and being in the things around me, so especially nature. Especially being out in the bush where there's no one — or being in an environment where I have to deal with being a human and being myself and not relying on other people — being busy.

Ross: So being very present?

Michael: Yup. Being very present, very absorbed, in the place you are, but particularly in nature?

Michael: Yeah, definitely. Even if death is near, it doesn't matter as much in those environments.

Ross: That's very interesting. Now for my final question — what, if anything, do you think makes your life meaningful?

Michael: May I tell you a theory I have about it? I think there's something fundamental to reality. I don't know if it's just particles or sub-atomic particles or some force or something like being itself, let's call it.

Ross: Yes.

Michael: But because there are these fundamental things, I believe that they're causing me to do whatever it is I do. And because of that cause or change, I believe that whatever meaning I ascribe to my life is truly meaningful because it's coming from this fundamental reality. So the meanings that I have about my family and my friends and experiencing good things and doing science and exploring nature, they're grounded in the idea that something fundamental in the world is causing me to feel that way.

Ross: Okay. So the things themselves, the meaning you find in relationships with family and friends, and in being in nature, and in pursuing scientific work, they are the things that give you meaning, but you're saying more than that. That you think there's a truth to that meaning in that it is not just conjured up by …

Michael: Yeah.

Ross: … by you.

Michael: That's right. It's not a trick. It's a truth from a fundamental reality that we can't fully understand yet.

Ross: That's very interesting, Michael. Thank you very much for your time today.

Michael: It's my pleasure.

Chapter 7

The activist

When a patient, returned to wellness, triumphantly leaves therapy it is a cause for celebration for all concerned. Watching someone climb their way out of the pit of despair and build a functional life is the greatest privilege afforded the psychotherapist. To be allowed into the private lives of others — to help create a path out of the pain, and to watch people bravely walk that path is what keeps so many psychologists enthusiastic in their work. But when the patient returns, years later, having fallen prey to another bout of illness, it can be quite disarming. It's like seeing an old friend who has gained a lot of weight since you last passed them on the street. The difference can be stark and sometimes shocking. Godfrey's two periods of treatment involved such a stunning change but, as you shall see, not in the direction that you might be thinking.

When Godfrey first presented, it was with a typical history of panic disorder and agoraphobia. His panic attacks had begun spontaneously one afternoon on an underground train when he was racing across the city to lodge a funding application for his activism. Godfrey was a freewheeling spirit who had done much to protect wilderness areas for future generations. He'd been involved in the famous campaign to save the Franklin River in Tasmania. And he'd rallied against other social scourges as well. A member of BUGAUP (Billboard Utilising Graffitists Against Unhealthy Promotions) in the 1970s, he would regularly paint over advertisements for cigarettes, making fun of these companies and highlighting the damage that they do to our society. He was, at the time, completely fulfilled by these activities. He was part of a movement that existed beyond the self, that would continue after his death. I had no doubt that this had once given him purpose and assuaged any fears of impermanence. However, by the time I met him, it was no longer serving that need.

After that first panic attack on the underground train, he gave a classic history of the development of agoraphobia, which had arisen as he began to worry about when and where his next panic would occur. He would do anything to prevent panic — including, somewhat unusually, implementing magical rituals and superstitious behaviours to ward them off. He believed that tapping his foot in certain patterns, or performing certain hand gestures, could ward off panic. He also engaged in checking behaviours involving stoves and locks consistent with Obsessive Compulsive Disorder, a condition that was clearly influencing the way in which he responded to panic attacks.

Godfrey had received treatment from various clinical services for nearly twenty years before turning to me. He knew what he needed to do to treat his anxiety-related symptoms, but a secondary depression had set in. His mood was low, and he was getting very little enjoyment from everyday activities. His sleep was particularly poor. He was suffering from middle insomnia, waking in the nights for hours on end staring at the ceiling. He lacked energy, was fatigued and tearful at times. How had the slide into depression begun? I asked him about changes in his life in the previous year and he told me that his mother had died. 'I don't think my depression is about anxiety, Ross,' he said. 'I think it's about mortality. It's somehow linked to my mother's loss. Somehow it's all about loss.'

Godfrey really had only one passionate interest that was still reliably giving him enjoyment. He expressed a deep desire to capture moments, particularly in nature, that would never return. He would wander into the 16,000 hectares of the Royal National Park in the dead of night and take pictures by the light of the moon and stars. 'It's bloody dangerous, Ross —

I've nearly walked off many cliffs and crevices in the blackness' he said with a laugh. 'But I capture things — magnificent things — that would never have been seen by another human if not for me'. And Godfrey wasn't exaggerating. His shot of a lightning bolt filling the night sky off the east coast of New South Wales, with a swirling wash of dark purples and reds against the blackness, was one of the finest photographs that I'd ever seen.

Treatment of Godfrey in this opening period was straightforward. On the depression front, we began to activate his behaviour, increasing physical exercise, pleasant activities and various goal-directed behaviours. He took up a walking program and deepened his interest in photography, bootstrapping up the passion with more and more projects. On the obsessive-compulsive front, ritual prevention seemed to do the trick, cutting his checking of stoves and locks and other items step by step. He began reading about Buddhism and focusing on living a present life, staying focused on the activities of the now. This combination of strategies started to give him reliable progress. Slowly the secondary depression began to lift as he gained more control over his life again.

After several months of treatment, most of his problems seemed behind him. He told me, 'I've had five great weeks, Ross. It's been effortless. The best I've ever felt.' For all intents and purposes, after more than two decades of anxiety, Godfrey looked like he was finding peace. His agitation seemed to have left him; he had built a new existence around his fanatical interest. He had moved to a small home in his beloved National Park, and his life was going exceptionally well. We terminated our sessions.

Three years later, at 52 years of age, Godfrey re-entered my rooms, a starkly different man. He'd lost weight; his hair was dyed, he was fit, and looked years younger than the man that I had originally met. He wore black, and there was a cool edge to the way he carried himself. Neat but nerdy had become unruffled and strong. It was like watching *Happy Days'* Richie Cunningham become the Fonz.

Though Godfrey had seemingly recovered in our earlier work, his concerns about mortality, he revealed, had never been far from him. Even his attempts to live in the present seemed to have been lost to the darkness of his mind. 'I was looking at the stars the other day' he told me, 'and thinking about the sun and the light that touches my eyes. Did you know that the light takes eight minutes to reach us from the sun? Everything I see is locked in the past. I'm imprisoned in the past, admittedly only milliseconds when light bounces off another object, but I can never really know the present. Even in this room, I'm seeing an ever so slightly dated version of you, Ross.'

He was clearly depressed again, and nothing seemed to be meaningful anymore. 'You die, and the essence of you dies at the same time,' he told me. 'Within two generations any sense of who I was as a person will be gone from the planet.' I was concerned by the depth of the darkness that had taken over Godfrey's thinking. 'Even Shakespeare, Ross, hasn't gained real permanence. What did he fight with his wife about?', he asked me. 'What were the irritants in his life? What was his personality really like? All these things are gone — the essence of him is forever lost.'

I asked him about his new appearance, complimenting him on how fabulous he looked. 'It's the women, Ross — the energy I get from the young women' he told me. Godfrey was less focussed on nature, turning his photographic skills to the female nude. 'Beautiful women, Ross. Women in their 20s that come to me and want their beauty shown. They know it's in them, and I bring it out — these beautiful young women who reveal their bodies to me positively and with great interest and passion. I'm living one giant wet dream, Ross,' he said, laughing, but with slightly watery eyes.

Godfrey revealed his journey through hedonism. This was his new solution to mortality. 'I cared too much, Ross,' he said. 'When you care about this planet, you end up hurt. So now I've turned to pleasure. I'm going to live every minute and enjoy every sensation.' He saw less meaning in his professional life, no meaning in his previous activism, and gained all meaning from his linkages to young people, sexual and otherwise, and the vitality of their existence.

Slowly over the course of the next year, he reduced his employment from full-time to three days per week. He bought the property in the national park where he'd been living and spent as much of his available time as he could concentrating on photographs of the female form, more and more sexual encounters, and deepening the intimate interpersonal relationships that now sustained him. With these changes, a semblance of repair seemed to slowly build.

I've continued to see Godfrey, at varying intervals, over the six years that have followed. His old fears of panic have re-emerged from time to time. For example, two years after his physical transformation, he returned for some brief consultations about fear of flying. His daughter wanted to travel and he wasn't sure that he could cope with the confinement of a long flight. But despite these occasional bursts of anxiety and agitation, Godfrey appears to have found a working solution to the mortality crisis that has plagued him across the bulk of his adult life. That first panic attack on a hot and dirty underground train 30 years ago had laid bare Godfrey's fragility, vulnerability and mortality. For more than 20 years he would live in terror. But, to his great credit, this charming, creative man continued to seek solutions and slowly assembled a toolkit, centring on mindful appreciation of sensory moments, to live the most functional life that he can.

His physical transformation and his hedonistic pursuit of younger women may, of course, be seen as a denial of ageing and death. Having said this, there is no doubt that the strategy has served him well. Godfrey is happier in the last five years than I have ever known him. As he ages, will another solution be required? Perhaps. For now, he continues to focus on sensate pleasures, interpersonal warmth, and being as present as he can, while admitting that the dark spectre of mortality is never far from his mind.

At the time of the interview I had seen Godfrey 34 times over 13 years.

Our interview with Godfrey

Ross: Thanks very much for agreeing to be interviewed, Godfrey. Can I start by asking you about your early life? Life at home as you grew up?

Godfrey: Sure. I was the third child that was born. My father was a clergyman, a Uniting Church minister, and my mother did a lot of unpaid work in relation to that as well, so their whole life was the church and the parish that they were in. The first four years of my life were spent in Wellington, New South Wales. It was a rural area, and I remember being a particularly adventurous child. I was always getting into trouble for running off, and at one stage, there was a railway line that ran down the back yard of our house, and I managed to find a way through the fence, and they found me, as a pre-four-year-old, sitting on the train tracks.

I had an older sibling, a sister who was four years older than me, and then there was another sibling born two years after her. Unfortunately, she died from meningitis when she was nearly two, and I was born not too long after that. I immediately followed this loss for my parents — this devastating loss of a child who was one of those perfect children, a little cherub. I wasn't aware of it at the time, but that was the context in which I was born. Looking back, I think that was actually pretty formative.

The earliest memory I've got is running away because there was a friend of mine who lived in the area, so several streets away, and I didn't know where that was, and so I went looking for him because his family had a TV set. It was the doctor's family, so they were the first people in the town to have a TV set. This was just the most incredible thing as you can imagine, as a child, actually finding a TV set and watching the Mickey Mouse Club and all these amazing shows. I went off looking for him and I got lost. I remember realising I was lost and becoming very fearful. Then I saw my father's car coming down the street and my fear just turned to elation. It's daddy, so I'm safe now, I thought. My father pulled the car up beside me, got out the car, came straight up to me and belted me.

Ross: Wow — I wasn't expecting that!

Godfrey: I went from being ecstatic to getting severely smacked on the bum, as you did to children in those days. It was just routine. I was talked to very sternly and aggressively because I'd been missing for some time and they were incredibly worried. They had just lost the previous child, I go missing, so it was a disproportionate response, but it made a massive impression on me. It really, literally, hit me hard.

Ross: What would you say your relationship with your father was like when you were growing up?

Godfrey: He was very stern and a very old-school father. Very removed most of the time. Sometimes I've got some memories of him in younger years, where we'd play games together, but not many. There's a few instances that I can think of, where we played backyard cricket. My main memory of him right up until my teenage years really, but certainly from birth to 10, was in his disciplinarian role, because I was a really adventurous child and so I was always running off and having adventures. We moved to Sydney when I was about five, four or five. We moved from rural New South Wales, where we could just run wild pretty much, within the confines of where we were and so on, to Enfield, in a city, a suburb. It was a parish of very old people mainly. Enfield was the polar opposite of where I'd come from.

            My memory of my mother at the time was she was very loving, but again, my main focus was my sister and my friends. That's where all my energy was placed.

Ross: But the relationship with mum was a positive one? She was loving and caring?

Godfrey: Very positive. I'd say it got so close as to almost feel like a co-dependency because I was always referred to as my mum's champion by dad, which was like if anything was going down, or anything was going wrong or whatever, I'd always stick up for her.

Ross: I see.

Godfrey: I was always with her because she was a stay-at-home mum, and I'd be doing the housework with her and I was in her company all the time when I wasn't with my friends. But what happened was that she had a major anxiety problem and depression, I recognise now, and she largely withdrew into her bedroom for long periods of time during this phase when we were at Enfield. I was about seven or eight, and so it went from being this co-dependent kind of thing to long periods where she was just not accessible. When I would go and see her, she just wouldn't connect with me. She was just locked in her own anxiety and stuff, so she wasn't available to me as a mother.

Ross: Did she ever talk about what was happening in those periods?

Godfrey: No. Absolutely nothing.

Ross: She would just come out of them at some point and be functional again?

Godfrey: Yeah, and then go back into them. She hated the parish at Enfield — she hated where we had moved. She was a country girl, so Wellington suited her fine, but she hated everything about the city and the new area. My father was just at a loss for what to do, and he was managing the parish and all these old people. I started school and was immediately subjected to this terrifying deputy, my kindergarten school principal, who in retrospect, was an absolute sociopath. So my first experience of school was like fear and terror of actually what would happen in the classroom because she just played these hideous games where corporal punishment was just normal.

There'd be one child who was causing havoc, and then there'd be others who she just wanted to send a message to the rest of the class, and so she'd get the child to hold out his hand and then she'd just cane him in front of everyone. Then she'd just arbitrarily pull out two or three of us, and then she'd get you to stick your hand up, and then she'd bring the cane down with all her might, and she'd just stop about an inch above your hand, to see what your reaction would be.

Ross: Oh dear.

Godfrey: If you pulled your hand away, then you got caned, but if you didn't pull your hand away, you wouldn't get caned. She would love that. She was just completely crazy. This was done to kindergarten children!

Ross: Oh my, that's terrible.

Godfrey: Kindergarten and first class and so on. She was crazy. The actual school, the experience in the classroom — you never knew when something …

Ross: … was going to happen.

Godfrey: When she'd go off. Then on the way to and from school, I had a
bully, and he just used to jump out from bushes and stuff like
that, and just beat me up. I never knew on the journey to or from
school, where I was going to get attacked. Of course, those days,
you didn't deal with any of that if you were a parent, so the way
my father dealt with it was to try to drop me off to school and
pick me up. But more often than not he couldn't, and he so
resented doing it anyway. So I just turned into this anxious mess
as a child; absolutely caused by this constellation of things that
came on me at the same time.

Ross: The movement from Wellington to the city was very critical in
your development. You went from being a very relaxed,
runabout sort of kid, to a terrified young boy.

Godfrey: Terrified of almost everything.

Ross: I wanted to ask about losses in your early life for you and your
parents, and you've already mentioned a critical one — the loss
of your sister. What impact do you think it had on their parenting? Did it make them very anxious and overprotective in their
parenting of you?

Godfrey: Actually, I feel it had the opposite effect because there were a
couple of instances where I have memories of almost neglectful
parenting.

Ross: Oh really?

Godfrey: I think unconsciously, so as not to become too emotionally
invested, given their experience of loss, they distanced themselves from me. I don't think any of it was conscious, but I was
almost neglectfully parented — it was so hands-off.

For example, I remember when I developed croup, and it was
horrendous. I would just cough and cough and cough for hours
and hours and hours. I just remember being alone in my room.
My mother didn't come to help. The only person I can
remember coming and visiting me regularly or the one who was
helping me was my sister. My older sister. She'd come in and

she'd try to help by distracting me, and she'd try and do things with me.

I do remember my mother reading me bedtime stories when I was young. That was a relationship highlight, but there were just hours as a child where I was just left on my own.

Ross: That's very interesting, Godfrey. Your parents lost a child and you think they unconsciously feared getting too close to anyone anymore because it can all be taken away.

Godfrey: Yeah.

Ross: Where there any other loses that were important in your early life?

Godfrey: Nothing springs to mind. No, throughout my life, until the death of my little sister as an adult, I've been untouched by death.

Ross: I see. I wanted to ask you about your parents and the extent to which they were worriers or anxious people. You've mentioned your mother clearly suffered from anxiety and mood-related problems. She didn't talk a lot about it, though.

Godfrey: Didn't talk at all about it. It would be 'mum's just 'having a turn''.

Ross: Right. In later years, would you say you were aware of the things she worried about?

Godfrey: Actually, interestingly enough, the strongest memories I have are less about her worrying about me, but my father — I'll get onto him shortly. But my mum's worries were generalised. They were mainly around being able to cope and being able to make a commitment and actually stick to it — being able to deal with life.

As to my father, I think he was more obsessional than he let anyone see. I remember sneaking into my father's study whenever he was out. It was like the forbidden realm. You weren't meant to be in there, but when I went in there, I remember even as a child, being fascinated that everything was taped down. He had a blotting mat on his desk — that was taped down. The paperclip tray, that was taped down, the telephone was taped down, the lamp was taped down. Everything had tape on it, as if you were living in an earthquake zone. Everything was taped and would not move, could not move.

Ross: Intriguing.

Godfrey: Everything was meticulously organised and compartmentalised.

Ross: Very obsessional.

Godfrey: In high gear! Things got a lot better when we moved again. Everyone was happier and calmer. We were in Sydney for four years and everyone hated it, and then we got transferred to Wollongong. That, for me … that was my golden period because I moved into an environment I loved. I had a group of friends, there was no anxiety, school was great, I was excelling at it, and there was no bullying. For me, it was just like complete freedom.

My mum still went into periods of time where she'd just retire into her room and wasn't around, wasn't available. Then she got pregnant again, so there are eight years between me and my next sibling. Now my next sibling was a high demand child, from the moment she was born. Incredibly anxious, incredibly insecure, and I remember watching, even as a child, the way both my parents parented her was as different from the parenting that I got and my older sibling got as you can possibly imagine. It was hands-on, it was fully engaged; it was addressing the insecurities, spending hours and hours and hours with this child, trying to help her become less insecure. It was recognising the need and doing a really good job of engaging with it. I cannot tell you the difference!

What I can't explain is what drove that process; what happened. Because it was then reproduced again six years later when my youngest sibling was born. She was even more intensively demanding than the previous sibling, but because mum was so practised now, she engaged. My father disengaged, and at 14, I stepped into the role of being a surrogate father to this high-needs child.

I remember we had a cot, and she would only go to sleep if you rocked the cot and rocked the cot and rocked the cot. You could then gradually decrease it. You could do that for two hours and you'd get down to a slow rock and then she might wake up! I did this as a 14-year-old, I did this for her, and you'd be about to stop, and she'd cry and wake! I'd just think I'm going to kill her [laughing]. But I always managed it, and I always was there for her in that role. My father just removed himself from all of us totally. It was my mum, my siblings and my friends during that period.

Ross: In your broader family, were there other with mental health issues? Clearly, your mother suffered and some of dad's behaviour's look anxiety-related.

Godfrey: Absolutely. Both of them, because my father, for the last 15 years, has had to deal with extreme anxiety and depression. He's just lost in it, completely lost in it. No one can reach him, and antidepressants, nothing has an impact on it. He's just slowly shutting down — he's just slowly shutting down.

My elder sibling and the sibling immediately after me have got no mental health problems whatsoever — no anxiety or depression. The last sibling was very anxious and depressed and eventually committed suicide. And in the extended family, I see similar patterns of behaviour in my grandparents — definitely anxiety and depression, and the same with some aunts.

Ross: So quite an extensive family history of mental health issues.

Godfrey: Absolutely.

Ross: I wanted to ask you about your earliest memories of your own anxiety, fear or worry. You've mentioned the period of coming to Sydney as a terrible period. Is that your earliest memory of anxiety — that period of your life?

Godfrey: Yeah.

Ross: Those fears included fears of various assaults from teachers or kids on the street. How did those early fears, of threat and harm from others, progress over time?

Godfrey: Well, the fears totally left me when we moved to Wollongong. It was extraordinary because it was so intense in Enfield, but when my environment shifted and it wasn't there anymore, I went back to my pre-Enfield self of just disappearing at dawn with the kids, and we'd do ridiculous things in terms of risk. I wasn't as extreme as some. I could see the consequences if you're swinging on a vine on a tree that you haven't tested, and there's a reasonable chance it's going to snap. So a couple of my friends nearly killed themselves and I didn't because I thought no, I'll wait for them to test out the vine before I go on. But that's just sensible.

There was nothing at all in those years, and there was nothing at all right up until my early 20s. I was engaged as an activist; I was regularly doing illegal things as part of being an activist, that got me arrested. I was involved in B.U.G.A.U.P. which was the billboard graffiti movement of the 70s against cigarette advertising, so we used to reface cigarette billboards all the time, and I remember — I probably was about 18 or 19 when I was doing this — I remember I was refacing a Winfield billboard with spray paint, and making it so funny. I remember I turned around and these two coppers just came up, and these were 'old school' police officers, so they just took us back to the police station and they just had fun with us. They were casually talking to us, and I remember one suddenly picked me up from the other side, and they just went racing with my head straight down toward the front of the cell. They would just stop you a centimetre in front of the cell. That was their fun. But I went through that sort of thing again and again and it didn't stop me. As soon as I got out, I was straight back to painting billboards again.

I did everything in those days. When I got involved in the campaign to save the Franklin River, flying all around Australia like 'it's Tuesday, we must be in Perth I guess'. It was that kind of frenetic political campaigning going on in the lead up to an election campaign and going down to the southwest wilderness of Tasmania, like totally normal. Probably more extreme adventure actually, I was becoming more towards the adventurous side of things.

But then I started getting irritable bowel syndrome, and that went on for a period of a couple of years. And then, out of nowhere, on October the 3rd, 1983, I had my first panic attack. From being in a peak of political campaigning, I went from my first panic attack to being housebound within six months. Couldn't take a step out of my house, in six months.

Ross: Extraordinary.

Godfrey: Then, for two years, I pretty much didn't put a foot out of the house.

Ross: The panic attacks start hitting you hard, you start restricting your movements for fear of having the panic attacks, then ago-raphobia kicks in and the whole thing deteriorates to the point where you're essentially housebound. Who were you living with at that time?

Godfrey: I had a partner, and so she was the only way I could sustain that lifestyle because she would go out and do the shopping and all that. But she had a whole bunch of her own issues. We were very co-dependent. She was physically sick, and I was emotionally sick. I looked after her physical needs and she looked after my emotional needs. It was a really destructive relationship.

Ross: What did you believe was happening Godfrey, when the panic attacks first started?

Godfrey: I thought I was going insane. I thought I was losing my mind, that this was the first step towards insanity. Because you've got to remember this is the early 80s, and so there's no internet, there's nothing, and mental health issues are just … like there's just mad people and there's sane people, and anyone who's stuck in their house is crazy. My whole being became centred around doing anything I possibly could to avoid the sensations of panic, and that just became circular. Every anxiety symptom I've had since then has been about avoiding panic. I associate panic with something, and if I do that thing, I'll have a panic attack, or if I do something to prevent it, I won't have it.

For example, even when I went into OCD, I didn't have any hygiene issues, it wasn't about that, it was about if I don't wash my hand 10 times and do the counting, I'm going to have a panic attack. It was totally circular.

Ross: Yes. All of the rituals got quite elaborate didn't they? There were foot movements; there were all sorts of behaviours.

Godfrey: Very elaborate.

Ross: They were all done to prevent panic because the experience of panic was so horrific.

Godfrey: So horrific. It was so extreme. The reaction to the sensation of panic, I couldn't tell you the number of panic attacks I've had in my life, but they have to be in the thousands. Literally. It's not like I would just have one panic attack for the day and that was it. There were nights where I would wake up, have a panic attack, control it, go to sleep, wake up with a panic attack, control it, go back to sleep, for days and days. Every single panic attack was like the very first panic attack. That's what's diabolical about it.

Ross: As the panics continued, you feared losing your mind. Certainly by the time you were housebound, you thought you were moving toward insanity. But what about that first panic? Do you recall what you believed was happening on that occasion?

Godfrey: Well, there's a very specific circumstance that day. I needed to get funding for a project associated with the activist campaign I was on, in order to sustain myself for the activist campaign, and also to provide the research that we needed to argue our case. I was right up against a deadline; I'd been working flat out on this project and this application. It became ridiculously important. It was like this is make or break. I had to lodge the application in North Sydney and I was in a hurry. I had about 20 minutes to get from Town Hall to North Sydney. I got on a train at the Town Hall Station, I felt terrible, the doors shut, and then bang. Panic. Absolute panic. I'm just gasping for air, and as soon as it stopped at Wynyard, the doors opened and I just threw myself off at the station.

Ross: You remember gasping for air … so in that first panic, it sounds like you feared not getting enough air. Is that what you were fearful of at the time, 'I'm not getting enough air, I'm not breathing'?

Godfrey: Yes, I think so. I haven't revisited this for so long. I'm trying to think about what I was actually thinking. I know I thought about having to get this application in. I have to get this application in. I don't recall thinking I was dying. I didn't think I've got to go to hospital, I'm dying. My thoughts were 'I've got to get back on the train, I've got to get on the next train. What was that panic about? What was that'?

Ross: I see. So you saw it more as some bizarre physical anomaly that had just happened?

Godfrey: Yes, out of nowhere.

Ross: And now 'I've got to continue' you thought.

Godfrey: Yes, I'm thinking 'I've got to continue'. I let a couple of trains go by, I calmed myself down, breathing stabilised, and I thought 'Am I right? Heart beat's normal now'. Then the train stopped, I got on the train, as soon as the doors shut, bang, it was on again. Now all I could think was, I'm at Wynyard, I've got to go all the way over the Harbour Bridge. Then the whole breathing thing and so on, but I managed to get the application in. I managed to keep going to North Sydney, got the application in, and then it was 'how do I get home? I've got no money; I can't get a cab'.

I can't remember how I got home. I don't remember whether I got back on the train. I think I did. Yes, I did. I managed to get myself back on the train, and the same thing happened all over again. Instant panic as soon as the doors closed, and so then I got off the train at Town Hall, and all I could remember thinking was I'm trapped. If the train stops, I'm trapped. When I got off the train, it was then how am I going to get home? Then my first thought was well a bus stops every few minutes, every couple of seconds it stops at a bus stop, so that's going to be all right, you can get on a bus.

Ross: A terrible day Godfrey. The panics were to continue, and as you say, agoraphobia developed and then obsessionality developed, and lots of rituals to prevent panic. Along the way, you also suffered in a completely different way didn't you — the existential issues? The issues around mortality, as I recall it, but tell me if I've got this timing right. It was in the period following your mother's death, in the 12 months or so following your mother's death, that you became very troubled by impermanence and wondering: What's life all about? And the fact that we all disappear and there is no essence of us left and so on. Tell me about all of that. When had that begun?

Godfrey: Well, actually, I remember that type of thinking going right back into childhood. I can remember having a confrontation with my father, probably around seven or eight years of age. We were meant to go off to this thing called Christian Endeavor, which is like a Sunday school in the afternoon of a weekend, which is a child's prime time. It was with these two hideous old crones, and it was all hellfire and brimstone. I remember thinking as a child that this is a fairy-tale. This is just nonsense, all this stuff, and I remember just thinking this is such a waste of my time and I could be going off and having fun. It was a complete rejection of the teachings.

Then came the Sunday where I was meant to be going to Christian Endeavor and I just said, 'I'm not going.' My father just blew his stack because if the son of the parish minister won't go to Christian Endeavor, then why should anybody else go? I just remember looking at him and thinking 'but it's all not true'. All this stuff about the afterlife is just nonsense. I remember thinking that even as a young child.

Ross: Wow.

Godfrey: Then it continued on into my teenage years, and that's partly what prompted my activism. I didn't feel there's any intrinsic meaning to anything. Therefore I'm going to make some meaning. I'm going to care about something. I threw myself into that, and it was very successful as a distraction from the existential dilemma. But it was always there. I remember writing school stories and so on, around these kind of themes.

Ross: Had you read, in those teenage years, any of the existentialists?

Godfrey: No, none.

Ross: It's extraordinary. You were thinking down a road that Sartre and Simone de Beauvoir were taking us at the time.

Godfrey: Never have read them, even today. I've never read any of the existentialists, but I just always had this belief, and it's strange because I was born into a house that although liberal in its theology and its orientation, was still focused on an afterlife. It never spoke to me, ever, once, whereas my siblings are all Christians, and they still buy into it. I don't know what my father thinks anymore because clearly his faith has done nothing for him whatsoever in the latter part of his life.

But I could just always remember thinking everything ends; there's no meaning to anything. When I was younger, I turned that into I'm going to construct me, and I've come full circle with that, and that's also now what I'm doing. But then for about a period close to 20 years, I was just immersed in utter despair about existence. I've got no fear whatsoever about death that I'm aware of, I've got a fear about dying. The process is frigging unpleasant, and why you can't just flick a switch and say, 'I'm out of here,' that's okay. The process of dying is frigging hideous and I'm not looking forward to that at all.

In fact, I've decided I'm not going to engage with it, so I am going to flick my switch when I need to. Because I've been into that space anyway, so that's quite a comfort in a way. It's not death itself — it's that death renders everything for a conscious entity, meaningless. Because anything you do, you're not going to know any of the benefits of that beyond your lifetime. The benefits from those things may go on, may not, but you derive no benefit from them whatsoever.

I remember thinking that people going on about Shakespeare and the fact that he never had one per cent knowledge of the genius that he was because all that followed him after his death. All that knowledge that he was this incredible anomaly that occurred 500 years ago, and is still, by far and away, the pinnacle, of literary genius, he can never know. He would have had a sense of 'I'm pretty good at what I do', but he would have no idea about how incredible he was because all that followed. Everything is like that. You may be an absolute genius, and you might get some recognition of that in your own time, but in essence, it's all rendered meaningless, and any action is, and therefore you may as well not care about anything.

Ross: That's very interesting Godfrey. You may not remember this, but many years ago, about seven years ago, you were talking to me about Shakespeare and you made another observation. You said to me that even if his writings remain, the essence of the man is gone, and you were talking at length about the idea that the essence of a person is soon gone, regardless of how significant they were. When I asked you what you meant, you said to me, 'Ross, what did Shakespeare and his wife argue about? What were their small moments about? We don't know any of it. We don't know.'

Godfrey: What did he say to her when he was having affairs with other people, and what was the quality of the connection of their relationship?

Ross: Yes, that bothered you a lot at the time. Who a person was, their essence — it goes anyway, and so it's irrelevant for the reasons you've already explained. Does that bother you now or not?

Godfrey: Yes, it does. It's just that I suppose I've had this relatively recent development, is that I've put all my eggs in the basket of hedonism. Most of my conscious thinking and planning goes into some hedonistic activity or another, or engagement with someone, and the immersion in the moment of pure pleasure. That takes up a lot of my time because I have a lot of hedonistic things I love to do. A lot of people who relate to me are much younger than me, they're girls in their 20s, and I just bounce off their energy and it just feeds me. I'm the older dude who gives them really good advice and acceptance and validation in a way. They've never got it from anyone before, so this thing cuts both ways.

Ross: Hedonism has become your solution.

Godfrey: What I'm saying is that I've used hedonism and it is now the treatment for my centre of gravity. My centre of gravity is always existential despair. That's my centre of gravity. If I don't consciously move myself away from it, that's where the ship keeps coming back to. What I believe is that the ultimate meaninglessness is that you think everything is meaningless! That's the most meaningless thing you can do — to believe everything's meaningless. There is nothing in that space. There is nothing of any value whatsoever to be got from that space or that belief system, but that's my centre of gravity, and I just pretty much put that down to a combination of things that happen to me and frigging chemicals in the day. I'm just serotonin deficient, and so my centre of gravity's going to go back there.

By effort of will, constantly CBT, constantly. I CBT almost everything in my life. It's to shift out of that space. Pleasure is a good motivator, it's a good trigger to do it, but life being the complex thing that it is, I'm starting to care about causes again. Because of the age of the girls that I'm engaging with, some of them are activists. One girl in particular, and we've become really close over the last 12 months, and she's 20, and she cares about everything. She cares about everything in the way I used to care about things. She really cares. She's vegan, and just every part of her life is like this.

You see, I'd tried to avoid the pain associated with caring, which is depression. When you care about the planet, the state that it's in, it's just horrendously depressing. Rather than dealing with the depression, I've just gone, 'Okay, I don't care'. I've shut down across the board, haven't been aware of it, I've just shut down across the board except for this tiny, narrow little community of people, and my two kids and my friends, I don't care about anything. But what this new young woman is showing me is that when you do that, you end up back in this place of meaninglessness. You've got to care. Even though it's going to be depressing, you have to care.

Ross: It's interesting Godfrey because caring was once your solution. The activism, for instance. Caring about the B.U.G.A.U.P. campaigns on smoking, caring about the Franklin-Gordon, saving that river system and surrounding wilderness. You cared a lot and achieved great things.

Godfrey: Yeah. We affected real change.

Ross: Absolutely.

Godfrey: Had real success.

Ross: Looking back on that period in your life where activism was your solution, do you not derive a tremendous amount of pleasure from the things you did and the contribution you made to the community, and on many lives beyond yourself?

Godfrey: There's a sense of it, but it's not particularly strong. When I look back on my life, my emotional experience seems to me, what's the word? I don't know, constrained or contained or something. I look back and I think okay, I'm now nearly 60, what are the things that are high points of a life? Childhood, things that I've mentioned, they're the high points. Then the activism, then the aspects of parenting and having young kids, but only aspects of it. I just feel something's missing all the time. Partly I've been circling around wondering whether I'm on the spectrum? Am I actually autistic in some respects, in that I don't seem to be able to derive the enjoyment that others can. The things that are negative, I get a disproportionate experience of, and the things that are positive, I get a small taste of. The hedonism — I won't bore you with the details — but there are aspects of my life that most men my age would just think unbelievable. Other guys would just kill to have a fraction of what I've had in my life.

Ross: It seems that you've been facing these existential issues from a very young age — you were thinking about the nature of existence as a child. And those topics are inherently disturbing and confronting and saddening, and you've sought solutions across your life. When you say, 'Maybe I'm on the spectrum,' I think a more transparent explanation is you've always been a thinker, and thinkers get so easily agitated. People that think about these themes, the nature of their existence, are troubled, and I guess the French existentialists were all about that weren't they? Each of them essentially said, 'My existence is absurd. I'm on a rock hurtling through space, with a thin atmosphere, in an unfair world with death and famine and cruelty, and I've got to create essence'. It's not easy being a thinker, Godfrey.

Godfrey: Absolutely. As soon as a sentient being comes into existence that is mortal, it's going to be fucked because it's the nature of sentience and the ego to want an open-ended existence. That's what its nature is. For some reason there's a group of us that think about all this, and it just gets worse and worse, whereas most people just enjoy it and think, 'hey, cruisy. I'm here, I'm aware, I'm going to have a pretty cool time.' But we don't do that. We look at all the objective circumstances, and one of the things that drives me insane is people saying 'everything happens for a reason'. It fucking doesn't. It doesn't happen for a reason. You look around the universe, random fucking shit happens all the time. The only thing, there is only one thing in the universe that is true, and that is change. That's the only thing that's true. Everything else comes and goes and everything else is just what you create to make it okay for yourself, that you're living in this state of total anarchic chaos, which even the physics is now suggesting came out of nothing like it's just BANG. It just happened. Well if bang, it just happened, then bang, it can just cease to happen.

That's how random and meaningless the whole thing is, and the only real thing is change. Then the thing is to embrace change, and this is so ironic in the context of what I'm going through at the moment, which is life's basically saying to me, 'You've been stuck in this cage you've put yourself in now for 10 years, it's going to change. Time's up.' I'm resisting that with everything that I can muster.

I've been trying to frame the way that I'm thinking about existence now, and I was thinking you've got the rectangle and then you've got this tiny little circle in the rectangle, and that's your comfort zone. You exist in that little circle. Then outside is where the magic happens, and it's change. I was thinking, yeah, that's all interesting — things happen outside your comfort zone. Then the other day, because I've been talking to a couple of girls who've got anxiety issues, I realised the buffer between the comfort zone and where the magic happens is the question 'what if?' That's the buffer — it's the big 'what ifs?' That's what stops people. The chaos of everything scares people.

But why is chaos so bad? Why is it necessarily a problem that everything changes, that there is no moral order to anything? When you look at animals — everything eats everything else. That's what happens. In terms of life, everything just feeds off everything else, often at its own expense. The first opportunity a species will get, it will over-consume and then deplete its resource and be wiped out. Then you have asteroids hitting the planet, wiping out all existence. There's been, I think now three occasions where 99.99 per cent of all living material on the Earth has been destroyed, and look at what we've got, this incredible biodiversity that comes out of that .01 per cent. Why isn't that enough? That's the issue that I'm now grappling with. Change is fascinating, change is dynamic, the whole universe is change, therefore I'm part of the universe, it's embedded in my DNA.

Ross: I see what you mean.

Godfrey: I'm going to die. Why is my existence and my insistence on trying to impose some kind of meaning such a preoccupation in that? Why can't I just accept that it changes? Enjoy that I've been in the fucking pinnacle of human existence, the safest country in that pinnacle of western existence, and I've set up this amazing life for myself, that other people, whenever I tell them about a part of it, only working three days a week, say 'Oh my man, you're living the dream.' 'What? You live in the Royal National Park near the water? Oh my god, you're living the dream. Oh my god, you've got two or three girlfriends who are all in their 20s and they're all really beautiful and they're all really intelligent? Oh man, you're living the dream.' But still, even given all of this, it's like I'm always just one millimetre away … away from …

Ross: The existential despair?

Godfrey: Yes … It's always my centre of gravity …

Ross: Can I ask you, Godfrey, in terms of reducing the fears and the despair, what is it in all the treatment that you've had that you think has been most useful?

Godfrey: CBT. For years I did every therapy under the sun. When I eventually got myself thinking I can't stay in this house, I've got to get out of this house, I've got to work with somebody, I started experimenting with psychological counselling. Because my whole orientation is alternative, I started all the alternative therapies, so I'd go and see this spiritual counsellor, and I did every permutation of every non-traditional psychological form that you could, and it was fascinating. The things I learned about myself and the piece that was flawed was absolutely brilliant, but it didn't make one ounce of difference to the anxiety or the depression. It changed every other aspect of my life for the better, but it didn't touch my anxiety and despair.

            Then I thought okay, that's all failed, so let's go conventional. Let's try this CBT thing. You know the story of that — that's when I started working with you. What I've found is I now apply it to everything, and there is almost no emotional state I can't manage the way out of. I manage anxiety and depression now, except grief. Grief seems to be in a whole quantum space of its own, emotionally. Fortunately, I've not really experienced it closely, but I've seen my son and my daughter, and I've seen what it's done to other people. I've been through periods where I've lost somebody in a relationship that was important to me, so love loss and grief is just in a realm of it's own. I tried CBT on grief and it didn't even touch it.

Ross: In CBT, has the C or the B been more important for you? The change in the way you're thinking, the attacking irrational thoughts, the trying to be an evidence-based thinker, so the cognitive side — or, the B part: I'm going to activate behaviours, seek pleasure, exercise, expose myself to my fears.

Godfrey: I'd say both. I'd say in equal measure. The awareness comes with the cognitive part though. I've got good at reframing things. I remember the first time I moved into a polyamorous relationship with a girl, and she introduced me to that world, and I'd never heard of such a thing, of non-traditional relationships, not being monogamous. I've had to deal with jealousy with that, and I remember applying the C part of CBT to that, and it worked like a charm, and it's worked ever since.

I remember one girl texted me at four o'clock in the morning, 'Oh my god, I just had the most amazing shag and I need to tell you about it.' First, it was just like 'oh no, somebody else was giving her this pleasure!' But then straight away I responded with 'she's just had amazing sex with this guy, and who does she want to text and tell about it?'

Ross: You were able to quickly reframe to situation.

Godfrey: Completely reframed it, engaged with her in it, and shifted the energy. So what I've learnt is I can do that with almost any emotional state. And then the B part of CBT — I've moved to a great location, live a balanced work-life, and sought out pleasure. But along the way, I gave up caring. Then this 20-year-old girl has just changed everything for me. She just cares without boundaries, and it was like, oh wow! Then I just realised, it just hit me like a freight train, that I'd put myself into this twilight zone of controlled emotional states, that I was confident I could control most of the anxiety, depression, and jealousy and all these other things with CBT, and not have emotional experiences. I realised that I'd painted myself into a corner. Now, the new cognitive strategy is to start caring and manage the depression associated with that.

Ross: It's coming full circle for you, Godfrey. It's going back to your earlier strategies when you were finding meaning in your existence as a younger man.

Godfrey: I'm aware I'm nearly 60. There is a deadline on how long I can get away with this shit, what I'm getting away with. It's only because I look so young, and then once they find out how old I am, it just becomes hilarious to them. It then becomes a thing of like, 'Oh my god, I'm with this incredibly old man'. But then they're like, 'That's so cool because you know all this shit, and you can help me with this'.

Ross: That makes sense. I want to turn to our last topic, which is death itself. What emotions arise in you at the thought of your own death?

Godfrey: Disappointment that I haven't found a better way of living. It's like the full stop. You've got this span to actually make some kind of peace with your existence, and I haven't done that. I haven't done that. I've got different strategies, but I'm not at peace with my existence. I can see me going right up to the finish line and never having really twigged or fully inhabited my own existence. That's the only problem I have with death — it's the finishing line.

It's also a motivator because it really is the finishing line. It's within sight now. I hope it wasn't and we can pretend it's not by who we're associating with, and living off that energy of 'anything's possible', and that's pretty much what I'm doing, but the finishing line's there. There is nothing beyond death. In my mind, there is absolutely nothing. If there is a soul then fine, but this ego, this thing that I identify with, this thing that I am absolutely 100% ceases to be at this point. There's no comfort associated with that.

Ross: I was going to ask you what do you think happens to you when you physically die and once you're physically dead? From that comment, I think I understand your view is you go to dust and that's it?

Godfrey: Yes.

Ross: Though you did mention a soul?

Godfrey: Yeah, I'm a little bit open-minded about the possibility that there are things we don't know. I don't hold out hope. Well … maybe it is hope. Maybe I'm not being totally honest. Yes, I do hold out a hope. I hold out a hope that there are things that we don't know. That there is something about life that is intrinsic. Despite all the evidence I seem to see in the universe, that there isn't, that everything's expendable and very temporary, and that it's all about diversity, in order for the diversity to exist, you've got to clear the decks. Logically, it doesn't make sense, but I hope that there is a sense that it's not all for nothing. That even if the ego dies, out of it, the experience of that life, something contributes towards something that might then re-emerge. Towards a higher degree of consciousness.

But then I take it through to its logical conclusion. Assuming that the whole point of existence and life and sentience is to go towards greater and greater complexity, the logical conclusion of that complexity and the increase in sentience is godhood. That's the logical conclusion of it — omnipresent, omnipotence. What's the only thing you can do of any interest as a god?

Ross: What would you say?

Godfrey: Cease to exist. Obliterate your consciousness. As a god, I think the only creative thing you can do is obliterate yourself completely because you've done everything. You've achieved everything. Everything's come to this place. There's nothing beyond knowing and doing and being everything, always, at all times, in all senses. The only thing is then to self-destruct, to see whether this would all happen again spontaneously.

Ross: How often do you think about those ideas, or about death itself? How often do you think about your passing?

Godfrey: Quite frequently. Yeah, quite frequently, and mainly as a deadline. I say to myself, 'What are you going to do when you grow up? You're nearly 60, what are you going to when you grow up?'

Ross: This deadline looming, of ageing and death, would you think about it daily? Would you think about it that often?

Godfrey: Yeah. Unless I'm really distracted. But even then I'm likely to come back to it very quickly because it'll be like, is this what I should be doing because the deadline is here?

Ross: I see. Then what relationship do you see between your thoughts about death and existence and your experience of life?

Godfrey: It's hand in glove.

Ross: You see death and your experience of living as having that close a relationship across your life?

Godfrey: Absolutely. It permeates everything. The neurosis of being a mortal sentient — it underpins everything, and it's ever-present.

Ross: It's coloured the choices you've made, the activities you engage in?

Godfrey: Absolutely.

Ross: You've mentioned the CBT paradigm for dealing with anxiety, depression and jealousy. But what have you found most helpful in assuaging your dread of impermanence? Is there any other tradition of thinking or any other philosophic position, or any other activity that has helped you assuage your dread of impermanence?

Godfrey: CBT has become a real foundation of how I approach life, but so has mindfulness. I think the Buddhist principle of mindfulness is the closest thing to hitting the nail on the head — to live a conscious life.

I've pursued hedonism to the most ridiculous extent, and what I've learnt with that is it's a drug, and the need for more is just getting ludicrous. Because it's not just hedonism, its sexual hedonism, it's purely sexual, and I'd built my whole life around it. Most of the activities I've been engaging in, one way or another, are setting up one sexual scenario or another. And what's needed to register on the radar now is ludicrous.

You could say that I was a basket case in my 20s, and I wasn't doing any of that. I've gone right back to it, but I've gone back to it with this awareness. But I'm starting to come full circle and realise that one age-old principle is true — even though it hadn't resonated with me for years — and that is about selflessness. It's making those connections, it's giving, it's turning your energy in those directions, but that means caring. When you start caring, then you're going to get disappointed and you're going to be let down. It opens the door to depression, so caring is a difficult space.

That's where I've come to — trying to pay attention to the age-old principles. Being mindful, doing unto others as you would have them do unto you, caring about other people more than you care about yourself because if you just go after ego-driven pursuits, you're destined to unhappiness. They're age-old truths of how humans have dealt with their neuroses.

Ross: That's very interesting Godfrey. My final question relates to meaning. You've touched on it across the interview with many of your answers, but what, if anything, makes your life meaningful?

Godfrey: Seeing what happens next. That covers a whole bunch of things, so one of the sub-parts of that is my relationship with these girls. It just gives me so much meaning. I make a clear difference to their lives. I've helped some who'd never even thought about going to university, now at university, getting high distinctions — helping girls who have been too terrified to leave home because their parents are so controlling and so on — watching them move out and making life work, to grow up. Those kinds of things.

But what happens next? I've started to care about them hugely, but they're young. They're experimenting with things. I'm not going to be this fixture in their life. I am going to be a stage. I am a transient part of their experimentation, and at some point, I'm just going to be made redundant. Then how am I going to deal with that fact? Everything is what happens next?

Ross, one of the things that changed my life was learning improvised theatre. You have to learn to work without a script, just as you do in life. You are simply working with material that's spontaneously generated between you and the other actors. The essence of improvised theatre is you never say 'No'. You always say, 'Yes … and'. You're in trouble if an actor says something to you and you think 'what the fuck do I do with that? That's just stupid'. You can't do that in improvised theatre. You don't say, 'No,' and block it; you have to, no matter what it is, no matter how outrageous and no matter how much you hate it, you have to say 'yes' to it. Not only do you have to say yes to it, but you've also got to build on it, and that's a cornerstone of how I now try to live. Say 'yes' and stay interested in 'what happens next'?

Ross: That's very interesting Godfrey. It's been a fascinating interview. Thank you very much for your time.

Chapter 8

The joker

'I'd love to be interviewed for your book' yelled Aidan, leaping from his chair. 'It'll make me immortal!' he said, chortling at his own wit. I smiled, somewhat uncomfortably, staring intently at the young man. In many ways, his reaction to the book discussion had summed up everything about Aidan. He was a man with an urgent need to survive, in any form at all, beyond the grave.

I first met Aidan when he was only 12 years of age — a thin and pale lad with a delicate frame heavily magnified by an anxious disposition. He looked like his bones could readily snap in two, like dry twigs broken easily underfoot. I imagined that he'd struggle in the jungle of junior high school, a boy destined to be brushed aside by bigger, bulkier youths with little respect for the weak and small. And this is how he presented himself — a weakling, stereotypical Woody Allen character sucking on an asthma inhaler.

Like Allen himself, Aidan used humour to connect to those around him. He was quick-witted and bright and had a self-deprecating style that was simultaneously admirable and irritating. He was a likeable boy, but only in small doses. He admitted that many friends were annoyed or frustrated because he didn't seem to know when a joke had been pushed too far. He was like a stand-up, vaudevillian comic who never got off stage.

Aidan had grown up with a range of factors contributing to his anxiety. His father had been an anxious man, worrying about his own health from a very young age. His mother had been overly protective of Aidan, having previously lost a baby at full-term. This type of loss can create particularly cautious mothering when the next child arrives, and Aidan was to be that child. Further, Aidan's younger brother would be born with a heart condition that required close monitoring across his development. The youngest sibling, Aidan's sister, also had significant health issues. Aidan, and all of his family members were well aware of the precariousness of life.

Finally, there was his Jewish heritage. From an early age, Aidan knew the details of the atrocities that had occurred to his people and the ongoing threats that his community lived with. The dangers, of course, were not just for Jewish people in Israel. Aidan attended a heavily guarded Jewish school in Sydney, Australia and was regularly exposed to 'lockdown training' — what to do and where to hide if an intruder managed to infiltrate the school grounds. It was in this atmosphere of personal, familial and community threat that Aidan would grow.

When I met him as a young boy, Aidan worried about many things. He was particularly concerned about the mental health of his family. He had a cousin who was suicidal, and he was continually affected by the fate of this girl. Could he go down the same path? Perhaps it was already happening? Was his mood deteriorating? Was he being slowly drawn to the cliff edges on his coastal walks with his father? Might he jump if he wasn't careful? Aidan would get lost in his thoughts and meander wherever his mind took him, dropping out of the present moment with alarming regularity. 'You are where your mind is Aidan' I told him many times, but he would barely hear me.

His fears of sudden suicidality were part of a bigger picture of fear of death. Suicide represented just one way in which he could prematurely die. He worried about heart attacks, strokes, cancer, embolisms, aneurisms and all manner of rare physical maladies. He was a regular at his local general practitioner and constantly sought reassurance from his mother about whether he looked sick. When in any doubt about his health, Aidan would refuse to go to school, and he became the master of a range of other safety and avoidance behaviours to protect himself. He would run at three-quarter pace on the soccer field rather than test the quality of his heart. He would avoid public transport, school camps, nights out with friends, plane travel, family holidays and anything that took him away from the safety and security of home. To make matters worse, he was generally noncompliant with the homework I set him. At the first sign of discomfort, Aidan would retreat from his exposure exercises, bunkering down at home.

Aidan turned to video games for distraction and would spend hours online rather than challenge or extend himself. In the safe world of gaming, Aidan could meet people without leaving his home and his isolation grew. Tragically, his addiction to games ate away much of his youth, continuing throughout senior high school and his undergraduate years at university. Aidan limped through his arts degree without distinction.

As the years grew, Aidan's fears crystallised around one central theme — not leaving a mark on the world. And, as a solution to this terror, he turned his attention to filmmaking. When he first told me that he was going to film school, I was encouraging but sceptical. By his own admission, Aidan had never really applied himself to anything, including therapy. And, more fundamentally, he'd never shown any real interest in film. He hadn't seen most of the major movies that I listed for him, and he agreed that no one who knew him would call him a film buff. He had made one short film in his undergraduate degree, but it was roughly put together with little attention to detail. Why would his attempt at film school prove different to his high school and university days?

However, right from the start, there was something different about this pursuit. Success in filmmaking, as unlikely as it seemed, would satisfy his need to leave his mark. He would create a product beyond the self — a permanent record of his time on the planet. Many social psychologists have argued that the desire to be remembered has driven creativity in man across millennia. Michelangelo lives on in the frescoes of the Sistine Chapel, a form of painting that is extremely difficult to master but offers the permanence of image since the watercolour is painted directly onto the wet plaster in the hours before it hardens. The technique, which does not allow for corrections and must be done under the time pressure of the drying wall, has attracted humans for thousands of years for one simple reason. It offers immortality. This is what motivated Aidan as he began his film studies.

Three months ago, Aidan sent me an online link to his first completed project at film school. I wasn't sure what to expect, but as I watched it, three times in quick succession, I was stunned. He had produced an extremely polished, professional and quite gripping short film that has now been recommended for international film festivals. With clear reference to himself, his film is about a young man in psychotherapy who is finally making progress.

Aidan looks stronger now. He is heavier, more muscular, and seems taller. He moves with greater confidence and wider stride. He is finally, both figuratively and literally, rising to the challenge of facing his fears. And for the first time in the 12 years that I have known him, he is winning. He is travelling, catching trains and ferries and driving the distances required to get to friends and small jobs on professional film projects. He has reduced his gaming and, for the most part, stopped checking the internet for reassurance about medical symptoms. He has dramatically reduced doctor visits.

Aidan is rapidly improving, but he has not fully recovered. He still has the capacity to get lost, listening to the threatening chatter of his mind. In the interview that follows, we see this at first hand as he grapples with the idea that he may be having a stroke as we speak. The irony of this, occurring during an interview to show his great progress, was not lost on either of us.

At the time of interview I had seen Aidan 112 times, over various periods of therapy, across 12 years.

Our interview with Aidan

Ross: Thank you very much for coming in. Could I begin by asking you about your family and life at home as you grew up?

Aidan: My family was always really close. Probably too close really, but always very nurturing and loving. People tell me that my dad was away a lot. He was always working up in the Hunter Valley or in some other place, and so mum was raising me mainly. Interestingly, all of my early memories were with both of them. I don't have any memories of just mum or just dad. I just have memories of both of them, unless those memories are implanted in the matrix [laughing]. But really, I had a really loving, nurturing, supportive family growing up.

Ross: Can you describe your relationship with your mother in those early years?

Aidan: She'd always been my closest companion or friend. She's always been there for me. It was particularly tough for her when I was in middle school, and I was having panic attacks every day, calling, crying to leave school, and she had to get to grips with the fact that she shouldn't pick me up, she should leave me there. That was difficult because she would always, whether good or bad for me, be willing to drop whatever, to come and help me. She is probably the most caring, loving mother I could have asked for, which is ironic, because it was most likely a hindrance to my recovery, having someone that was always there that was constantly within my reach.

Ross: Right. You see your mother's support, and always being present and always being willing to meet your needs, as maybe …

Aidan: It stopped me from fending for myself. It stopped me from getting over my fears. I've only realised that as I've gotten older. Ross, you told me once how men in the 1960s and 70s had to get over their panic and agoraphobia. They had to go to work to support a family. They didn't feel they had a choice. They would have panic attacks in the car or train, but because they had to go to work, they just did it. And so the frequency of agoraphobia in men was a lot lower than women. But my mum, by being so loving and supportive and always being there for me, stopped me fighting for myself. Of course, it's not her fault.

Ross: Tell me a bit more about your relationship with your father.

Aidan: Well, that guy's a shit head [laughing]. No, really, I love my dad. He is an interesting one because he's always struggled with anger. I'm pretty sure he's borderline autistic…and borderline everything really [laughing]. I tell this to him all the time; he is the nicest, most generous man. He thinks of everyone but himself, but he can sometimes get really angry, and I have to remind him that, 'Listen, you do things for everyone else, why are you so angry?' So often, he gets frustrated because I don't do enough, but he's the one that's unusual. I have memories of my dad when I was younger, growing up, he always worked hard and did everything he could for us. He's always been that kind of guy, and everything he's ever done, whether it's working far away like my mum says, constantly traveling overseas, he's doing for us. It's not easy for him — he has his own anxieties. He worries about his own heart, and he's been struggling with anxiety his entire life. He still struggles with it quite a bit. He's terrified of flying — he flies because he has to. He does the things he has to do when he needs to do it, and I have crazy respect for that because I know how hard it is for him, yet he goes and does it. That's something I have not yet learned how to do, just to put my feelings aside and do what has to be done because it has to be done.

Ross: Can I ask about any early losses in your life, and the impact these may have had on you?

Aidan: I've generally been very, very lucky in my life never to have had to experience the loss of a close family member, relative, loved one, or friend. I have no excuse to be as mentally messed up as I am because I've had just the easiest time so far. Everything's been given to me. But I lost my goldfish.

Ross: Your goldfish.

Aidan: My goldfish. I remember coming downstairs one day and seeing it floating in my old house, and I was like, 'Why is it floating?' Then we buried it, and I remember that was the first time I really, really cried about something.

Ross: How old were you?

Aidan: This is back at around age 10.

Ross: It's memorable to you?

Aidan: I remember, I definitely remember it. I remember we buried it in the backyard, in a plastic bag. I think five or six years later, I came back and I tried to find the plastic bag but it was gone. Then, I remember a couple more fish died, and dumb as I was, I believed my mum when she told me that a bigger fish just ate him. 'Where's the other fish?' 'Oh, this fish ate him.'

Aidan: For years, I was telling people that this fat fish over here ate my other fish. What an asshole. But in actual point, he just died and my mum …

Ross: Protected you from knowing about the natural death.

Aidan: Yeah, it's probably something I haven't told you, I didn't think it was relevant.

Ross: No. Aidan, it's very interesting to hear that, that at maybe 15 years of age you were digging around in the yard for the plastic bag with the fish.

Aidan: I wanted to see it again. I couldn't find it.

Ross: I see. Again, it says it was memorable; you were aware of it still at 15.

Aidan: Well, I remember it. The other loss was when my grandpa's sister died. I would have been about 10. It was the first time I cried when a family member died. I don't even know why I cried about it, I didn't even know her. I'd never met her before, and I remember going to her, the sister's grandchild's place, and it was a sombre kind of mood. I just remember going to the bathroom and crying, and I don't remember why.

I think it was just because … the idea of losing someone … I guess it's that idea of anyone can lose someone, probably the first time that idea became clear to me. Then, there were two other occasions, one where I cried, one where I didn't. One was after a cross-country race. I was running with a friend and we both did really well. Then I couldn't find him. When I did he seemed sad and I said, 'What's up?' He said, 'My grandpa's dead.' I remember going to prayers and I was really sad. I went to prayers for someone, which Jews do.

On and off, I started thinking more about death. I remember one night we were away and I was hugging my stuffed dog Spotty — I carried him everywhere. I started crying because I just thought, 'What would happen if my mum or my dad or my siblings died'. I didn't want to lose them, and I started crying.

Ross: Are you aware of any losses in your parents' lives? You've mentioned one relative, but perhaps even before you were born, are you aware of any traumas and losses in their lives that affected them.

Aidan: I mean, they have grandparents that died, but none that ever affected them too much. No, not really.

Ross: I see. I wanted to ask you about your parents and their anxieties. You've already covered it a little. Is there more you can tell me about that, the things your parents worry about?

Aidan: My mum told me many times, till this day, she was pretty much like me, bloody worried about every little feeling she'd get in her body, everything. She got panic attacks. She had panic attacks all through her 20s. So, she tells me she completely understands, and she says she was lucky to have my dad because whenever she'd panic, my dad would be there for her. So, she had really bad panic disorder, I think, when she was growing up.

    I asked her recently, 'Well, when did you stop worrying about your body?' She goes, 'The day you were born,' because — back to what you were saying before — she couldn't afford to worry about herself anymore. She had someone else. So, I feel like I should just knock some girl up and fix my issues [laughing].

Ross: So, was she implying that her anxiety transferred? She could no longer worry about herself, as she was worried about you? Or was she saying that her own problems with anxiety stopped?

Aidan: I think she blames herself for my anxiety because of how anxious she was when I was born because she'd had a miscarriage before.

Ross: I see. So, she was an anxious mum, an anxious first-time mum who had previously lost a pregnancy.

Aidan: Yes, and the baby was nearly at full term. She had to give birth to a dead baby — that's definitely been haunting her for years. She wouldn't let me see a photo of the baby until I was much, much older and she did some artwork about him recently. So yes, if I had to think about losses that have had a long-term impact on one of my parents, that's definitely been it for my mum. Maybe so for my dad, but he's not as open with his feelings as my mum is.

Ross: You said she blames herself for your anxiety. Is she saying that because of that loss she was so anxious when you came along, and you were so precious …

Aidan: That she transferred her worries to me.

Ross: I see. She'd had such a loss, and you were so precious that she didn't want to lose again?

Aidan: Yeah, yeah. I think so. She blamed herself. Then Adam was born, my brother with his heart condition, and he almost died. So, it's like she doesn't want to lose another kid. She does everything to protect us.

Ross: So, she worried about you as the firstborn, having lost a child, and then she worried about your brother because he had a heart condition. Were you aware, when you were growing up, of your brother's heart condition?

Aidan: Yes, indeed.

Ross: Do you think it had an impact on you?

Aidan: Probably. I don't know. I'm not going to say yes or no, but probably yes.

Ross: Do you remember people talking about it?

Aidan: I remember mum telling him he was a miracle baby. I remember seeing him in an incubator. I remember visiting him in hospital a few times and hating it. I hated hospitals, the puke and death — I hate hospitals still. I never like going into hospitals. It's ironic, I won't go anywhere that doesn't have a hospital nearby, but I won't ever go to the hospital.

Ross: Right.

Aidan: I like knowing that it's there, but I don't want to go there.

Ross: I understand. Tell me Aidan, is there any other history of mental health problems in your family?

Aidan: One cousin has tried to hurt herself a few times. That was a difficult confronting thing to hear. Another cousin is also depressed and anxious, and I've tried to help him through it. I'm pretty sure my brother's got severe anxiety. One grandpa and both grandmas have definitely been depressed. And my younger sister is anxious about some things. Mental illness definitely runs in the family tree.

Ross: Both anxiety and depression by the sound of it, and quite a big genetic dose through the family.

Aidan: Oh yeah. If I think about it like as a board game, I was dealt the money card, but then I was given the mental health card. It's like, 'Hey, you have all this money, but the downside is, you're not going to be happy.' So, mental health has definitely been a factor in my family. My whole life, my dad's been terrified that I'd turn into his father. His father's a gambler; he's always been terrified of me turning into a gambler. I must admit, I also love gambling. I think it's fun.

It's amazing how my brain works — I always believe in the tiny odds. It's the same with gambling and my fears. I'll go out gambling because I think, 'Oh, the tiny odds of me winning is enough — I'm going to win.' Then, in just the same way, I'm so terrified of dying from a disease that people only really get through saliva in kissing or whatever, and I don't do any of that shit. It's like, 'Oh, I'm going to get it.' My life's a big gamble. I always believe that the tiny odds are going to come through, which is funny because that's dumb. What a stupid way to live my life? I'd be so disappointed if I died before you, Ross, no offence. No offence to you. You know what I mean? Because ...

Ross: Because you haven't lived fully yet?

Aidan: Yes, because I haven't done anything yet. I mean, if you die today, Ross, you can rest peacefully in your grave knowing that you've done everything that you could have possibly done. What the fuck have I done? I haven't travelled. I haven't done anything noteworthy. If I die, I'm just another dead person that might be in the news for a day and then forgotten. You won't be forgotten. Your work will live on. I don't get that, but that's an omen to be talking about. What was the question again?

Ross: That's fine. You've covered the mental health problems of your family. I want to turn from family now and focus on you. Aidan, what are your earliest memories of your own anxiety, of being fearful, worried or afraid?

Aidan: I will never forget my first proper panic attack — I was on a trip. I flew into Melbourne and I got a bad ear infection. So, I couldn't fly home and I had to go on a camp the next day. So I had to catch an overnight train back home. Fuck! This is so vivid, this memory, it's crazy. I remember boarding a train. I even remember what movie we were watching — it was National Lampoon's Vacation with Chevy Chase. My dad had the top bunk, I had the bottom, and I just remember the train being so rickety and I remember getting off, and I was dizzy and feeling nauseous, but, I have to go on this camp. So, I went. On the camp, I was a bit vulnerable, I didn't really realise it, but on the camp, I was terrible. First, this kid behind me on the bus threw up! First straw broken.

Ross: He threw up near you?

Aidan: I was a bit further back. He just threw up in the bus. Then, we got to the camp, I was feeling very vulnerable, I didn't know what it was, and then I went to the bathroom and I don't know what it was, but I think there was just vomit on the floor of the bathroom, second straw broken. So, I really started to get anxious, didn't know what it was. Then, when we went to bed, I was lying in bed and I couldn't sleep, and I was trying to sleep, and I'll never fucking forget this, I still blame that piece of shit for what happened, this kid walked past the room saying, 'I feel sick. I feel like I'm going to throw up.' And when he said that, something clicked and I just had a panic attack — a full-blown panic attack.

Ross: Right.

Aidan: As he said that, that was the last straw. I freaked out.

Ross: How old were you?

Aidan: Fuck! This is Year 4, so around 9 years old? That's my first panic — I remember it vividly. But I was already fucked with anxiety before that.

Ross: This was obviously a very big scene and your first experience of full panic.

Aidan: This is huge for me.

Ross: But you think you already were anxious about things before this?

Aidan: I was anxious before, I didn't know what the feeling was. I had no idea. But it really went bad from that camp. When I got back home, I told my mom, and it was then I remember, I think I was depressed, I must have been depressed then, because every day, I just remember I was never happy. I was always feeling down. Something was wrong, definitely wrong.

Ross: Aidan in the camp scene you described, two people had already been sick. Do you remember if you were worried about getting sick?

Aidan: I probably was but …

Ross: You don't remember.

Aidan: I don't remember. I just remember worrying. I probably was worrying about getting sick.

Ross: The worrying about getting sick did become a prominent fear for you. You've worried about that on and off over many years.

Aidan: It's become my personality. I'm always that guy that's worried about getting sick. I've made self-deprecating jokes about it all the time and people get fed up with the jokes. One of my good friends said to me, 'Do you really want to identify as the guy that's got anxiety instead of identifying as Aidan?' I think he's got a point there. There was probably stuff beforehand, but this is the main trigger for me. My mum tells me there was stuff before, but I think I really just went downhill from there. I think that's when I started going to different psychologists and trying different medications, and that's when I actually stumbled upon you.

Ross: Aidan, your friend's comment about you and your jokes about getting sick is interesting. What do the jokes do for you? Do you think it's your way of dealing with it? Do you think it's the way in which you …?

Aidan: I don't know, I've never thought about it. I just make them. I find them funny. There probably is some deep-rooted self-deprecation, 'I joke about it, so it's okay' kind of thing. I joke about it all the time. I've always made self-deprecating humour. I don't know if it's been a way to ... I don't know ...

Ross: Communicate it to your friends maybe, in a safe way? Communicate how you're feeling?

Aidan: I've always been good at communicating my feelings to my friends, so I don't think that's it. I've always been very good at communicating my feelings. I don't know. I think it's because I like to make people laugh, and I know that making fun of myself is funny. There's probably a variety of reasons.

Ross: Indeed. You've worried about getting ill, and that has stayed with you — almost, as you said, become part of who you are. You've worried about illness a lot. At first, it was about getting sick or throwing up. Can you tell me the range of illnesses you've worried about getting?

Aidan: Well first, it was all vomiting. I think the reason why I hated vomiting is because when you vomit, you can't breathe. So, there was always this thought in the back of my mind that when I threw up, what if I didn't stop throwing up and I couldn't breathe? Fuck! That's a revelation.

Ross: I see.

Aidan: Yes, I think the reason why I didn't like vomiting is because when I did it, I couldn't breathe, so it was like I was choking. Choking definitely is a big one. All these things at the back of my throat. I'm always worrying about blood happening and me choking on my own blood, which is funny because I'm worried about choking on my own blood, but I'm not worried about choking on food. I'm very worried about vomiting blood not just because of choking, but because of what it would mean. Some sickness - something that could kill me. It all started to become illnesses or medical incidents that could kill me.

Ross: Like stroke.

Aidan: Stroke, yeah ... Do you know, I'm actually having thoughts about that during this interview! It's crazy. I'm fucking scratching my head at the moment because there was a pimple on my head and my arm's feeling a bit tingly. I'm lucky that my brain only worries about one illness at a time. I don't understand why, but when I'm worried about meningococcal, I'm not worried about my heart. When I'm worried about my heart, I'm not worried about meningococcal, when I'm worried about my stroke, I'm not worried about my heart. They interchange, but they're never at the same time.

Ross: Aidan when you came in today, before we started this interview, you mentioned that you had been having a difficult time of it in this very recent period, because you'd come across somebody dying of meningococcal, and you were very thrown by the suddenness of it all. Can you explain that?

Aidan: Yes, the girl just had a headache, and then, hours later, she was dead! The idea of just dying, just something so quick, I think has always been what scared me.

Ross: And so you're worried about stroke, and heart attack.

Aidan: It's a stroke, heart, meningococcal, anything …

Ross: With meningococcal, where did you see this report on the girl who died?

Aidan: I was just taking a shit. I was on my phone taking a shit. I was about to go to the gym, because I felt like I've been feeling a bit anxious recently, because I haven't been going to gym because I've been worried about my heart and stopped going to gym. Taking a shit before going to gym, and I scroll on my phone, and I see a healthy girl died of meningococcal.

Ross: When was this?

Aidan: A week and a half ago. I've started reading into how it happened. The girl had gone on a ski trip with her friends, she came back, she felt unwell, she had a bad headache, she went to the hospital, they gave her Nurofen, and they sent her back home. Then, by the time she realised something was wrong she'd already had bleeding on the brain, her kidneys had failed, and she died. Then, I looked up, how do you get meningococcal?

Ross: You googled this?

Aidan: I decided to do the dumb thing [laughing]. Why I did it, I don't know. I guess I googled it to put my mind at ease. But as often happens, it made it worse. I know you've told me again and again that I have to stop reassurance-seeking, and I've been doing much better at it over recent months. But this time I gave in. I googled it. I found quite a lot of doctors saying, 'I've seen patients healthy in the morning and dead at night.' Then after reading that, I had to go down more, I started thinking 'what are the symptoms?' The symptoms are a stiff neck. Well shit, my neck's a bit stiff recently, because I've been probably playing video games when lying down. My neck's been stiff recently.

I had this worry about meningitis before because I had a rash on my arm. Basically, a meningococcal or meningitis rash is like blood spots that appear when you press on your arm, but they don't go away. There's a whole lot of that, and I had that on my arm once. We actually called a doctor to come to my house a few years back, because I was so terrified of it. Then, I had it again a few weeks ago. So, it was lingering at the back of my head. So, this made the whole situation worse.

I was looking it up, and it said, the rashes, sometimes you don't even get it, and when you do get it, it's only a sign that it's too late. But a high fever, sudden onset high fever, vomiting, neck stiffness, joint pain, joint stiffness, and it's like, they're just such broad terms. I've had joint stiffness and neck stiffness while feeling nauseous at the same time before. So, it's like it said, if you have any of these, rush to hospital.

That's what's so scary. These are such broad terms of things that people can get. So, if I feel a bit nauseous, maybe I get a temperature, and my neck starts feeling stiff, I'm going to fucking run to the hospital because it's like, 'Well, shit! Better check this out.' Then, I read more things. I saw this meningococcal testimony site online, and it told me stories of this guy, he went on this trip with his wife, he was feeling fine, and he started feeling a bit sick. He thought it was food poisoning, and then it just got worse. By the time they got to the hospital, which is 10 minutes away from where he was, he was already throwing up blood and dead within the hour. Holy shit! Holy fucking shit!

So now, I get my neck feeling a bit stiff, or I start feeling nauseous, I'm always checking my temperature, and I'm thinking, 'Well, if I have that, I'm going to fucking die in an hour.' I almost threw up the other day, I was feeling nauseous, and I almost threw up, and I think I'd have the thought, if I threw up, I would have fucking had to go to the hospital, because what if I started throwing up blood. It's terrifying to me. It's absolutely terrifying to me.

Ross: As you said Aidan, you know after the treatment you've had, that reassurance-seeking on the web is a very bad idea.

Aidan: Still did it.

Ross: Yes, you went down the rabbit hole of reassurance-seeking again. Is that because tolerating the anxiety just felt too tough this time? It just proved too hard for you to live with the doubt?

Aidan: It's my gambling brain that goes, 'Well, most likely it will make me more nervous, but there's a slight chance that it might put me at ease.'

Ross: I see.

Aidan: That slight chance of putting me at ease can still sometimes outweigh the opportunity cost — it's greater than living with the fear of having it.

Ross: I see.

Aidan: I've always said to myself, I might try to live in blissful dumb igno-rance rather than know everything about these illnesses. I've had a conversation with someone, we had a philosophical conversation, and I said, 'I'm going to try to be happy and dumb, rather than unhappy and smart'.

Ross: Yet you keep searching.

Aidan: Yet I keep fucking searching. Not always. These days I rarely search, but I still give in sometimes.

Ross: So, you've feared a lot of illnesses, but also other things. What other things have you feared?

Aidan: I watched *The Truman Show*, boy did that fuck me up for a few years. If you're reading this or listening to it, don't watch *The Truman Show*! It will fuck you up. For years, I was worried after seeing the movie that I was living that same life. I don't know if it's just OCD or narcissism or a mixture of both, but it was everywhere. Part of me has always known that this is bat-shit farm crazy.

I even thought my dog was a camera for the show. Once I had a stud-finder, nail detector thing, and I put it to my dog's neck and to my dog's face, and it beeped.

Ross: So, you believed there were studs supporting a camera inside the dog?

Aidan: Or that the dog was a camera itself. I eventually just put the stud finder down, thinking that maybe it was interfering with the chip in the dog's neck but, either way, that bothered me for years.

Ross: So you had the thought that the dog might be a camera and decided to check it out with a stud finder?

Aidan: No, it was accidental.

Ross: You accidentally put a stud finder on the fur of your dog?

Aidan: I was holding the stud finder in my hand, and I was just doing it around the room.

Ross: Right.

Aidan: [Laughing] You got me. I probably did it on purpose to check it out.

Ross: Can I ask whether there have been happenings in your life that have made your fears more intense? You've mentioned your brother, for example, and his heart problems, you've mentioned the origin of the vomit fears, that was happening. Have there been other things that you think contribute or have intensified your fears?

Aidan: Can you repeat? I was worrying about the fact that not only my right eye twitches, now my left eye's twitching, both eyes.

Ross: Right, you were worrying that your eyes were twitching, which took your attention away from the question.

Aidan: A lot of the times when you speak, less now, but much more when I was younger, I think the first half of the sessions I ever spent with you, I don't remember shit because I was just thinking about myself and you were just talking to an empty wall.

Ross: Well, that's good for me to know [laughing].

Aidan: Sorry about that.

Ross: No need to apologise. I was asking, have there been other things in your life that have made your fears more intense? For example, we know your brother's heart condition probably made more of your fears intense.

Aidan: My Jewish background probably intensified my fears somewhat. It's always been drilled into us that people are attacking Israel. Jewish schools are heavily guarded, even in Australia. I went to Israel once, and as we went there, the Gaza War started. So, that was fun. We were meant to go to the city by the border of Gaza, but there were rockets flying over, so you couldn't go.

Probably, definitely, hearing about all these atrocities that happened to Jews, hearing about all that. Maybe as a little kid who obviously had some anxious tendencies to hear all these things that happened to Jews and identifying as a Jew and knowing all of that — I think it did have some impact.

Ross: At your school, you did have regular drills on what to do if there was an attack on the school?

Aidan: I do remember being terrified when there were lockdown drills. I remember all those. I'd always get terrified. It ended up getting to a stage where I would actually ask the principal, 'Can you just tell me the drill is coming because if I'm in class and the drill goes off, I'm going to have a panic attack'. I remember one day we had a little prayer group in the morning, and the lockdown drill happened. We had to close the blinds and be quiet. So, we closed the blinds, but they only closed up to ankle height. Through the intercom a voice was saying, 'This is a lockdown, this is a lockdown.' They didn't say it's a drill. So I'm like, 'Oh God! What's happening?'

Then, I saw these feet walking by outside, outside the room. I just freaked out! I thought it was really unfair. I'm still pissed off with the school for doing that although I understand why they did it.

Ross: Your school was very security-focused.

Aidan: Yes. They've even upped the gate security now, but I always knew that going to school was a target. Thank God I didn't go to school in the US. Could you imagine? I wouldn't go to school. I would refuse to go to school because of all the gun shit happening in the US. I just wouldn't go. That's actually the one thing, not the one thing, but one of the things that makes me not want to go to LA and pursue directing, because I don't trust America. I really don't.

But yeah, I remember that lockdown drills terrified me. You talked about restricted egress with me many times. It's very relevant to my fear in lockdown drills because you couldn't leave. You were locked down. You were stuck. The idea, what if I need to go to the bathroom, I need to go outside and get some air, I can't because I'm fucking stuck in this room. That's what scared me most, the fact that I couldn't move. We're locked down. We're stuck in this room for hours, I hated it.

Ross: So, the lockdown drills and the security …

Aidan: Didn't make me feel safe; they made me feel less safe.

Ross: They made you feel less safe. You said you grew up knowing the history of your people, and knowing and being taught from an early age about the atrocities that had happened.

Aidan: Oh yeah. When we went to Israel, we went to Yad Vashem just for the Holocaust memorial. We have the Holocaust drilled into us. Never really cared or thought much of it when I went to Yad Vashem. My dad told me when he went there, he cried the first time, and it bothered him. So, I was ready for more when I was walking in. I walked in. I was so desensitized to all of it, mainly because I play a lot of violent video games. I'm sure that has something to do with this, but also because it just didn't bother me that much.

If I went there now, probably it'd have much more of an impact on me. But maybe it did have some psychological impact, learning about the Holocaust and all this shit. I just realised, maybe going to a public school would be better.

Ross: Well, that's an interesting idea. Can I ask how you first came to treatment?

Aidan: I think I went to a few different people. Mum brought me to a whole bunch of different places.

Ross: At quite a young age.

Aidan: Quite, I've been going to therapy for a long time.

Ross: Perhaps soon after the vomit experience at camp?

Aidan: Very soon, very soon. I think it was a couple of weeks after the vomit experience. I remember having a chat with my mum and telling her, 'I just don't feel happy, I just don't feel right.' Then she's like, 'Okay, something's off here.' The fact that I was even at that age articulating those feelings, I think is pretty impressive in itself.

Ross: I agree. Can I ask, either within or beyond treatment, what do you think has been most helpful in lightening your fears? We've heard about the things that might have intensified fear, but what has most helped reduce your fears?

Aidan: To be completely honest with you, time. Time. I'd like to say that it's going to Ross Menzies, listening to him that has helped me most. The truth is I've been very, very slack and really not even tried to do the CBT homework to get better until very, very recently.

Ross: Do you mean time to mature to do the CBT work needed to recover, or do you mean time itself is a healer?

Aidan: Both. Time is a healer, definitely. Time has beaten some fears. Time has shown me that I'm not actually going to kill myself — what a dumb thought that was. I was so worried about killing myself. I didn't want to die, and I was worried about killing myself because I get these aggressive obsessions. Thinking back on it now, what a dumb thought.

Ross: You haven't mentioned those obsessions, but you had them from the first time I met you at 12 years of age. On the one hand, you were terrified of getting ill, 'I'm going to catch something, I'm going to die' and on the other hand …

Aidan: On the other hand, 'I'm going to kill myself'.

Ross: Yes. 'If I don't get sick and catch something and die, maybe I'll get sad because I'm so anxious, and end up killing myself'. As I taught you early on, your fear surrounded death, one way or another. You were terrified you would take your own life or that something would externally take it. So, time you're saying, has shown you that it isn't true, that living a decade and more …

Aidan: Living a decade or more in fear has done nothing but hinder me. The bad things I've feared, and I've feared so many, have never come true. You often asked me to think about all of those predictions that never came true — to write them all out and reflect on that. I know you wanted me to change the way I listened to my mind. But I'm a gambling man, and I'd think, 'What if it's right this time?' And I still struggle with that sometimes.

Ross: I asked you before, do you think that time has let you mature to now finally face the work that has to be done?

Aidan: When I was young, I had an excuse. My excuse growing up was 'I'm still a kid, I'm still a kid'. As you so rightfully put it last year, 'You're not a kid anymore, Aidan. You're an adult now. You're 23 next week. Time to step up.' It was at that point that I realised, 'Okay, I can't keep hoping that something's going to magically happen. I need to take charge of myself.' So, time to mature and realise that this isn't going to fix itself. It's easier because anything's easier when you live with it for a long time, you just get used to the pain.

I'm now getting to the age where I don't want to leave this world and have done nothing. One of my first cousins still lives at home, got bad anxiety. I know it's a very Jewish thing to live at home until you're much older, but I don't want to. It's more time to change.

Ross: In this last period, particularly in the last six months or so, you've been far more active in doing exposure-based work, confronting your fears, getting on public transport, going out with friends.

Aidan: Totally. I've been much more active. While I still don't do it enough, it's a fact that a few weeks ago, I was able to catch a train by myself to the city, hang out with my friends, even though I was feeling anxious and faint and lightheaded, and I stayed with them and then hung out with them, caught a train back and then instead of going home, I went back to my mate's house, and we hung out till three o'clock in the morning. That was fantastic.

Ross: So, you can see yourself improving as you confront your fears?

Aidan: Yes. And I don't want to admit this, because I hate admitting it, because I fucking love them so much, but stopping playing video games was helpful too. I was hiding behind the gaming — the video games were stopping me from facing my fears. I justified to myself — I don't want to go out because it's fun to play video games. It's more fun playing video games than going out. In actual fact, playing video games just didn't make me anxious — going out makes me anxious. So I stopped playing video games, and I started forcing myself to go out more, doing more things.

Ross: So the video games had become almost a replacement for the stuffed dog you used to carry around everywhere. They were your comfort, a security blanket almost. It gave you a reason to be home, and you felt very secure and safe with them.

Aidan: They also stopped me from worrying about myself. So, when I'm playing video games, I don't worry about anxiety. I've recently — which is not good — gotten back into video games occasionally because they numb my brain. I know when I'm playing this game, I'm no longer worried about having meningitis. It's a drug. I don't take Xanax anymore, but I do take Valium very occasionally. I have the same box, like it can last me for a year. I don't take it all the fucking time. I don't take it all the time, but I do take it. I try not to take it, I try to stew and live with it. But when I'm having a very bad day, which I still sometimes do, it's take Valium or play video games or both. What was the question? I started ranting.

Ross: No, that's fine. I was asking about things that have lightened your fears, and you've said time, a willingness to confront the fears, and being sick of getting to this age and not fully living. So, you've thrown yourself at your life and you've seen it improve.

I'm going to move to our last set of questions, Aidan — on the topic of death. We've talked about it indirectly along the way, but can I ask, what emotions arise in you at the thought of your own death?

Aidan: What's funny, it's probably very subconscious, but right now I'm freaking out because I had like a tic or twitch on my right eye. I'm getting it in both of my eyes, and I really want to blink both of my eyes, and I think it's because I'm talking about all this stuff — it's probably subconscious. I've had some thoughts that I'm having a stroke, and I'm a bit scared right now. Well, what's the question?

Ross: Thoughts of your own death, what emotions arise in you at the thought of your own death?

Aidan: Regret. Done nothing. I've fucked around for so long doing nothing. If I die now, I wouldn't have had a chance to make up for that.

Ross: I see. In this question Aidan, I don't necessarily mean if you die right now. I just mean, the concept of your own death, it could be later in life. I just want to know how you feel about the idea of your own future death.

Aidan: I don't like the idea of nothingness. I wish I believed in God and the afterlife, and I don't know. I spoke to this guy who tried to fucking convert me to Christianity. I was having a philosophical conversation with him about life, the guy I told you about earlier when I said 'I'd rather be dumb and happy'. He said, 'I'd rather know the truth.' Then he tried to convert me Christianity, and he goes, 'if Christianity isn't real, then it doesn't matter. But if it is real, it's the most important thing ever. Because, if you don't believe and strive to be like Jesus, you go to hell.' That made me think, 'Oh shit! Maybe I should start believing in Jesus, because, can I be a Jew and still …?' Apparently, it's not about believing in Jesus, it's about realising that you'll never be as good as that man, and striving to be like him.

So, I can be a Jew and be like that. But instead of thinking of Jesus as some mythical creature, just think of him as some guy that I want to strive to be like. I'm having these thoughts in my head, all because I don't want to die. If I die, and there is an afterlife, well, fuck me, right?

Ross: So what do you think will happen to you as you physically die, and once you're physically dead?

179

Aidan: I don't know, and that's terrifying. It's like an uncertainty, and I don't know what's worse, the uncertainty of not knowing, or knowing that nothing happens. I feel like coming to grips with the fact that if you die, nothing happens, can be freeing for some people, as you told me once. But at the same time, you can say that because you've done what you needed to do.

Ross: You've mentioned this a few times. Clearly, it's an important part of your fear — living a life where you don't feel you've achieved what you want, and suddenly it prematurely ends. That's clearly an important issue for you.

Aidan: It is very important. I don't know why.

Ross: How often do you think about death? How often do you think about the possibility?

Aidan: Every day.

Ross: Even in this interview, you've made it clear that you've been thinking about physical symptoms and death while we've been speaking.

Aidan: Many times. I know I'm basically asking for reassurance, and you probably won't respond, but did you notice that I blinked like a million times just then?

Ross: So it really can come quickly upon you, thoughts of death, and then grip you. You think about death many times a day on most days of your life.

Aidan: Yes, but they don't always grip me. Sometimes, and I'm getting better at this, I don't care about my thoughts. By the way, I notice you didn't reassure me [laughing].

Ross: Indeed [laughing]. To an extent, you've covered this next question already, but what relationship do you see between your fears of death and your experience of everyday life? How dominant or how important have your fears of death been, do you think, in your everyday life?

Aidan: It's interesting because my worry about not doing anything or being remembered is always on top. But my death fears have stopped me achieving. They've stopped me from travelling. They make lots of places scary. I don't want to go to hospital even though I need to be around one.

Ross: It's influenced you going out.

Aidan: It's influenced me going out if I'm feeling a little bit off. Even if I'm not feeling sick, I was feeling fine this weekend, and I went out with my mates. I knew I was feeling a bit anxious and I'm like, 'I have to go out with my mates.' So, we drove and we went out, and I was feeling a bit lightheaded. I was getting really worried about being so lightheaded, and I couldn't sit down and enjoy the dinner with my friends.

Ross: So, it affects your daily enjoyment, but it's also restricted terribly what you've done in your life, where you've gone in your life, what you've seen in your life.

Aidan: Totally. I'm such a lucky, privileged piece of shit that if I went to my dad tomorrow and said, 'Dad, I want to travel the world,' he'd book me a flight in an instant. That pisses me off even more, the fact that I know I can do anything, and I choose not to because I'm worried about it. That upsets me more than anything in the world. When I have all these options, everything, and I fucking choose not to do them, for one reason or another. I could go travel the world, see everything, do all these beautiful things, but I wouldn't enjoy it. It upsets me. It really upsets me.

Ross: This might be hard to answer because your dread of death is still very large in your life, but I wanted to ask, within therapy, or outside of it, what have you found most comforting in assuaging any dread of death, in reducing any dread of death? What have you found most helps you with fear of death?

Aidan: Exercise helps. I don't know why or what it is, but there's a brief period of the exercising where I'm actually not worried about it. When I'm playing video games, it's also reduced.

Ross: So, distraction? Exercise helps, distraction helps, and video games.

Aidan: Whether it's good distraction or bad distraction, distraction helps. Seeing you, for some reason, this office is like an aura of comfort. The second I leave it, the aura trails with me for a few days or even weeks, where I'm not worried about it. I remember I was having a huge panic attack about death, and you said some things that made me feel so good, I went to the casino, I'm like, 'I feel amazing.' Then I went home, and I'm like, 'I feel amazing.' Then ten days later, 'I think I'm dying.'

Doing things that will slowly get me towards the goal of, in my head, being remembered, I guess. When I make my film, when I'm working on my film, I'm still worried about dying, but I'm like, 'I'm always there, I'm closer to not having any regrets.'

Ross: That's so interesting, and it relates to the last question, about meaning and where do you find meaning. What, if anything, makes life meaningful for you or is giving you meaning and purpose?

Aidan: Filmmaking, yes, it gives life meaning. I wish I believed in God, and I had religion because then, that would be my meaning, that would be my purpose. I know the hard part of life is making a purpose.

The purpose at the moment is to make a feature film, make a movie, make a good movie. My dad's like, 'What are you going to do for money?' I have no idea. I'm not thinking that far ahead. I'm just thinking, I just want, I don't know. I just want to do something.

Ross: So leaning toward that goal gives you meaning and purpose.

Aidan: A goal and a purpose. I'm making a short film at the moment, about mental illness and a lot of the things the character says are based on me. He goes, 'I want to wake up in the morning and have a purpose, other than to go back to bed.' That is me one hundred per cent. I wrote that thinking of me, because a lot of times, that's what I do, I wake up, and it's like, 'Well, I just want to go back to bed because I'm worried and I don't want to be worried. When I'm sleeping, I'm not worried, so, why would I just not want to sleep?'

Ross: As you start film making, and you're making this product at the moment, and you've made the short films, and you're striving towards making a feature film, is it taking away the dread of death?

Aidan: Not yet sadly. Whenever I go on set to film, I need to take Valium in the morning because I know that I may panic. I know I should-n't. I know it's a safety behaviour. But I worry about panicking on set. I'm just worried if I feel a little lightheaded. I had a panic attack on set once because I felt dizzy. Ever since then, every time on set, I feel dizzy, every time I feel dizzy and lightheaded, that worries me like crazy. I don't know what it is. I don't know what it is. I enjoy being busy, having something on my mind to think about, other than anxiety. The past week, I've been so focused on my film. When I'm worried about my film, I'm not worried about myself.

But then, when I'm worried about the film, I'm still worried. Then when I stop worrying about the film, I worry about the threat of death. So, I just need to keep my mind occupied, get other things to worry about other than this whole dying thing. But at the moment, the film doesn't make my dread of death really go away. I really hope that one day I can just not feel afraid, not … Fuck! I accidentally just quoted one of my lines on the film [laughter].

Ross: It's a very nice place to finish Aidan. It is interesting to hear that while you get meaning and purpose from making the films, it's not making the dread of death go away at this stage. I'm reminded perhaps in finishing, of a wonderful quote from Woody Allen, who famously said, 'I don't want to achieve immortality through my work. I want to achieve it through not dying'.

Aidan: It's a great quote.

Ross: And a nice way to finish the interview. Thank you very much.

Chapter 9

The architect

W hen I first met Bruce, he was closing his business. He'd been an architect his entire working life, and it was finally time to shut down the office. He had 15 staff and was feeling the pain of walking away. He was a reflective man, one of the gentlest souls I've met in 30 years of psychotherapy. It was always a pleasure to talk to Bruce. A good man, a solid man — someone who could genuinely be referred to as the salt of the earth. He had provided for a family, now well grown and living independently. He had a lot to be proud of.

But below his warm, gentle patina was a sadness — a deep blackness that he couldn't shake. From our first meeting, he talked about feelings of loss. He was losing his business, his father had died, and his life was constantly changing now. Things were passing him by. 'Why haven't I achieved more?' he asked. 'If there was a report card on my life it would read 'done okay, could've done more" he told me sadly in an early meeting.

While he longed to have been more successful in his professional life, he also saw it as futile and pointless. I wondered, often between sessions, why Bruce hadn't recognised his triumphs as an architect. He had built fine buildings, and not just houses that come and go, knocked down by a younger generation with fresh ideas, but public spaces that continued to be used. Why hadn't these achievements resonated with him? 'Ross,' he told me, 'when you design a building and walk away, it's no longer yours. The inhabitants change it. They occupy it. It's their space. I never feel a lasting link to the buildings I create. They're never really mine.'

Bruce was in the middle of a significant depressive episode. His mood was low, and there were feelings of futility and pointlessness, an absence of meaning and purpose. Our sessions continued for over six months, and slowly his mood improved. He came to think about the human condition in somewhat different ways. He could recognise the contributions that he'd made to the lives of his family, to the community through the spaces that he'd designed. He came to experience mild satisfaction (or, at the very least, not despair) about his impact on others. Over a period of four months, his mood scores improved on standard tests of depression. He was exercising more, attending Pilates classes and looking for activities to give him pleasure. He became a fan of epicurean delights and got better at finding small pleasant activities that he felt enhanced him. Bruce was on the mend.

This is not to say that his journey over these months was an easy one. Along the way, events had occurred that had thrown him back into a dark abyss. His attendance at his school reunion, 50 years after leaving, had been particularly confronting. Everyone around him was old, and he realised, perhaps for the first time, that he was old as well. But he worked hard on his existential issues. He had always been a reader, and he was eager to consume any book I suggested. He demolished volumes by Yalom, the Stoics, Epicureans and other philosophers, and became more interested in such diverse topics as history, physics, mathematics and exploring the nature of existence. By the time our first set of sessions was complete, a year had passed and his mood had normalised. His depression had left him, and I was very confident about Bruce's functioning.

It was five years later that Bruce returned to treatment, and it was not with good news. He had received a diagnosis of advanced prostate cancer, the cancer that had killed his father. And now, with a personal sense of being much closer to death, he feared the re-emergence of his existential issues. He wanted to check in — to get an objective assessment of how he was travelling.

Facing one's mortality is much easier at a distance. In our youth, death can seem an abstract notion — something that happens to old people, but not to us. Like the worst of a cold winter to come, it can be laughed at from the warm, long nights of the preceding summer. In the opening quarter of a life there are more pressing matters — how do I ask that girl out at the bus-stop that I see every day? Is this floral shirt too colourful for the party? Should I get a tattoo, or perhaps just change the colour of my hair? But when the hair starts to grey, and the joints start to ache, and one's vision is notably weakening, the chattering voice of consciousness quietly redirects our attention toward impermanence.

Even at this point, death can still seem far away for many. Carl Jung argued that the early signs of ageing can actually help psychologically prepare us for our death that still lies over the horizon. But what happens when death is closer again? When specialists have told us what is likely to kill us? How do we cope with clear and present danger? This is the hardest of all of the existential challenges. And this is what troubled Bruce. How well had his earlier psychotherapy prepared him for this? Would any evidence of resilience be present?

In the gap in our treatment, Bruce had done some exciting things. He'd travelled to the Americas, Cuba and other exotic lands. He'd taken up running and other positive pursuits. He'd remained a scholar, consuming new writers from the various philosophic positions that we had explored together. But what stood out above all else was his gentleness of spirit. Bruce was still a tender man, a measured man facing the very likely decline in his health and functioning over the period ahead.

In the opening meetings of his return, he was naturally preoccupied with decisions about his health. What treatments to select? How to approach the final hurdles? But given all that he'd read, and all that he understood, I found him in surprisingly good mental health. In many ways, I felt deep admiration for Bruce. He was in better shape than I could've imagined as he faced his own impermanence. It was as if our earlier work had been fated for what was to come at this challenging point years later. He had not mastered death, but he was certainly doing better with it than anyone I'd met in my clinic over the previous thirty years.

At the time of the interview I had seen Bruce 25 times over 6 years.

Our interview with Bruce

Ross: Thank you, Bruce, very much, for coming in and being willing to take part in this interview.

Bruce: Pleasure.

Ross: Can I begin by asking you about your early life, your family, life at home as you grew up? Tell me about those early years.

Bruce: I was the oldest of four children. I was a baby boomer. Both my parents had fulfilled their duties in World War II. That's how they met. My father worked in radar, in air radio. My mother was working in very top-secret work in Sydney. After the war, my father briefly moved to Lord Howe Island and was an air traffic controller. My mother and I joined him when I was less than two. In fact, that's where my earliest memories are, living on Lord Howe Island at the age of two, for a year or so, and then back in Sydney, living with my mother's parents. That's when dad built a house in Eastwood.

My brother and sister arrived, twins, in 1949, and then Dad was posted to, or moved to, Central Western New South Wales as an air traffic controller in about 1950. A couple of years later, my younger sister was born. It was a pretty happy family life, with both my mother and father striving to improve themselves, both working pretty hard. My father did a lot of shift work as an air traffic controller. We went to the local schools and eventually, he built a fairly comfortable home in the northern part of town which we moved into in about 1960.

I had my education there, but generally, it was a fairly happy household with the emphasis being very much on self-improvement, and improvement of surrounds, and education. There weren't any major glitches in family life that I was aware of. And, both my parents seemed to get along fairly well.

Ross: Okay. Tell me about your relationship with your mother? How would you describe, in those early years, your relationship with your mother?

Bruce: She was my primary carer. Because my father was often absent due to shift work, it fell upon my mother to look after the four children, all of them being under the age of five. So basically my mother was the main carer. She was a very caring woman who was not tough but strong. She had very strong religious beliefs and encouraged us to join the local church, which we did. My father was not quite as strict when it came to church and religion. He had a more philosophical approach to life. However, we did follow our mother's footsteps and go to church and became part of a local church community. This formed a part of my life, probably up until the age of being a young teenager, when I started to rebel against it for various reasons.

But my mother was very caring. She did a marvellous job looking after us and also working when I think about it. And she loved her sport, playing golf and tennis. So, she was very much a strong, compassionate, caring mother.

Ross: And your father? Your relationship with your father?

Bruce: He was a little bit more … remote. He was working a fair bit and also, his interest in sport and social activities wasn't as strong as my mother's. He was a bit more thoughtful. He could be pretty tough at times when we misbehaved, but generally, I think he was very caring.

Ross: In your early life, were there any losses that you experienced?

Bruce: Ah, yeah, there were. My maternal grandfather died when I was about 10 or 12 years old, and that came as a bit of a surprise, not a shock so much, but a surprise to me. He was a naval officer — a very strong man, an Englishman from Lancashire who lived in Sydney. Very strong and calm. When he died, we were asked to go to the funeral, and I was a bit shocked and surprised to see his open coffin.

Ross: Right.

Bruce: With him lying in it. And that became … a bit of a jolt. It had an impact. There was sadness, but also questioning. I became quizzical as to why people had to die. He was my grandfather, and I was pushed forward to the coffin to see him. My parents knew that this was the done thing. It was the 'right thing' to say goodbye. So yes, that was a bit of a loss. Other losses? Well, family pets involve losses. We did rely on having a cat and a dog at home as kids, those cats and dogs lived under the house, never inside the house. They used to wait for us to come from school, and they were very protective of us when we were young kids. So, the loss of the family dog was something that we … we took it sadly as small children as we realised that you don't … you know … family pets don't stay around forever. My mother constantly used to say, 'we're never getting another dog because I'm so sad to see it go'. And she was saddened probably more than us.

Ross: It affected her. Were there any losses in your parents' lives, perhaps before you were born, that had an impact on them?

Bruce: There were always little whisperings, here and there, about losses, but never brought up in front of us as children. We were shielded from it.

Ross: I see.

Bruce: My uncle died at a young age. He was much younger than dad. But there was never any great explanation about how and why he died, except that he passed away and we didn't go to the funeral for some reason. So there are little question marks about some of these things that were never quite cleared up because we were shielded.

Ross: Would you have said either of your parents were anxious people?

Bruce: No, I don't think so, Ross.

Ross: What are your earliest memories of anxiety yourself — of being fearful, worried or afraid?

Bruce: My earliest memory of anxiety was when I was a preschool child, and across the road from our house was an open paddock on the edge of town. A large tent went up and being a young child and inquisitive, I scurried off one afternoon to see what was in the tent, thinking it might have been a circus. Which it almost was in one sense, because when I opened the flap of the canvas door, there were a couple of fire and brimstone preachers in there.

Ross: I see.

Bruce: Having an evangelical meeting. A lot of people had been rounded up and on the walls were large drawings of the Tower of Babel, various other Old Testament buildings, and on a stage, in front of everyone, jam packed in, was this man with a Bible in his hand, bashing it on the table, and scaring the bejesus out of everyone in there — talking about fire, brimstone, and what happens when you die.

Ross: Right.

Bruce: You either go down to hell or up to heaven he was declaring. As a preschool child, this scene had a major impact on me. Because suddenly I associated death, for the first time, with pain and worry and fire and eternal burning in hell. I snuck out feeling quite worried and concerned about my future because I knew that if I didn't tread the line, I would be in eternal heat. A blow torch on me!

Ross: How did that fear develop over the years?

Bruce: It sort of lingered, Ross, I think, in some ways, when I look back on it, my mother was encouraging about me going to the local Church of England, and her beliefs were quite strong. I had this lingering thought about what might happen when you die, which is what Church tended to be all about. And I couldn't quite link, you know, superimpose these two things. My Mother saying that the church is a caring place to be, God is love, but on the other hand, you go into the tent and God is all-powerful and there's fire and brimstone. That nagged at me, and it seemed a contradiction to me. My father was never greatly religious. In fact, he used to talk about how religion was the opium for the masses.

Ross: I see.

Bruce: He had a much more relaxed, philosophical approach to religion, and we'd have discussions about these sorts of philosophical topics at home, and my mother and father would retreat to their opposing views. It left me with doubts, and so by the time I was about 12 or 13 years old, I decided to finish this whole business of being in church. I became a bit more removed from the whole thing and started to cast my gaze wider.

Ross: What other things have caused you worry or anxiety over the years? When I first met you, the big questions seemed to be about what you had achieved in your life. 'How well have I lived?' 'What's my professional contribution been?'

Bruce: From an early age, I wanted to make something of my life. Going to a local school was fine — I knew nothing else. There was only one high school in the town, and I was surrounded by people who were pretty keen to get on. There was very much a work ethic when it came to school life. I threw myself into school and then started to take those subjects which I wanted to make sure gave me the best opportunity to go on. I was encouraged by my parents, especially being the oldest child, which seemed to warrant some sort of special expectations. I was encouraged more than my sisters, and even perhaps my brother.

Ross: Right.

Bruce: Encouraged to do really well. So, there was quite a fair bit of pressure, I think, on me, to excel. And when I finished my schooling, in my final year of school, I became very philosophical about it all. I didn't see the point — I didn't want to do it and didn't study for my first leaving certificate. After it, I decided I would leave home, buy a car, and forget about the whole thing. For some reason, as a teenager, I had started to revolt against that whole thing. So, I lived in Sydney, played guitar, and just bummed around. But then, after a year, I started to realise that life was bigger. I realised that I did want to go to university. I did want to pursue a career as an architect. So, I went back, and I sat those exams again and got a scholarship.

Ross: How did you choose architecture?

Bruce: Well, from an early age, I'd watched my father build houses. For some reason or other, my father had become interested in building, and he built three or four houses when I was a child.

Ross: I see.

Bruce: And being the oldest, I helped him build those houses. I was up early, at the age of ten, driving with him to a building site in another part of town.

Ross: Right.

Bruce: Helping stack bricks, mix mortar, make sure the tradies were there, check materials, and physical labour. And during that time, I started to form, you know, an idea, about what it was to build and create something. I realised pretty quickly that it was much easier to think about it and create it, then it was to be carrying bricks.

Ross: Of course.

Bruce: Although, it was good fun and it earned me a bit of pocket money, which I spent. However, I could never see labouring as being a full-time commitment for me. I could see something beyond. I like diagrams. I love diagrams and maps.

Ross: Right.

Bruce: I created maps and diagrams when I was a little kid. I joined the Boy Scouts and did more of that as I got older. So from the beginning, I guess, I had encouragement to build, my father was a part-time artist, he used to paint, and somehow I put together art and building. I was encouraged by my grandfather, maternal grandfather, and my father, to study architecture.

Ross: When I met you, you were going through, what one could think of as an existential crisis. You were closing your business after all those years as an architect, and there was a sense of, not only 'what next?', but 'what has this all been about?'

Bruce: Absolutely.

Ross: Tell me about that. Tell me about how you felt about your career and what it was all about.

Bruce: Well, I'd spent, at the point, when I came to see you, Ross, I'd spent, pretty well the whole of my life up until that point, either working for, training for, or working as an architect in my own business. And I set myself goals from a very early age to do as well as I could, and to achieve as much as I could, and to a certain extent, I felt I'd achieved what I set out to do. My life had a purpose and a meaning in architecture. But in closing my practice and finishing work, I was closing down that meaning.

Ross: I see.

Bruce: Closing the business led me to consider, more so than ever in the past, what am I here for? What am I doing? What's it all about? Does it have a meaning? Is there any meaning to life? Do any of these things coincide with the point of geometry or structure to my life? What takes me forward from this point? Is it finished? I felt a deep sense of sadness that wouldn't go away, and it became deeper and deeper. As I started to postulate some of those philosophical issues, it got harder. Although, being fairly well read, studying philosophy and art, and so forth, it somehow saddened me to think that one could lead one's life to the point of no purpose. And then I started to look around, and think well, is there a purpose in my life? Does it mean that I've done all this for zero?

Ross: Yes.

Bruce: And Marcus Aurelius' words struck hard that when you die, you go to nothing and nobody remembers you, and soon you'll be dust and be blown away.

Ross: Yes.

Bruce: So it all started to weigh heavily on me.

Ross: It did indeed. In our early meetings, even the things you've done, the wonderful things you've done professionally, didn't seem to matter. I remember you saying to me, 'if there was a report card on my life it would say, 'done OK, could have done more'.'

Bruce: [laughs]

Ross: Yes, Bruce, I distinctly remember you telling me that. It had quite an impact on me at the time. Nothing you'd achieved was enough — the things you'd built and the things you'd designed — some of which, you know, were prominent buildings. Why do you think that was?

Bruce: Well, I feel a lot different now, thanks to you and your help. At the time, I had an overwhelming feeling of loss, of professional loss, of sudden awareness that it will all be gone. It's a bit like chaos theory, I suppose. Scientists and mathematicians stumbled upon it in the 1920s, or quantum physics, where they realised there is no structure except what nature throws up and beyond that, there is no more.

Bruce: I started to look at truth, what truth was and started to explore how others saw truth and meaning and it just hit me very subtly, I suppose, that the only truths I could see at that time, and I guess even now, are mathematical truths. Or truths of nature. And that's it. My life and my achievements started to diminish, compared with the bigger picture of life, and also compared with what other people have done. Although, I think when you start comparing yourself to other people, you're always going to be in an awkward spot.

Ross: I agree.

Bruce: Because people have done worse and people have done better. So, it wasn't a comparison of myself with other people; it was really a self-assessment.

Ross: Indeed.

Bruce: A self-assessment of what has this person done? They've worked hard up until this point, but has it been worth it? Is there any purpose and meaning from this point on? Because it didn't appear to me, at that point, that I had done enough.

Ross: You were also struck by ageing at the time. You had gone to a 50th school reunion around that period, and you came back and said to me, I was catapulted back into 1963.

Bruce: Yes. That was an astounding experience. I walked into this reunion, up the stairs, and I looked around, and I thought, I'm in the wrong spot. These are all old people — I've come to some sort of gathering of old codgers.

And then just as I was about to walk back down stairs to find the right meeting room, to find my group of old students, somebody said, 'Hey, Bruce!' I turned around and there was this person waving a name tag at me.

He happily pinned it on my chest. And I thought, my God, it just became a shock. But we'd all suddenly aged so much. And I was catapulted back into 1963, amongst all these kids my own age, and here they were, all those years later, and now they're decrepit. And what's more, I realised that I was really looking in a mirror of sorts. Suddenly, it hit me that I was looking at myself as an aged man for the first time.

Up until that point in time, I had never really considered myself as old. So, I had to accommodate, somehow, that truth of ageing compared with what my mind was saying.

Ross: Yes, it was quite a challenge, I remember, at the time. But over those months of treatment, you did very, very well and your mood improved, and your scores on depression tests improved, and things looked much brighter. You were enjoying your existence far more.

Bruce: Yes.

Ross: And you were engaging in a lot of positive activities, you were running, and lots of pleasant activities with friends — all sorts of things happening. This second period of treating you, of course, has been occasioned by health issues. Tell me about that and how this has thrown up old challenges again.

Bruce: Yes, well, thanks to your help in confronting existential issues and being a bit more epicurean, rather than simply stoic, although the Stoics have a lot of good things about them. Stoics appeal to me through their self-discipline and purposeful approach to life. Epicureanism is something that I find very hard because of my nature, I suppose. I tend to like to work hard at something, and set a course of action and go for it. Whereas to sit around, peeling grapes, sipping wine, that's something I have to work at.

But with your help, I'm leading a bit more of a relaxed life and seeing myself differently. In a different context, it would have been fantastic. I mean, it had been going really well. Except that I did go to see a doctor about a month ago, or a bit more, because I decided to do some running training and prepare for a big race. I wanted to make sure that I didn't have any medical issues, and in particular, a friend of mine had had a heart attack and was in hospital, and he recovered, but I thought, well, this was a bit sudden, so I'll go in and have a health check. And, I went to see him, and he had the health report in front of him, which involved blood test results. He went through each one and said 'these are fine. Your heart's good, your various other things are good,' and then he got to the last page and his face went white.

And he looked at me, and he was obviously very upset, and he said, 'look, your PSA is 55', and I said, 'well, is that a good score? Or a bad score? What is it?' And he said, 'no, no, it's a very high cancer scale that you're in now, you've really got a high rate of cancer in your prostate, and there's nothing that I can do for you except pass you on to a specialist,' which he did.

So, following some weeks of PET's and MRI's and so forth, and various other scans, including biopsies, it was determined that I had high grade prostate cancer, and this was starting to spread, and something had to be done about it, some form of intervention. Surgery, of some type, had to be carried out to deal with it. This was quite a sudden thing because I've never really had any physical ailments before, and I realised that if I didn't deal with it, things wouldn't be good.

Then I reflected on my father's death, some ten years previous. He died of prostate cancer but had chosen not to tell anyone about his state of health until six months before he died. In fact, my mother was sworn to secrecy for eight years, when he was first diagnosed, and he decided, in his 70's, to refuse treatment and allow it to take him away. Why did he do that? He did that because he did not want to burden his children and grandchildren with the fact that he was passing away, slowly, and gain their pity or concern and affect their lives.

So, I thought it was a very brave thing that he did. So, suddenly, I can relate to the position that my father was in and in my case, I told Susan, my wife, and she unequivocally said, 'you are not going to do the same as your father, are you?' So I was in the position of a no-win situation because I couldn't let it carry me away because the cat was out of the bag.

And Susan was different from my mother. I guess my mother was a bit more respectful about his wishes and my father was strong about not saying anything. So, I was then faced with a decision, again, an existential one, of how do I then deal with and manage the rest of my life? The end of my life is now closer than it was when I last saw you.

And the cause is now well-chiselled. But, surprisingly, I was able to think it through with a bit more logic than I had some years previously when I had seen you. And with discussion, I found to my own surprise, that I've managed to think through a way of managing this a bit more successfully than it could've been.

So, I simply took my iPhone, and I wrote a very simple but clear, but not highly coloured version of what situation I was in to my four daughters. And I spelt it out clearly, and unemotionally, and positively, and said, I'm going to have treatment, and I've been diagnosed with a high-grade cancer but don't worry, things will be okay, I'll deal with it. And then all hell broke loose because the four daughters were on to me in various forms, various ways of communicating their concern. One daughter jumped in the car and arrived soon after in tears. So, I couldn't take the lead of my father at that point. I had been pushed forward with another course of action.

But, I quickly booked into see you because what was concerning me, at that point, was I had no symptoms.

I had no physical symptoms, but I had been told by experts, that I didn't have all that long to live if I didn't have fairly serious treatment. So what was I going to do? My head was saying, I'm fine, I'm still running, enjoying things, no symptoms, no pain, no physical difference, but my head was saying, as I woke up in the morning: You've got a disease and it's about to kill you. And it's in there, you can't see it, you can't feel it, and it's sneaking in, and every day you go on, this is going to get you.

So, I must say that the disconnect between my mind and my body was something that I knew I needed help with before it got out of control and one thing started to affect the other. That is when I saw you. It was very helpful in seeing you again because that helped me knock off the rough edges of where I could go if I'm not careful.

Ross: I think I've said to you that I agree with your assessment — because you've worked through many of these issues years before you are dealing with the situation remarkably better than you might've. But also, remarkably better than most people do. It's been very impressive, Bruce.

Bruce: Thank you, Ross.

Ross: Can I ask what emotions arise in you at the thought of your own death? How do you feel about death — a topic that we all inevitably have to think about?

Bruce: Quite differently to when I first met you some years ago. I feel now that I can face death a bit more easily, positively, shall we say? It's inevitability and confronting nature are both there, however, I'm a bit more focused on the inevitability rather than the terror. So, although it's a concern and it's not a comfortable thing to think about, its shape and form aren't a nightmare. I don't wake up thinking 'I'm going to die'. My concern now is what I best can do with the rest of what I've got left. What other truths can I uncover to my own satisfaction about life and death between now and when I do go?

It's probably, not so much a feeling of inevitability and well, it's going to happen — I have to go. It's more like a building in a square that you don't want to visit. You go into this beautiful square, and there's a series of buildings around that square. They've all been constructed for people, and one of them you don't want to go into, but you're doing a tour of this group of buildings, and each one has its own delight and interest and characteristics, and whatever happens, you're going to go through that building to complete the tour of this square. And that's where you're going to be, and it's waiting for you, and it's there, and you're going to have to progress towards it. It's not going to come to you. It's me going to it.

Ross: That's interesting Bruce. It puts you in a more active role — you're controlling where you're going on your tour. You're seeing the buildings as you wish to see them on the way. It's not haunting you every second.

Bruce: It's not haunting me every second — that's a good phrase actually. That really sums it up quite well.

Of course, one of the big issues with me with death was, what happens after? I reflect back to opening the tent in that country town. That biblical meeting and seeing fire and brimstone and the Tower of Babel and people slipping off the edge and a lightning bolt pushing people down to their peril because they haven't led a good life. That now becomes the question.

Ross: I wanted to ask you that, Bruce, what do you think happens to you as you physically die and once you're physically dead? What are your current thoughts on that?

Bruce: Well, having read a bit of science, and just thinking about the creation of life, no particles can be either created or destroyed, they always are there. So, nothing can be created or destroyed; there's always going to be shifting energy and particles. So, there are now studies that link particles with wave motion. So, if you look at Nano technology, a science being able to detect atoms in incredible detail, they realised that light behaves in a very strange way, particles and wave lengths, but we're all made of particles and those particles, when you start to examine somebody's skin, aren't hard edges.

Filtered particles that drift off into space ever so gently. So, when life leaves, there must be, well, I believe, there must be some particle or energy change that converts that energy that was once a human being, into another form of energy, with a different, not necessarily consciousness, but with a different particle combination that exists somewhere.

So, it may just dissolve into a series of particles or energy waves, but it can't be destroyed or created.

Ross: Yes, I see.

Bruce: It's always there if you look at physics.

Ross: So there's an existence of a sort?

Bruce: An existence of a sort, or if you like, a presence or a sort. It may not have consciousness. It would be good if it did. It would be interesting to have a different consciousness without a physical body, that would be interesting.

If one thinks of life as a series of raindrops falling through the sky, eventually they're collected and shatter and form part of the bigger sea or ocean. Now, that ocean is perhaps called the sea of life or the river of life, and you're a particle in it. It's a bit like the universe. Well, we used to think that the universe is mainly empty space, when, in fact, it isn't. Take a cubic metre or even a cubic centimetre of open space and there's a lot of dark matter that they're discovering. So, there's a lot of space and particles out there, and maybe that's what happens.

Ross: How often do you think about these sorts of issues — about death or what happens after, or what you become? How often is it on your mind?

Bruce: Very often. Very often. The more I read philosophical books, the more I read, the more I understand, the more I talk to people, the more I consider how other people have lived their lives, the more, I guess, unfortunately, when I see friends or colleagues die, the more I then reflect on their lives, my life, and the bigger picture. So, it's a fairly constant thing.

Ross: Do you see that as a good thing? Or a bad thing?

Bruce: I think it's a good thing. Honestly, I think it's a very good thing because one can lead one's life in a state of stupor. Maybe it's fine that some people just lead their lives thinking, 'I'm never going to go... it's going to be like this forever' and then suddenly they go. In my case, no, I've always been to a point of questioning and trying to understand where this all goes. The point of philosophy and religion, and so many other institutions and activities is to understand these issues. How do people live knowing that they've got to die?

Ross: For what it's worth, Bruce, I agree with you. You and I think similarly, as did many others before us. I love Seneca's writings on this topic. He reminds us that you only get one go at dying, so you'd better prepare for it if you want to get it right. If you want to master making lasagne, you can have as many attempts as you like. You can wreck your first 20 attempts in your effort of mastering lasagne. But if we're dying only once, Seneca argued, you better be thinking and preparing across life for how to do this right — you're not going to get a second or third go at it!

And I'm also reminded of George Harrison's wonderful song, The Art of Dying, where he sings, 'nothing in this life that I've been trying, could equal or surpass the art of dying' and even more poignantly 'but if you want it, then you must find it, but when you have it, there'll be no need for it'. George is telling us that death is the hardest journey, but that it is solvable if we search. So, I agree with you Bruce — thinking about death has got to be better, staring at death, has got to be better than trying to stay ignorant of it.

Bruce: Absolutely, and do you know Ross, being a Freemason has also helped me in taking a more global view of life. In particular, the third degree of Freemasonry prompts and enables people, if they want to, to contemplate these bigger picture issues and confront them. And that's been an interesting philosophical journey in itself.

Ross: That's interesting, Bruce. I remember a conversation, years ago, in which you said to me — I'm not sure that I have this right and you might have to explain exactly what you meant — you said to me that the Freemasons spend a lot of time thinking about death but perhaps not enough thinking about how to live. Do you recall this or can you explain what you might have meant?

Bruce: Yes, I think I can. Freemasonry — being not necessarily a philosophy, certainly not a religion or a cult — is an organisation of thinking people. Great thinkers have been Freemasons. George Washington, Mozart and Mark Twain were Freemasons. Anyway, they spend a lot of time in social structures that actually pose questions. And there is a focus on self-improvement, and if you look for help, there will be people around you in the organisation to help you. It's a nurturing organisation, and it does look at all aspects of life. It allows you the opportunity to explore the thoughts of these supportive individuals. Whereas a religion or a cult, is based on a single person, you become a follower of a single person. You're given answers, and you follow doctrines.

That can be good for people who want a quick answer to difficult questions, but if you want to think about things, you'll probably go through a bit more pain. Freemasons don't offer simple answers on how to live.

Ross: I see. Can I ask you what relationship you see between your thoughts about death, death itself, and your experience of everyday living? Does death dominate your activities of the day?

Bruce: That's an interesting question. No, it doesn't dominate. It's something that I've confronted with your help, and I've been able to perhaps get a better perspective of where I am, within my own life, and other people's lives, and life in general. And, it's there, it's a part of what I do, if you like, a component of my everyday life but it doesn't prevent me from doing things. It doesn't hold me back, it slightly saddens me sometimes, but I don't allow that sadness to take me into deeper thoughts that prevent me from thinking logically.

Ross: Within treatment, or in anything you've ever read or come across, what do you think has most helped you assuage any dread of death?

Bruce: Well, for me, it's very obvious that the biggest breakthrough was having you determine pretty rapidly the reason for my deep sorrow. You were very quick to identify existential issues that were causing me to feel that pain. Before that point, I could only see deep sorrow and concern, which was starting to slide out of control a bit because it was starting to be ever present and totally determining what was happening in my life. I had to haul myself from one moment to another, with difficulty. So that was a good turning point because you were able to firstly identify what was going on. Then you helped me through some of the books you suggested I read. You pointed me in a direction that was very positive because I could then see my sadness in a context. And then, I guess — I haven't really thought about this — you were able to help me to confront some of those issues, perhaps ever so gently, to make me aware of them. But certainly, all the books were good — I've since gone on to read other great philosophers, and this has all helped.

Ross: So, the first important step was recognition.

Bruce: Identification.

Ross: Identification that your suffering was existential in its nature. From there, you began a journey of reading and consuming people's thoughts on these topics — the great writers that have examined these issues over centuries, well, thousands of years. And that has served you well.

Bruce: Oh, it has. Identification was so important. Also, having the self-awareness to say, 'look this is an issue that I have, and I want to do something about it'. And I guess you've led me through those steps and have got me to this point.

Ross: Thank you, Bruce. My final question relates to meaning. What if anything, makes your life meaningful now? What gives you a sense of meaning?

Bruce: Very good question. Well, if I had to sum it up, I would say that I still lead a morally disciplined life, not in a religious sense, but in a sense that's it's only going to help other people around me and the world in general if I have a disciplined moral life. Because an undisciplined, unregulated life can lead to social chaos. That's the first thing.

The second is to continue to unravel some of the mysteries that other people tried and failed to unravel. To grapple with them, try and understand truth, get to the truth of matters, rather than accept what's around — to continue to do that, to search for truth. Continue to care for my children, my wife, and grandchildren and help them as much as I can. To be there for them, to help them if they've got difficulties. Try and provide that care for people who are coming through. I've had an art exhibition and written a book last year, which has been a good focus on creative output and I continue to do part-time architectural work. So, writing, art, architecture, in admittedly smaller components, but still achieving something, if you like.

Achieving little goals that I've set myself and challenges. Continue to be fit by running, eating reasonable food, trying to relax a bit more when it comes to things around me — and trying to do all this while still aiming to lead a good life.

Ross: That's a very thorough answer. Thank you very much, Bruce, for coming in.

Bruce: Thanks, Ross.

Chapter 10

All you need is love

When I first met Matilda, she was most concerned about sound sensitivity. She would become quickly frustrated when she heard chewing, swallowing or cutlery scraping on plates. Her reaction to noises, commonly known as misophonia, had grown over the years and the range of sounds that angered her had slowly increased. Now 24 years of age, even the faint noise of a cup being placed on a table could move her to anger. But as I assessed her in our opening meeting, it became very apparent that a much larger problem was interfering with Matilda's wellbeing.

Matilda saw death and the threat of death almost constantly around her. 'What if the bus explodes that I'm in?' she told me. 'What if the stove blows up?' and 'What if I've left the gas on and it kills us all in the night?' The threats seemed to be ever-present. 'What if someone sneaks up behind me in the street with an axe?' She experienced images of trams cutting people in half and fears that she'd be framed for murder. 'Anyone could impersonate me, Ross. They could kill someone and I'd be blamed!' Matilda was a very scared woman, and she found being out in public extremely difficult. She also worried about illnesses, and these varied depending upon what she saw on the news or read in a magazine. Death could come in many guises, and at any moment.

The origin of her fears was complex. She had experienced severe bullying throughout her youth, a known contributor to the development of anxiety disorders. She had a sister who had developed meningitis and had also been to hospital regularly for other operations, all of which terrified Matilda. And then at 11, she experienced a trauma in a hospital herself. A poorly inserted IV line began to leak. She saw her own blood pouring from the puncture site. It was to be an event that would haunt her over the years that followed. 'The image is still really, really clear in my mind. I thought I might die, just bleed out' she told me.

Matilda's fears were complicated by chronic low self-worth. Although she was scared of death, she also didn't believe that she really deserved to live. In one extraordinary session, she admitted to me that she felt guilt for having a shadow. 'I'm nothing, Ross, and I don't deserve to block the sun's rays that have travelled all this way.' She didn't believe she had any skills, abilities or redeeming personal qualities. 'I'll never amount to anything,' she once told me, 'and no one will ever want me. I consume space, I take up space, and I don't deserve to.'

Her original problem of misophonia needed exposure treatment. She began to listen to noises on recordings to slowly desensitise to chewing and scraping and other sounds. But her fears of death and harm clearly needed the most attention. The more I talked to Matilda, the more I saw how deeply seated these fears were. She admitted to me that as a high school student she had taken biology in order to learn how to prevent illness. She would research food handling and food poisoning to learn about bacteria and how to prevent them from attacking her. She would watch documentaries about serial killers to understand how they managed to choose and trap their victims. She had been preparing for years, in so many ways, to ward off countless paths to death.

As we began exposure to possible threats, I knew it was not going to be easy. Recovering from such a chronic history of the threat of harm that was so ever-present, in every footstep, down every street, would never be a simple task. Her anxiety-related disorders had emerged very early in life, and she had strongly held beliefs that her fears were reasonable. In addition, she didn't simply have a single anxiety disorder. At a minimum, she met DSM-5 diagnostic criteria for OCD, Generalised Anxiety Disorder, Post Traumatic Stress Disorder, Illness Anxiety Disorder, and Body Dysmorphic Disorder. Unsurprisingly, the first seven sessions were hard going with only minimal gains made on any of her fear reactions and threat beliefs. Because she saw her fears as protective, Matilda was reluctant to drop her safety and avoidance behaviours, and so her compliance with exposure homework was less than ideal.

And then, almost overnight, her fears appeared to stunningly leave her. She arrived for our eighth meeting and announced that the intrusive images had disappeared. I hadn't seen Matilda for a month, and she declared that she was in the best mental health she'd ever experienced. Diligently, one by one, I listed all the fears she'd previously reported. To each and every one she smiled and told me that she simply didn't worry about it anymore. Not only did she not believe that the events would occur but, even more surprisingly, she reported that she had no thoughts about the topics. She was no longer experiencing intrusive images of stabbings, muggings, assault, nor of exploding stoves, cars, trams or buses.

'How has it happened?' I asked. She hesitated briefly, 'I'm in a relationship now, Ross' she told me, beaming from ear to ear.

Many theorists have suggested that attachment can assuage the dread of death, but I'd never seen such a dramatic example before. A new relationship that was functional and fulfilling, and very quickly the centre of Matilda's world, had seemingly wiped away years of chronic fear. Notably, her fears and intrusions were absent even when her partner wasn't with her. Her misophonia, though improved, remained, as did some general worries about money and her capacity to fund her lifestyle. But there was no doubt that her fears of death had all but vanished.

It is now 12 months since that stunning eighth session in which Matilda announced her recovery. I have seen her four times across that period and monitored her thoughts, behaviours and emotions closely. While interpersonal issues have arisen, largely relating to family relationships, her death anxiety remains at bay. At least in Matilda's case, John Lennon was right — all you need is love.

Our interview with Matilda

Ross: Thank you, Matilda, for coming in for this interview. Can I ask you firstly to tell me a bit about your family and life at home as you grew up?

Matilda: Right. Well, my life at home was very different from where I am now. My mother and father were still married. My sister was born deaf in both ears, which was difficult, but, at the time, nothing seemed to be wrong with me.

Ross: Was it a happy home most of the time? In the early years?

Matilda: I think so. I'd say it was pretty happy but like, mainly because it was just comfortable. My parents weren't fighting all the time. But growing up I had some really bad friendships. I was bullied my entire life. My parents didn't really know about it because I never used to speak to anyone about it because I thought this is how people treat people. I didn't know anybody because I went to a really small school. It was a Christian school next to a church. So we had weekly scripture readings, and it was very religion-based. My mum did not approve of any of that, so I was a bit conflicted on what to believe. So home was okay, but school was awful.

Ross: Can you tell me a bit more about each of your parents? Let's start with your mother. Can you describe your relationship with your mother in the early years of your life?

Matilda: Early years, it was a very good relationship. She was really nice and encouraging. She supported my interest in drawing and art.

Ross: So she was positive growing up.

Matilda: Quite positive, yeah.

Ross: And your father?

Matilda: Very positive but … I can't really remember much about that time, sorry.

Ross: That's okay, Matilda. Were there any early losses in your life? Any deaths of aunts, uncles, grandparents, pets? Anything that you think had an impact on you?

Matilda: Not really. I do remember when my next door neighbour died and my parents made a big deal out of it. I didn't know how to feel because I really liked her, and now she was gone. I didn't really feel anything.

Ross: How old were you?

Matilda: About three or four.

Ross: So you were very young. It's interesting that you remember it.

Matilda: I know. It's strange. I do think about it often.

Ross: Okay. Are you aware of any losses or traumas in your parents' lives, perhaps before you were born? Did they ever talk about any traumas that could have had an impact on them?

Matilda: Yes, indeed. My mother never really spoke about any of it when I was very young. But at around 15 she told me that her father had been really abusive and used to steal money from her. And her mother died very young of ovarian cancer which scared me. I still don't know the whole story of my mother's early life because she's very sensitive about it. I've never met anyone from my mum's side of the family, other than her sister. We don't know where her father is. And my dad's father died of cancer as well. But he never really spoke about that either.

Ross: Wow — that must have been a lot to take in.

Matilda: Yes, I know. And so I have two dead grandparents. I've only met my grandma on my dad's side, and my mum has a really strained relationship with her.

Ross: Would you say that either of your parents are anxious?

Matilda: I'd say my mum is really highly strung. She gets stressed out about really tiny things. She's always nervous about something. She's sort of a perfectionist.

Ross: I see.

Matilda: When she was younger, when her marriage was more stable, she was a bit more carefree. My dad, on the other hand, doesn't seem to be anxious.

Ross: So your mother is highly strung and worries, but she wasn't when you were young. You wouldn't have called her an anxious woman when you were at school, for instance?

Matilda: I suppose there were times I'd get anxious around her, because I feared her reaction, especially if I've done something that I knew would stress her out and make her angry.

Ross: What sort of things would stress her out?

Matilda: Well… I don't know if I can differentiate if it was really anxiety or she was just mad at me. You know, if my grades were poor, or I'd forgotten an information slip or some detail about homework. She'd get really, really stressed out and really angry about stuff like that.

Ross: I see. Can I ask, is there any history of mental health problems in your family?

Matilda: Yeah. When I first got diagnosed with OCD my dad suddenly said that a lot of his relatives were admitted to an infamous mental health institution. My mum actually had no idea about that. He'd never spoken about it before. He didn't state the reasons why they were admitted. Frankly, it just came out of nowhere. My mother sort of confronted him about it afterwards. 'You never told me this' and 'Didn't you think this would have an impact on me?' and 'Didn't you think this might have something to do with our daughter?' So I don't know the details of what conditions they had. That's all I can tell you about the mental health of my family.

Ross: Let's now focus on you rather than your family and their lives. Can you tell me about your earliest memories of your own anxiety, of being worried, anxious or afraid? Your earliest memories of being fearful of anything? What was it about?

Matilda: I have, like, so many — they predate my happy memories. I was afraid of being called to the principal's office when I started school. I was afraid of forgetting things. And I always worried about being hurt in some way.

Ross: Hurt?

Matilda: Hurt in lots of ways. Hurt by my friends or hurt by other people. There was this one guy in my school who was huge, like a massive bully and just really strong, built like a brick shit-house. And he just used to beat up a lot of kids, and I used to be one of those victims too. He wouldn't really beat them up as such, but he'd just sort of push them over or hit them, and it really hurt pretty bad. And I know the teachers didn't really do that much about it. So I changed schools. It had been a very poor school, and it didn't get a lot of funding.

I also worried whenever a new student came into the school. My friends and other kids would always make a point to tell all those students that I was a disgusting person. 'Do not be friends with her' they'd say. I don't know why they did it. I think it was because I used to do kind of these gross things. Like pick my nose and stuff and let my finger nails get very dirty. And obviously, everyone made fun of it. The kids latched onto that and I'd get bullied a lot. So I still get anxious with new people coming into my life. I always think I'm going to be a target again.

Ross: I was going to ask how those fears progressed over time. You're saying that the fear of being treated badly has stayed with you across the years.

Matilda: It has stayed ever since. The bullying was intense and continued through high school. As the years went on some people started to treat me nicely. And I started thinking, 'Wow, no one has treated me like this before. Maybe this is how people are supposed to be treated.' And I started to think, 'maybe my old friends aren't really very nice to me.' And eventually when I was in Year 9, say 15 years old, I brought it all up with my parents and the school counsellor. The school counsellor insisted that I wasn't to talk to these people any more. I wasn't to go near them. The bullying stopped, which was great. It was miraculous. But unfortunately, it didn't end there. I became lonely and was still fearful. I agreed to date a boy that I didn't like, just because I was lonely. Eventually, I had to end that and he became nasty. There was always someone being nasty to me.

Ross: So there's a lot of stuff that went on in your social life as a young person and the bullying and bad treatment certainly affected you. Just so that I've got it completely correct, when you meet new people now, or you're in a new workplace, do you think you've recovered from all of that? Or are you saying, 'No, I still anticipate the world will treat me badly'.

Matilda: Well, it's not as bad as it used to be, but it's still there. I now know, as you've taught me, that it could be my mind being an enemy — the wolf in sheep's clothing. Absolutely. But there's always this tiny little voice saying someone is going to hurt me.

Ross: So you still fear new people or certain social situations. Over the years, what other things have you worried about? Have the worries changed? What did you become afraid of as you grew?

Matilda: I've had lots of other worries. I've worried about getting attacked or stabbed or assaulted — people jumping out of the bushes or shadows with axes. I've worried about the bus I'm on blowing up. I've worried about attacking others — all sorts of death stuff.

Ross: When did the fears of physical harm and death develop?

Matilda: I think it began after intrusive thoughts of myself hurting, inflicting harm upon other people. I think it was in early high school. I would have thoughts and images of stepping on someone's foot or pushing someone. They just kept coming and getting more and more advanced. I so wanted to be friends with nice people, and I was terrified I'd do something horrible to mess it up. My mind kept thinking up things that would wreck everything with them — that would make them hate me.

Ross: I see. How did you react to these thoughts? Were you scared that it would happen and that you would do them?

Matilda: I was very scared, yes. When I met my best friend, Meredith, I would stand a bit away from her. I would always keep at a distance just to avoid the possibility of me accidentally pushing her. Because I really wanted to be friends with her and I didn't want to accidentally hurt her and ruin our friendship somehow.

Ross: You were worrying that you were going to harm others. And then at some point you developed fears that somebody was going to harm you. Someone was going to step out of the bushes or out of the shadows or come up behind you. When did that happen? How old were you when you started having those fears?

Matilda: I suppose in high school. I was just so afraid of people or me getting hurt. I felt like I deserved pain itself. I think it started soon after my parents gave me independence, allowing me to go out on my own. Without someone protecting me I started worrying about tragedies, like 'maybe I'll get hit by a train, or run over by a car.'

Ross: You mentioned in session that around this time you also became obsessed with harm coming to family members.

Matilda: Yeah. I'd worry that I'd come home and the house would be on fire. Those fears were definitely there by high school.

Ross: Some of the images and thoughts were quite graphic. Of axe attacks and trains cutting people in half. Were the images disturbing?

Matilda: Yes, very disturbing. If I was happy, it would just kill that mood immediately.

Ross: Another fear you mentioned was that someone would impersonate you and kill someone. And you'd be held responsible for the death. It's a fascinating fear — very imaginative.

Matilda: Yes, lots of them would make great movies [laughs]. I had that one in high school. And I started to worry more and more about illnesses that could harm or kill me. I even took biology at school to learn about germs and illnesses so I could prevent getting sick.

Ross: I see.

Matilda: Illness fears were almost always with me, ever since my sister started going in and out of hospital. She had meningitis. And she had several operations for her cochlear implant, and for all these different reasons. She just kept going in and out of hospital and I would say to myself, 'dear God. Please let this not happen to me.'

Ross: Right.

Matilda: I became very afraid of germs, afraid of unclean things. And then I became really afraid of food poisoning. I started constantly researching food poisoning and other illnesses to prevent them.

Ross: And this was still in your teenage years?

Matilda: Yes. I still think about it now and again. I went to a restaurant the other day, a Chinese place that was really nice, but afterwards, I was like, 'What if I got poisoned?' So it still occasionally happens, although maybe only once every few months now.

Ross: That's interesting, Matilda. Can I ask you, have there been events in your life that have made your fears worse? Now you've mentioned some of them — bullying, and illnesses and conditions that your sister had. Are there any other things that happened that intensified your fears — made you more frightened of the world?

Matilda: Yes, there is one other incident. I was about 11 years old and I was misdiagnosed with meningitis. So I was in the hospital and they gave me an IV, but for some reason, the doctor doing it was very unstable. And it broke, and I bled out completely from the bed. And it was, like, a really horrifying scene.

Ross: Oh, wow.

Matilda: Like, I don't know if I ever described that to you.

Ross: No, I don't think you have.

Matilda: But because I was so young, I was really distraught at the time. I was like, 'Oh my God, is this supposed to be happening. Oh, my God, oh my Goooood look at this. So much blood coming out of me'. The image is still really, really clear in my mind. I thought I might die, just bleed out.

Ross: Do you think about that event these days?

Matilda: Yes, quite often. Yeah. I don't know why? It just comes to my head every now and then. I'll suddenly think, 'Wow, I nearly died'.

Ross: So you have this huge trauma in hospital — as a young girl that would be extremely distressing. The fact that you still think of it regularly tells us a lot about how important it was. Tell me how the scene ended?

Matilda: They sorted it out in the end. And I was in the fucking hospital for two days during which time it was really unpleasant. Like I would be in constant pain a lot of the time. And yeah, I'd just wake up in terrible pain and I didn't actually know what was happening to me. I know at one point I had to get my spinal fluid extracted, which was with this humongous syringe plunged into your back. And it was really terrifying. And it felt so bad, and I still think, 'my God, I never want that to happen to me ever again.' They took it out and showed me the spinal fluid. They thought I'd like to see that, but I was like 'you just took that out of my spine!'

Ross: It sounds like this was an awful experience for you.

Matilda: Yes, it was actually.

Ross: And may well have played a role in the origin of your death-related thoughts. You were in primary school at the time, so it was before all your thoughts of hurting others and being hurt on the streets or in buses and so on.

Matilda: Yes, perhaps. The timing is right. Ever since then I've never wanted to go into a hospital. I'm really afraid of IVs, and I think the bleeding out happened before the graphic images of death.

Ross: I see. So that's a really interesting event to add to the bullying and your sister's illnesses that could have contributed to the development of your death and harm obsessions. Tell me, Matilda, have there been any happenings in your life that have done the opposite? Have there been any happenings or situations that have reduced your fears? For example, your relationship.

Matilda: Oh, yes, absolutely. Ever since I started to see my boyfriend, my fears on the streets stopped. Suddenly I wasn't afraid of being murdered or attacked or assaulted.

Ross: Tell me a bit more about it. What do you think it was about?

Matilda: I just felt safe, like, protected. Also, one of my earlier worries was when I was with my friends that I'd push them onto train tracks or something like that. But I didn't seem to worry about that with him. I suppose it was because we were always holding hands and I felt like now that we're holding hands, I'm not going to suddenly push him into the street. I don't know. It just made me feel safe, I suppose. It's corny, I know.

Ross: Not at all. Not at all. So this first really significant love attachment seemed to wipe away both fears of harming others, and fears of being harmed by others.

Matilda: Yeah, I felt protected. It was great.

Ross: Do you mean that you felt safe only in his presence? Or was it the fact that you were in the relationship. Let's say he wasn't there one afternoon, and you were walking down the road. Did you still feel safe? Even on your own?

Matilda: Yeah, still safe. He didn't have to be with me to feel safe. Even when he's overseas, I'm not worried walking down the street anymore.

Ross: Suddenly, in a relationship, many of your fears leave you.

Matilda: That's right. Even though he's away a lot I'm not afraid. I just don't think about people jumping out from the shadows, or attacking me with axes or anything.

Ross: That's fantastic, Matilda. Just wonderful.

Matilda: I know. It's amazing.

Ross: Can I ask you, how did you first come to treatment? Can you tell me about that?

Matilda: I'd been dealing with the mental health problems on my own, all the way through the last years of high school. Terrible anxiety, terrible. And very low self-esteem. Even though I had good teachers. I never spoke to my parents about it. I knew they probably wouldn't take me seriously because I had mentioned in the past that a friend had been having some anxiety and they said she was doing it for attention.

But anyway, early last year was the point where my mum found out some really dark things I had said to my friends. I had confided in some friends about wanting to kill myself because of how bad I was feeling. They told mum, and she came to me. I opened up about so much stuff, and she said, 'my God, I had no idea.' That's how I first came to treatment. I was diagnosed with OCD and put on medication. Dad and mum both came to the psychiatrist with me. That's the day my dad opened up about his family being in institutions.

Ross: I see.

Matilda: And at that point I realised, I have to take this seriously. I think my mum felt bad for not realising it all much earlier in my life. My dad didn't really talk to me about it at all. And still doesn't. It's strange.

Ross: He doesn't know how to talk about it, perhaps?

Matilda: That's right. I don't think he knows how to talk about it. But basically that's how it all happened. That's how I came into treatment.

Ross: I want to turn to our last topic now, which is death. We've talked about death and fears of harm to you and others, but I want to know how you feel about death. What emotions arise in you at the thought of your own death?

Matilda: It depends on what kind of death. An early death — I'd obviously be upset by that. And it depends on the circumstances. For example, if there's an important event coming up in my life and I suddenly die, that would be horrible.

Ross: I see.

Matilda: But the thought of death when I'm happy and old, and I've lived a good life … that doesn't bother me. I'd like to die peacefully and painlessly. I don't like pain. Recently I burned myself on a stove and that made me think about being burned alive because it was, like, so painful. I can't imagine the pain all over my body for a really long time. I think about these things sometimes. For example, my sister recently spoke to me about wanting to be an organ donor when she dies. And I was like, 'that's cool', but inside I was thinking that being an organ donor really weirds me out.

Ross: I see.

Matilda: The thought of people touching my corpse after I'm dead is a really strange thought. I think it's really gross. And people taking my organs out and putting them in other people — it's a very bizarre thought to me. I'd love to help people, I suppose. There's just something very strange about people doing things to me after I'm dead.

Ross: And you think about these things?

Matilda: Quite often, but usually it's my dead young body, I suppose, that I'm afraid of people touching. I don't think about my old dead body.

Ross: What do you think will happen to you as you physically die? And once you're physically dead? What are your current thoughts about what actually occurs to a person when they die?

Matilda: I think your consciousness just immediately goes to another person. Like snap, as soon as you die, you're reborn but not as the same person. When I was in high school, we did a drama play about what happens after you die. And we acted out possibilities which were reincarnation, ghost, heaven and hell, and nothing or limbo and stuff like that. When I was in the Christian private school, I always believed that there was heaven and hell. And I always thought, 'Oh, we're going to go to hell.' But my mum told me this is so stupid. There's no such thing as heaven or hell and stuff like that, but she would never tell me what she thought happens after you die. So I can't be certain.

Ross: But if you had to bet right now, you're saying you think your consciousness goes to someone else — a type of rebirth.

Matilda: Yes.

Ross: So you see some sort of continuation, but with no awareness of who you were before?

Matilda: That's right. But it's definitely another human. It's not like you become a dog or another animal.

Ross: How often do you think about death? You've mentioned thoughts about burning alive, and you've mentioned thoughts about people touching your dead body. How often do you think about death, dying and these related topics?

Matilda: Pretty often. Quite a lot without even realising, like, I'll just be doing something and realise, 'Oh, I've been thinking about dead bodies'. So, because I like fiction and stuff that's related to death, sometimes I think about that stuff a lot.

Ross: Tell me about the death-related fiction.

Matilda: I really like horror movies and stuff. My mum never used to let me watch that kind of stuff until I was about 15. She just wouldn't let me, and if I hid them on any media, any gore-related material, I'd be grounded or punished. She just wanted to keep me away from any of that kind of thing. But now, I'm liberated. It's like, 'Wow, my mum can't control me anymore, I'm going to watch movies with horror and with blood and gore and stuff like that.' But after a while, I realised that pure gore just didn't really interest me. And now I like more suspense and plots and shows like *Black Mirror*. So I still like creepy stuff, but with more subtlety.

Ross: Yes, you like things with a dystopian edge. But you also like shows about the undead and vampire-related shows?

Matilda: Oh, yeah. Vampire-related things I really like. And also crime fiction. Lots of murders, unsolved cases and so on. True crime.

Ross: It's interesting because you've been afraid of murderers and people attacking you and you pushing people in front of trams and trains. When you were afraid of those things, would you still want to watch shows about serial killers and horror, or is it a more recent thing?

Matilda: No, I think I always had an interest in it. I've had some curiosity just because I just wasn't allowed near any of it. And I wanted to know how their minds work. It helped me feel safe to understand them.

Ross: Can I ask you what relationship do you see between your fears of death and your experience of everyday living?

Matilda: Oh, it's affected everything. It's influenced the things I've done right across my life. For example, I think it's affected how much shit I let people get away with. I let all the teasing go on because I was afraid of losing them, killing them, them dying, and so on.

Ross: I see.

Matilda: And I've avoided so many opportunities in my life because I was afraid of dying. It held me back from the stuff I could have done. It's kept me sheltered. It's taken so much from me.

Ross: But since the relationship with your boyfriend that has all improved — that's been the one thing that radically changed it. It killed many of your fears.

Matilda: It absolutely did.

Ross: What else, within therapy or outside of it, has helped you reduce your dread of death?

Matilda: Well, obviously help from you and the medication.

Ross: In treatment, has there been anything specific that you think you can pin improvement to? Is there anything that you've done in treatment, or heard in treatment, or thought about that you think might be a part of how you got past your fears?

Matilda: Well, when you taught me not to trust my mind. That my mind is like a wolf in sheep's clothing. That's really helpful. Realising that consciousness can be a disguised enemy.

Ross: Not to trust the chatter of your mind.

Matilda: Yeah, exactly. And also, just finding special interests. Things that I've invested my time in. My art and creating things. When I was young, I was told to focus on school. But now I am free to do what I really want to. I love the animated shows I watch and some other TV shows. They're a great distraction for me. Stuff like that has helped a lot.

Ross: That ties in nicely with the last question I have for you Matilda. I want to ask you about a meaningful life. What, if anything, do you think makes your life meaningful?

Matilda: It's like a Venn diagram with three things — relationships, creative outlets, and having the ability to enjoy those things without fear of anything, being able to enjoy these creative outlets or these animations and TV shows without anyone telling me to stop or that I'm wasting my time. It is being able to do these things without fearing illness all the time.

Ross: These things create meaning in your life. And do you think living a meaningful life diminishes your fear of death?

Matilda: I think so, definitely, yes.

Ross: Well, thank you very much, Matilda. That's been fascinating.

Matilda: No problem. Thank you for asking me.

Chapter 11

Purgatory

For the ancient Egyptians, only a pure heart that weighed less than the single 'feather of Maat' would guarantee passage to the heavenly fields of Aaru. Hearts heavy with evil misdeeds that had caused harm to others would fall from the scales into the mouth of the crocodile demon Ammit, dooming the soul of the dead to restlessness in the underworld for eternity.

It is now more than 4000 years since Maat, goddess of truth and justice, was first described in the Pyramid Texts of Unas. Though belief systems have changed radically across the millennia, fear of judgement has remained an integral part of the human psyche. Across time, country and culture people have worried that the actions of their lives will be weighed in the balance to decide their fate after death.

Melissa, a 35-year-old woman from Brisbane, was obsessed with how she had lived, and whether she could be judged to be a 'good person'. She was constantly caught in reflections on her past. 'Have I caused harm to anyone I've met, Ross?', she would ask relentlessly. 'Is someone suffering, or even dead, because of something I've done?' The origins of her fears lay in her early engagement with religion. As a young girl raised in a Catholic home, she'd heard of the painful purifications of purgatory and had become terrified that she would not make it straight to heaven. The fear was so present during her school years that she wore a red and white braided cord under her tunic to connect her to the virgin martyr Saint Philomena. She believed that Philomena would intercede if she suddenly died and she could avoid purgatory completely. She wore a medal to Philomena for the same reason, a small charm to avoid any separation from God upon her death.

Her knowledge of the concept of purgatory was rudimentary, based on a single flyer that her mother had brought home from a church meeting. But chronic fears can begin in simple ways, and the brief description of punishments in the crumpled leaflet was enough to set Melissa's mind searching. What had she done that could be called into question? How would God judge the collected moments of her life? Had she forgotten something that the heavenly father would focus on — a brief lapse, a moment of disregard for others, a small action that would have a negative impact that she couldn't have known about?

Her life became ruled by the fear that she would be held wanting, firstly by God and then, when her religious faith left her in adulthood, by the norms of her community. Her fears began to focus on the fundamental question of whether she was a good person or an evil-doer. Between sessions, her mind would remind her of old moments in which she may have damaged others, even unwittingly. For example, years earlier, Melissa had worked in bars, and for a time, she became obsessed with the amount of liquor she had sold. 'Perhaps, I poured a drink for someone,' she said, 'who really didn't need another. How do I know what happened to them, Ross? How do I know that they didn't go out on the road and die? How do I know they didn't become an alcoholic?'

She was particularly terrified of causing damage to young people:
'What if I'm wearing clothes that can be seen through in bright light. Perhaps it could mess up a child?' She took to wearing dark-coloured tights under everything, even under denim jeans, to prevent the possibility. She feared picking up bottles in chemists and putting them down in the wrong place: 'What if somebody picks up something I've misplaced and buys the wrong medicine? It could kill someone!' she told me searchingly. The list of her fears was endless — an infinite register of the ways in which one

person could bring another down.

Wanting to know that one is blameless can feature prominently in Obsessive Compulsive Disorder (OCD), a condition often marked by inappropriate guilt. As I explained to Melissa across several sessions, she was seeking a degree of certainty about her past actions that no-one can achieve. Can anyone really know that they have caused no harm? Can you, the reader of this book, truly know that you have never injured another? Have you ever taken advantage of anyone? Have you ever taken credit for somebody else's work that could have led them to better things? Have you ever, perhaps in your school years, laughed or teased another who might have been altered by the experience? Have you ever excluded another from a game or social activity? Have you ever ignored a screaming voice in the distance? Have you ever poured one more drink for the friend that had already had too many? Have you ever ignored the needs of another or the plight of a troubled friend? Have you ever spoken harshly to a young person, potentially damaging their sense of self? Even a moment's reflection on these questions is, in my view, a moment too many. And lingering or ruminating on them can be a disaster. It can take you down a dark rabbit hole that can be difficult to escape. This is precisely what had happened to Melissa across the decades of her illness.

Slowly over treatment, Melissa came to realise that one simply can't have certainty about the outcomes that she feared. None of us can ever know how our behaviours and choices have rippled out across the lives of others. There is nothing a human can do but learn to accept their past and live with the doubt that harms, small and large, may have occurred to others as a result. Learning to live with doubt was the foundation stone of my sessions with Melissa.

Over time, Melissa gained more skill in letting go of her thoughts. Her mind would continue to throw up moments from her past, but she would no longer be gripped by them for days or weeks on end. Increasingly, thoughts could come and go, the doubts unanswered, the moments from her history accepted. Perhaps, most importantly, she came to have a better and more accurate understanding of who she was as a person. Melissa was a kind and gentle woman desperately trying to do her best for the people around her. The irony of Melissa's case, as in so many like her, is that the dread of hurting others had created its exact opposite — a positive, caring, careful woman in all of her interactions with her fellow travellers.

At the time of the interview, Melissa's treatment was incomplete. I had seen her 38 times over 18 months. She had improved considerably, but the little girl who feared purgatory still resided somewhere in her psyche. She still wondered about her goodness, and at times her mood and functioning would deteriorate badly. On balance though, I was hopeful. She was finally starting to see that the feather of Maat is too hard a test for any of us.

Our interview with Melissa

Ross: Well, thank you Melissa for coming in. I want to begin by focusing on your family. Can you tell me about life at home as you grew up?

Melissa: Sure. I had a mother, a father, and an older brother. We moved around quite a bit. I think I moved seven times before I was 13. My parents never argued or anything. They almost broke up when I was about eight. But then they got back together, and they stayed together until I was 15.

Ross: A lot of movement though, in those early years. Did that make it difficult with schools and friends?

Melissa: It's funny. Since my brother has had children, he's been very dogmatic about it, saying that moving was a really terrible thing for him, but I didn't notice it at the time. I was disappointed to leave friends behind, but I liked going to new schools and new houses.

Ross: I see. Can you tell me about your relationship with your mother in the early years?

Melissa: Yeah. We were very close. I've always been close to my mum, but it was hard when the marriage broke up. They still argue about it today — they can't agree on what actually happened. I had some anger about that period, but I went to see various new-age therapists and they encouraged me to talk about my feelings, and mum was very good about it. She was fine to talk about it, and stuff. But then when they broke up when I was 15, I lived with just my dad, and that was very hard.

Ross: Tell me about your relationship with your father before that period, and then after the break-up.

Melissa: I have a good relationship with my dad. He's a very hands-on father. He wasn't one for going to the pub or anything. He always came home. He tended to work quite far from where we lived, so he wasn't around all the time, but he was there a lot of the time. I never got smacked, and I didn't get in too much trouble.

           We weren't that close, until my mum and he broke up, and then I lived with him. And then our relationship became closer, and I suppose I became quite dependent on him in a way because my mum went straight into a relationship with someone else whereas I felt like he was the only one I had to rely on. It became a dependent relationship, and when he started dating again, I didn't cope with it very well.

Ross: I see. Other than the separation of parents, did you have any other losses in your early life? Any deaths that you think had an impact on you?

Melissa: Three of my grandparents died when I was too young to remember when I was one or two. My aunt died when I was about seven. I remember that. I remember taking the phone call from my uncle because we lived in Adelaide at the time and they were in Sydney. It was at the time when my parents' breakup thing was happening. It just so happened that she died.

Ross: You took the call?

Melissa: Yeah. I don't know why. I have a really bad memory generally, but I do remember that. I answered the phone. My uncle didn't tell me what he was calling about. I passed on the phone to mum. I just remember in retrospect that I answered it.

Ross: Yeah, right. Do you think any of these deaths had an impact on you?

Melissa: Only indirectly. Like, my mum has said that my dad changed a lot after his father died, and that was one of the things that changed their relationship. In that sense, yes, but not that I ever noticed personally.

Ross: I see. Well, I was going to ask you about any losses or traumas in your parents' lives, perhaps even before you were born. You've mentioned losses that had an impact on them. Any others that you're aware of in their younger years that you think may have altered them?

Melissa: My dad's never gotten over being made to move to Australia, even though he was like 13 when it happened. You can tell when he talks about it that he's still angry with his parents.

Ross: Really?

Melissa: Despite the fact that he doesn't want to live in England, so I don't really understand what he wants to have happened out of that.

Ross: He felt that no one listened to him, or what he wanted?

Melissa: My grandmother was one of three sisters, and they all moved over to Australia and brought their families. My grandfather apparently had quite a good job in England and they had a nice house and stuff, so he didn't understand why they moved. The other two sisters' husbands were in lower-income jobs and not doing very well.

Ross: I see. Are either of your parents anxious people?

Melissa: My mum is.

Ross: What sort of things does she worry about?

Melissa: I don't know. I guess I didn't understand at the time, but now looking back, I would say she was looking for a reason for her existence or some kind of meaning because she came from a difficult start. Her father was an alcoholic, and he killed himself, and her sister was a paranoid schizophrenic who died, and then their marriage wasn't going well. She turned to religion, and I developed a religious mania I think, in retrospect, by default, through going to all these meetings and things.

Then, as she got older, she turned more into alternative therapies and stuff and was following the harmonic convergence of 1988, and stuff. Now, I think she's just spiritual, but she doesn't discuss it with me because she knows that I am fairly ambivalent about it.

Ross: I see. She was anxious but she also wondered a lot about existence, the nature of her existence, the meaning of her life?

Melissa: I don't think I understood it at the time, but looking back, that's what I think it must have been.

Ross: Before I focus on your own mental health issues, I was going to ask if there is any other history of mental illness in the family? You've mentioned some of it.

Melissa: Yeah. As I said, the alcoholic grandfather who we now think was schizophrenic. My aunt was schizophrenic, my cousin, well two of my cousins are bipolar, one has Asperger's. My cousin and I were actually in hospital at the same time together!

Ross: Quite an extensive history of family mental health issues. And a range of different problem areas. Now I want to turn from your family to you. What are your earliest memories of being anxious, worried or afraid?

Melissa: I guess the first time I can remember was when I was about nine or so. I used to worry that I was going to die in my sleep. Or that I wouldn't sleep at all. My mum would have to sit by my bed until I fell asleep. That was around the time when mum was searching in religion, and I became very superstitious as well. I was 11 and going to church with her. I started to wear a Saint Philomena cord wrapped around my waist, under my uniform, and a scapula, and all manner of holy bits and bobs that are supposed to protect you.

Ross: Right. You were worried about dying in your sleep, you were worried about harm, you had religious, iconic things to protect you, and some of that was at your own instigation, or was that coming from mum or the church? Do you recall whether you wanted to wear them?

Melissa: It was definitely me who was wanting to wear these things.

Ross: I see. Can I ask you to clarify those early fears? You mentioned that one fear was dying in your sleep, and another was that you wouldn't sleep at all. Some young people fear that not sleeping could cause death. 'If I don't sleep and it continues for days, could I die that way?' Do you remember ever thinking that?

Melissa: I don't think so. The not sleeping is still a fear that is present for me, but I feel very differently about it now than when I was a kid. You have no responsibility as a child — there was no consequence to not sleeping. It was just that I wouldn't sleep, I guess, lying there in the night by yourself, staring at the ceiling.

Ross: I see. Now the wearing of protective religious icons and so on was because of your own fears that something could happen. These were to protect you from something bad suddenly occurring?

Melissa: Yeah.

Ross: Do you remember what sort of things you feared could occur? Do you remember what you were worried about in those early days?

Melissa: I just remember being scared of dying. Actually, that's not quite true. I was scared of dying, but what I was more scared of was purgatory. From one of the meetings that my mum had gone to, I got a look at this leaflet on purgatory. I don't know if it's still current in the church, but the belief then was that you go through a period of getting punished in purgatory and stuff before you can go to heaven — if you deserve to go to heaven, that is.

After that, I was just really worried that I was going to go to purgatory, and that it would turn out that I'd done something wrong.

Ross: I see. You'd go to purgatory and you'd be punished, and your fear was just the experience of purgatory, or that you might never get to heaven?

Melissa: I was worried about hell. But mostly I was scared of going to purgatory.

Ross: What was the thing you mentioned that you wore around your waist?

Melissa: A red and white, like, braided cord, that's supposed to connect you to Saint Philomena. And then I had a scapula, it's like a necklace but with these little felt pictures of Mary. But supposedly if you died wearing these objects, you would go straight to heaven, and that was my protection. And a miraculous medal for the same reason, a little charm thing.

Ross: So these devices specifically were to treat your fear of purgatory — 'if I'm wearing these and something happens, I get straight into heaven'?

Melissa: Mm-hmm (affirmative). I would say Hail Marys before, as I was worrying, trying to go to sleep, I would say 'em.

Ross: For the same reason?

Melissa: Mm-hmm (affirmative).

Ross: Because that will get you straight to heaven if something happens?

Melissa: Yeah.

Ross: Those early fears of death — dying in your sleep, purgatory, judgment, having done something bad — how have they progressed over the years? What happened to them? Are they with you at all? How have they changed?

Melissa: Well, the fear of not sleeping has stuck with me, but now it's a fear that I won't be able to cope with whatever is happening the next day. Or, more so that if I have a job that I'll somehow let people down at that job through my lack of concentration or attention 'cause I haven't slept, and that I'll cause bad things to happen.

I guess all of my obsessional thoughts stem back to, 'Have I hurt someone in some way?' In that sense, I guess I'm still always waiting to be judged to see whether or not you can go to heaven or not. Even though I've been agnostic for maybe 10 years after going to Catholic school, it's not until the last 18 months or so that I've really actually believed that nothing happens to you after you die.

Ross: I see.

Melissa: But being scared of being judged in some way for doing something bad still seems to have a hold on me. I'm finding it hard to shed. Thinking that there's nothing after death has also coincided with a new threat. Before, I never would have considered killing myself, now I think about it quite frequently. In the past, when I was a believer in Catholicism, suicide is a sin, and you would be judged for it and all the rest of it. Whereas when you don't believe in that, and you just think you're going to be mulch, you don't have to worry about the sin aspect of taking your own life.

Ross: So it introduces a new threat.

Melissa: A new possibility.

Ross: So your fear of doing something wrong started because of a fear of being judged and going to purgatory. If I'm understanding you right, you're saying, 'even in the period since I've become a non-believer, in which I don't believe in a purgatory or a hell or a heaven, I keep fearing that I've done something wrong'. Can you give me examples of the wrongs you might have committed, or that you fear committing?

Melissa: As time has progressed, it started being more concentrated about worries that I could have been a paedophile and I would think of any interactions I have had with children in the past and worried that I might have done something. Or, something may have happened.

I guess as I got older, it's become more all-encompassing. It just took over other places of my life. Now I worry if I put a bottle back in the wrong place in a chemist that someone will be looking for medication for their child and won't be able to find it and then it will be my fault. Or I'm thinking about a cigarette butt of mine and was it completely out because I'm terrified that someone's going to stand on it and burn themselves, or a dog will stand on it and hurt himself, and that'll be my fault.

I can't go back to working in libraries, because I'm terrified that I will either not put a book back correctly, or I won't check it in properly, or I won't check it out properly, and someone will need it, and that will somehow make them fail an exam, or miss an epiphany they're meant to have in their life, because they haven't read the correct book.

Ross: You've had fears about so many things that you have had no evidence for at all, haven't you? 'What if I've walked into that child? I don't have a memory of it, but what if I did do it?' That's happened across many years, those sorts of fears. 'What if I've done something that's bad and I've forgotten?'

Melissa: I've forgotten, yeah. I don't remember exactly when they started, but they've been around since I was at least 18. When I first got noticeably sick, and then ended up going to see doctors and getting diagnosed. That was the first time that I really remember it.

Ross: Have there been any happenings in your life that you think intensified the fears? Happenings that you think made you believe in the fears more, or made you believe that they could happen more — anything at all? It could be news reports; it could be things at school, accidents, loss, bullying, anything that you can think of that fed the fears?

Melissa: I think in general, when I'm stressed out, they're worse. I first got sick when I first went to university, so that was a big change. I went from being a big fish in a little pond to being a teeny, tiny fish in a big pond and I didn't cope very well. Other than that, yeah, anything and everything seems to provoke them or make them worse.

Sometimes I go out and I see kids and I think, 'Oh no, I don't need to worry about these kids, because I feel very benevolent towards them,' but then another child will walk past and I'll feel ambivalent towards them, and then I get nervous again.

Ross: Mm-hmm (affirmative). Melissa, how did you first get treatment for your anxiety?

Melissa: When I was 18, and I was at university, I started having trouble sleeping. I saw a sign on the back of a door at university, in the toilets saying, 'If you don't sleep this many hours a night, then come and participate in our sleep study.' I never really thought how much I did or didn't sleep was unusual before, but then I started obsessing over that, and then not being able to sleep.

I went to a GP who then referred me to … I can't remember if it was a counsellor or a psychologist, but he diagnosed me with anxiety, and my mum was worrying about me and was chasing doctors around, and eventually got me an appointment with a psychologist who I saw for a while. She diagnosed me with OCD and then subsequently I went to hospital for a little while, and have been re-diagnosed and treated since that time.

Ross: In treatment, what are the things that have been most helpful in lightening your fears?

Melissa: It's a hard question in a way, because I've been sick for a long time, but only debilitated by my illness for the past three years. Things that have helped in the past don't help now. When I saw the first psychologist, I used to see her twice a week. We talked a lot. I think it's psychotherapy?

Ross: Mm-hmm (affirmative).

Melissa: Yeah. I didn't realise that was unusual at the time. That helped, talking through things helped. Although there was a limit. You can only discuss what your mum did when you were seven so many times before you run out of …

Ross: … things to talk about.

Melissa: Yes, that's right. Certainly, medication has made a difference. What else? I don't know, being in hospital, when I was in there.

Ross: Being in hospital helped because it gave you respite or because of the things you learned?

Melissa: I think more just the respite. I mean, the first time I was in hospital, when I was around 20 years of age, I don't remember there being any classes or really learning anything. But when I returned to hospital more recently, I did lots of classes, and they do try and teach you things. But I don't know … it's very much showing you what you should do, rather than what you actually do. It's like knowing you should eat fruit and vegetables, but then eating a piece of chocolate until you start feeling that you're over-weight and then you eat fruit and vegetables. They teach you lots of things, but in the background, until I feel really horrible, I didn't really do any of the tasks.

Ross: Yeah, okay. There might have been things that would be useful, but you've found it hard to keep them up?

Melissa: Mm-hmm (affirmative).

Ross: I want to ask you some more direct questions about death. What emotions arise in you at the thought of your own death?

Melissa: That's changed a lot in the last couple of years. I used to be absolutely terrified of the thought of dying. I think that's why I was
mentally unwell for so long. Now, I mean, for the most part,
whilst I don't welcome it, it is funny when you sit and think about
it for a while. We all know that at some point we're going to die.
It's a weird, human condition to be in. But generally speaking, I'm
fairly okay about it now. I'm not scared about it or anything, and
there is a big part of me that is quite looking forward to not
having to deal with my thoughts and obsessions and stuff.

Ross: That's understandable, Melissa. Can I ask, what do you think will
happen to you as you physically die and once you're physically dead?

Melissa: I think that when you die, that's it. I mean, I believe that your
energy or whatever probably goes somewhere else in the universe
to be used by something else, like plants, when you decompose
and stuff. But the intrinsic thing, your personality, the thing that
makes you you, just goes. I just think that's it. Once you die, then
that's it. You cease to exist.

Ross: How often do you think about these sorts of things, about death
itself, your death or the death of others?

Melissa: Again, it's changed a lot, but quite frequently. Some days not at
all, but certainly like five days out of seven, it would cross my
mind, or I think about it.

Ross: The death of yourself, the death of others, the concept of death?

Melissa: Myself quite often. And both of my parents, I do think about now,
just because they're getting older, and my dad had cancer a couple
of years ago, so that makes you aware of people's mortality.
Because I'm self-obsessed, it's been more in the last few years, as
I've realised that at the moment, I'm really dependent on them,
and if I was by myself, I don't know what I would do.

Ross: I see.

Melissa: More about worrying about how I will cope, rather than just
thinking of them not being here.

Ross: What relationship do you see between your fears of death and
your experience of life, of everyday living?

Melissa: Well, all my fears of death came from being raised a Catholic and thinking of all the things, the ideas of sin and heaven and purgatory and all the rest of it. All my life I've lived like there's a huge tally sheet being made up of your actions, good and bad, that you will be called to account for.

Now that I don't fear that so much, it's in flux. It's only been in the last couple of months that I've really gone, 'hang on, if I don't believe in God, then why am I so worried about so many of these things?'

Ross: Certainly, that's been my experience of you, Melissa. In the time I've known you, it's as if you're still keeping a tally sheet. You come into sessions saying, 'Oh no, what if I did this thing and it hurt someone? Is it a bad thing? Have I done a bad thing or not?'

Melissa: Very much so. I'm realising that. And I know that I shouldn't be seeking reassurance… but…

Ross: It's hard to stop.

Melissa: There's just always a part of me that expects to be punished. There's still that fear that there's a God up there that's going to throw some lightning bolts. It's crazy — I don't even believe anymore.

Ross: I asked you before what has helped reduce your specific fears, but what about the dread of death that you once had? Within therapy, or outside of it, what if anything reduced your dread of death?

Melissa: I don't think anything in therapy, up until recently, talking with you, which has helped me start clarifying the 'hang on if I don't believe in God, what am I doing? What am I even scared of now?' But prior to that, it's just been my own evolving sense of what I believe in.

Ross: I see. To finish, I wanted to ask you about meaning and building a meaningful existence. You mentioned earlier that your mother was seeking some sort of meaning earlier in her life. What if anything, makes life meaningful for you?

Melissa: I don't know. Meaning always seems like a very Western, first-world concept when you're not in the middle of being ethnically cleansed, or in the middle of a famine, or anything. For poor people meaning just has no currency.

In that sense, I don't believe in a plan or anything that I do has any greater meaning. I just think we all exist on a rock hurtling through space, as the saying goes. But I guess for things that are personally more meaningful; I don't know. I'm just very self-absorbed. This illness has made me very self-absorbed. Really it's my family — my mum and my dad — they are the only things that still have meaning to me personally.

Ross: So family relationships?

Melissa: Mm-hmm (affirmative). Just mum and dad. That's all I need.

Ross: Mum and dad, okay. That's a good place to finish. Thank you. Thank you very much, Melissa.

Part 3

Reflections

Rachel E. Menzies

Chapter 12

Lessons from our clients

A s a clinician and researcher in the area of death anxiety, I believe there is much we can take away from the remarkable stories of the individuals interviewed in Part Two of this book. It is rare that one gets the opportunity to learn so much about a person's life, either within therapy or outside of it, in a space of time as short as these interviews. As a reader, it is hard not to be struck by how fascinating these individuals are, how compelling their histories have been, and how hard they have fought to overcome their difficulties, bravely wading their way through the murky territory of the same existential dilemmas we all must face.

When reading and reflecting on these cases, a few questions seemed especially worth discussing: What factors or experiences contribute to an individual's fear of death? Why do some of the people interviewed show a miraculous and speedy recovery in their dread of death, while for others, their quest for death acceptance may be a lifelong journey? What strategies seem to be the most effective at keeping the spectre of death at bay, and why? At the heart of it all, when it comes to fears of death: What are the problems, and what are the solutions?

What Contributes to the Dread of Death?

Researchers in the area of mental health have found that individuals who experience anxiety disorders often have experienced some form of confrontation with death earlier in life. These confrontations with death may involve the death of a loved one, or the threat of death, such as through suffering an illness or being physically attacked. These interactions with death may occur at any point across the lifespan, but for many of the individuals discussed in this book, they stretched well back into childhood. There are a multitude of ways in which children may first catch glimpses of death. For many children, their earliest encounter with mortality is through the loss of a pet. For Aidan, the death of his pet goldfish when he was ten years old appears vividly etched into his memory. He recalls that loss being 'the first time [he] really, really cried about something', and remembers his mother lying about his pet's death to hide the natural reality from him. As Aidan recounts in 'The joker', his pet's death had such an effect on him that, half a decade later, he found himself digging around in his backyard, trying to find the plastic bag in which the goldfish was buried.

At around six-years-old, John would often see his domineering father returning from a hunting trip covered in the blood of slaughtered animals, with his rifle over his shoulder. At this young age, John would watch his father string up the dead animal, remove its skin, and slice open its stomach, causing its intestines to spill out all over the garage floor. In 'My father's son', John also describes witnessing his father's violence towards his family members. First, he describes seeing his father beat his mother, including once pointing a gun in her face. On a second occasion, John saw his brother suffer an allergic reaction after being stung by their father's bees. While watching his brother's eyes swell up, John's father simply laughs. Just one of these experiences could easily be a sufficiently traumatic event for a child to develop lifelong fears associated with death.

For some children, they may first experience death through the loss of a close family member. As a child, Bruce was made to see his deceased grandfather in an open coffin, an event that he reported finding confronting, as would many 11-year-olds. Although not all children will witness death firsthand, their learning of a death in the family may also have surprisingly powerful repercussions. In 'Dinosaurs are hiding', Rose notices that her compulsive washing increased following the recent death of her grandfather. In 'Bring me back', Michael describes how, when he was a child, he learned that his cousin had suddenly died of a heart attack while out on a walk. Later in his life, Michael became plagued by fears of suddenly dropping dead, fears which seem almost undoubtedly linked to this loss as a child. Similarly, in 'The caveman', Berat recounts the violent death of two cousins, one of whom was hit by a truck, and the other who was reportedly murdered and cut into pieces. In 'Eating in emergency', Mary describes seeing a dead man lying on the road while she lived in Darwin. Further, as a result of the frequency with which her family would recount stories of death, she says she 'started to fear any symbols of death or loss or departures.'

Aidan's childhood was, perhaps indirectly, heavily impacted by the loss of his sibling, who died in the womb near the end of his mother's pregnancy. After this horrible experience, his mother's own anxiety naturally increased, causing her to be an extremely cautious mother when Aidan was born. A multitude of studies show that overprotective parenting is a known risk factor for childhood anxiety, and this likely contributed to Aidan's later worries. On the other hand, the loss of a child may also manifest in an altogether different style of parenting. In 'The activist', Godfrey recounts the way that his parents' approach to childrearing was forever altered by the death of his infant sister: 'So as not to become too emotionally invested, given their experience of loss, they distanced themselves from me. I don't think any of it was conscious, but I was almost neglectfully parented.'

Unfortunately, for some children, they may find themselves staring death in the face. In 'The caveman', Berat recounts how he nearly drowned at a beach when he was just eight years old. Immediately following this near death experience, from which he only narrowly escaped, his mental health began to decline. To this day, simply drinking water can prove troubling for Berat, as it reminds him of the same sensations he experienced on that horrible day. Matilda was similarly traumatised when, at the age of 11, she was admitted to hospital after being misdiagnosed with meningitis. In 'All you need is love', she describes how an intravenous line began to leak, and she witnessed her own blood pouring out onto the bed. 'The image is still really, really clear in my mind. I thought I might die, just bleed out' Matilda says. 'I nearly died.'

Of course, while these sorts of losses or confrontations with death in childhood may prove particularly formative, experiencing a loss in adulthood may also significantly impact one's wellbeing, as well as their responses to death. In 'The activist', Godfrey's slide into depression begins after his mother's death. 'I don't think my depression is about anxiety,' he reflects. 'I think it's about mortality. It's somehow linked to my mother's loss. Somehow it's all about loss.' In 'The architect', Bruce finds himself directly faced with death after he is diagnosed with the same illness that killed his father. Naturally, he fears that his suite of previous existential concerns will re-emerge. Despite this, he ends up handling his diagnosis with impressive skill.

Across the ten cases presented, some form of early experience with death is described in all but one interview. These confrontations with mortality, interwoven through these individuals' childhoods, seem likely contributing factors to the worries and fears of death they went on to develop. Some other shared experiences across the cases also seem noteworthy. Nearly half of the people interviewed reported experiencing bullying during their school years, including John, who described extensive bullying both at school and at the hands of his own father. Other social factors, such as intergenerational trauma, also feature across the cases. For Aidan, his Jewish heritage likely played a role in the development of his fears. Since childhood, he had heard the atrocities of the Holocaust being recounted to him: 'As a little kid who obviously had some anxious tendencies to hear all these things that happened to Jews and identifying as a Jew and knowing all of that — I think it did have some impact.' On top of this, the frequent lockdown training at the heavily guarded Jewish school he attended arguably contributed to Aidan's sense of perceived threat. In 'Eating in emergency', Mary's story offers a striking example of the impact that the trauma of previous generations can have on an individual's worldview. Mary's grandmother was part of the stolen generation, and seven of her siblings died at an early age. The trauma associated with living as an Indigenous woman through the stolen generation had understandably permeated her perspective on the world, and as a result, the way in which Mary was raised: 'My mother made the world around me a very unsafe place. She frequently told me, from a very young age, how dangerous the world was … The shadows of the stolen generation were never far from her mind.' Mary's mother lived in fear that her daughter would be taken away from her by child welfare. On one occasion, Mary was made to hide in a neighbour's cupboard, when her mother panicked that the police would remove her from her care. In Mary's words: 'The trauma was passed down — it infected my mum … My family wander around believing they are in an unsafe world where they don't fit in'. It is perhaps unsurprising then, that Mary went on to develop such severe fears of death, reporting the highest scores on a standard measure of death anxiety that her psychologist had ever seen. 'They talk about death a lot — death has clearly haunted them', Mary adds. 'I don't think they've ever really processed the big losses in their lives.' If a child's first experiences of mortality teach them that death is sudden, unpredictable, or all-encompassing (such as it was for Mary, when stories of death and the threat of separation surrounded her at all times), it would be nearly impossible for anyone to reach adulthood having successfully evaded the dread of death.

The 'Givens' of Human Existence

Benjamin Franklin once famously wrote that there are only two certainties in life: Death and taxes. However, world-renowned psychotherapist Irvin Yalom, echoing the thoughts of the 20th-century French existentialists, might disagree. In his book *Existential Psychotherapy* (1980), Yalom proposed four ultimate concerns, which he considered the 'the givens' of human existence: death, freedom, isolation, and meaninglessness (p. 8). According to Yalom's framework, much of human struggles can be viewed through the lens of these four themes, based on their inescapable nature. These themes permeate to various extents the ten cases presented in Part Two. A reflection on the way in which these existential concerns at times formed either a problem or solution for these ten individuals grappling with their fears of death may illuminate their relevance to both clinical practice and our own lives.

1. Death

The existential concern that requires the least introduction, at least to the readers of this book, is that of death. It should come as no surprise that Yalom viewed our awareness of death as a central part of human existence, as we each must grapple with our knowledge of death's inevitability, along-side our desperate wish to live. The nature of death as a driving force of much of human behaviour across history has already been explored at length in Part One. In Part Two, we are presented with 10 individuals whose fears of death have dramatically shaped the course of their lives in one way or another.

In 'Eating in emergency', Mary was so consumed by her worries of death by choking or anaphylaxis that she refused to eat most foods. Of the meals that she did eat, she would often only do so in hospital emergency departments, so that she could be revived if something 'goes wrong'. In a similar vein, in 'The caveman' we learn of Berat, who was so terrified of being poisoned that he regurgitated most meals. Berat had also developed complex magical rituals in order to prevent harm, such as needing to return to a destination in the exact way he had come. Ironically, his rituals landed him in a particularly dangerous situation when he ended up on a pushbike dodging cars while riding the wrong way through a busy tunnel, in order to alleviate anxiety caused by an incomplete ritual 10 years prior. In 'My father's son', John's fears of death manifest in distressing images of himself attacking other people, and equally, ending his own life in violent ways, such as by worrying that he would throw himself into a tree mincer. In 'Dinosaurs are hiding', Rose recounts how when she was just seven years old, she was terrified of sleeping because she was convinced that her mattress was actually filled with rotting human corpses. In 'Bring me back', we learn that Michael is so overwhelmed by the thought that he could drop dead at any moment, that at one point he is visiting the hospital emergency department every second day. Later in his life, Michael becomes obsessed with religion, in a desperate attempt to know which faith is 'correct' in order to prevent eternal suffering in the afterlife. In 'The activist', we meet Godfrey, who struggled with anxiety and 'existential despair' for more than 20 years, before experiencing a severe bout of depression after the death of his mother. In his interview recorded in 'The joker', Aidan's worries about dying manifest in front of our own eyes, such that he speculates out loud whether he may be having a stroke in that very moment. In 'The architect', Bruce's decision to close his business makes him question the pointlessness of his lifetime of achievements, given that 'when you die, you go to nothing and nobody remembers you.' His worries about leaving a mark on the world are challenged further after he is diagnosed with advanced prostate cancer. On the other hand, Matilda sees death everywhere around her despite her own good physical health, in 'All you need is love'. She experiences a myriad of dark fears including being murdered on the street, suffering a fatal illness, or even being framed for murder. Lastly, in 'Purgatory', Melissa's dread of death presents itself through her worries about the possibility of eternal punishment in the afterlife, and her desperate searching for any harm she may have unwittingly caused another.

Themes of death and loss are interwoven throughout the lives of these ten individuals. Like all of us, they must navigate their awareness of mortality, and try and find a path through the shadows cast by our inevitable fate, using whatever tools they can find.

2. Isolation

Another existential concern proposed by Yalom is isolation. Existential isolation refers to the idea that each of us both enters and leaves this world alone. That is, although we may be surrounded by a plethora of loving and beloved friends and family, there will always be an unbridgeable gap between us and them; we can never truly know anyone, no matter how much we may seek connection with them.

In addition to this existential isolation that all of us must grapple with, one may also experience the loneliness of *interpersonal* isolation. Such experiences of being cut off from others can create significant distress, and, as we will soon discuss, may play a particularly noxious role in driving the dread of death. It is likely no coincidence that soon after being isolated by those around her, Mary described a sudden surge in her fears of death — specifically, a sudden worry that she may have a brain tumour.

> Things had been going so well…I was not afraid at all. But then…I had a situation where I was coerced into sexual activity with a man who was much older than I was. It was straight after that my fears returned, although I've never believed that it was the sexual encounter itself that caused it. I think it had more to do with feeling let down by people around me. You see, I told everyone what had happened, and they made it sound like I just wanted attention and that I'd wanted to have sex with this older man. Everyone I'd trusted turned against me. So maybe that was it. Soon after that, I remember getting the thought 'I have a brain tumour'.

Mary suddenly found herself abandoned by people she had trusted. This isolation led to the escalation of anxiety that had previously lay dormant in the background of her life. This incident was not Mary's only experience of isolation. She described severe bullying and exclusion throughout high school, a known risk factor for the later development of anxiety disorders. In 'All you need is love', Matilda also identified a long period of 'intense' bullying, the memory of which 'has stayed [with her] ever since'. Even after the bullying stopped, her devastating sense of isolation persisted: 'I became lonely and was still fearful. I agreed to date a boy that I didn't like, just because I was lonely. Eventually, I had to end that, and he became nasty. There was always someone being nasty to me.' In fact, Matilda's experience of loneliness and isolation appeared to directly contribute to her symptoms of OCD, as her intrusive imagery of harming others was clearly associated with her underlying desire to connect with those around her. 'I so wanted to be friends with nice people, and I was terrified I'd do something horrible to mess it up', Matilda admitted. 'My mind kept thinking up things that would wreck everything with them — that would make them hate me.' Matilda's observation here is very insightful, as she notices that her mind was playing on her own vulnerability and targeting her weak spots, to torment her with the threat of even further isolation. At the heart of her mental conjuring, of her distressing images of stepping on friends' feet or pushing them onto train tracks, was the devastating possibility of being forever lonely.

If isolation is a key existential concern, then regaining one's sense of belonging and connection with others seems a likely solution to managing existential dread. In fact, numerous studies serve as a testament to the protective function of close relationships when it comes to fears of death. One thing that seems to play a central role in either reducing or heightening our existential concerns is our own attachment style. This can be understood as one's personal framework for engaging in close relationships, such as with parents in early childhood, or romantic partners in adulthood. According to decades of research first pioneered by John Bowlby and Mary Ainsworth in the 1950s, each of us can be broadly categorised as having one of three styles of attachment: (1) A secure attachment style, in which one feels reasonably comfortable in close relationships, as well as feeling content with both relying on others and being independent; (2) An ambivalent attachment style, in which one seeks high levels of intimacy in relationships, and frequently fears being abandoned by others or that others may not reciprocate their own desire for closeness; and (3) An avoidant attachment style, in which one is uncomfortable with the level of intimacy typically desired by others, and instead desires independence. One early study found that individuals with a secure attachment style are significantly less fearful of death compared to those with an ambivalent or avoidant attachment style (Florian & Mikulincer, 1998), suggesting that individuals who tend to view their relationships with others as reliable or supportive seem better equipped to fight off worries about mortality.

Other studies have demonstrated that death anxiety may drive us to seek security from others through various behaviours related to attachment and relationships. For example, reminders of death have been shown to increase individuals' reported attraction, trust, and love towards their current romantic partner (Florian et al., 2002). Other findings reveal that after reflecting on their own mortality, people are more likely to choose to sit next to other participants in a staged group discussion, rather than sitting alone, compared to those who had not been reminded of death (Wisman & Koole, 2003). Similarly, reflecting on death seems to make us think more about connecting with others, as simply being subliminally presented with the word 'death' (that is, with the word presented so quickly that it would not have been consciously detected by participants), has also been shown to increase the mental accessibility of words related to relationships, such as 'kiss', 'hug', and 'closeness'.

Collectively, these results suggest that not only can death anxiety motivate us to seek meaningful and satisfying relationships with others, but that such relationships may indeed successfully ward off our existential concerns. Across the cases described in Part Two, the importance of fulfilling relationships in shifting the trajectory of one's life and keeping fears of death at bay is palpable. Matilda's story, aptly titled 'All you need is love', unquestionably provides the most striking example of the transformative power of relationships. When she first presented for treatment, Matilda had experienced almost a decade of chronic mental health difficulties. She met criteria for at least five disorders, with symptoms stretching back to her high school years. Matilda saw death everywhere she went, and almost everything was viewed through the lens of having the potential to kill.

Bacteria in food may make her deathly ill. The bus she caught may explode, and so too may her home stove. Illnesses she heard about on television may prove the end of her. Passersby may try to murder her. If she wasn't murdered herself, perhaps someone would frame her for murder. She may in fact unwittingly murder a friend, by pushing them onto train tracks. As a result of all of these fears, simply going out in public had become unimaginably terrifying for Matilda.

Yet despite this extensive and complex list of worries, Matilda's anxiety miraculously disappeared almost overnight. As if by magic, all of her myriad of fears — her fears of stabbings, illness, assaults, and exploding vehicles or appliances — suddenly vanished. This stunning evaporation of symptoms is an outcome that therapy itself, no matter how good, rarely achieves at such a striking speed. So what was the silver bullet that produced this incredible result? The answer was clear to Matilda: 'I'm in a relationship now,' she explained. 'Ever since I started to see my boyfriend, my fears on the streets stopped. Suddenly I wasn't afraid of being murdered or attacked or assaulted'. What's more, the addition of her new partner didn't serve to ease her worries about death only in his presence. As Matilda described in her interview, even when her boyfriend is overseas, her fears of death no longer plague her, suggesting that the relationship is doing something more profound than simply giving her an understandable sense of physical safety alongside her male partner. Matilda's case provides a stunning example of how a meaningful relationship in and of itself can prove a powerful force in alleviating concerns about mortality.

Of course, while long-term monogamous relationships may be the norm in much of Western society, many varied forms of interpersonal connection may also assuage existential dread. For Godfrey, his burgeoning focus on pursuing intimacy with numerous younger women appeared to serve a similar function. After nearly twenty years of anxiety and a more recent slide into depression after the death of his mother, Godfrey had lost much of his sense of purpose in life. By deepening his connections with others, such as with the young women he photographed nude, and investing more time into building fulfilling relationships, Godfrey was slowly able to rebuild an enjoyable life, despite some occasional surges in anxiety. His relationships with women mark a notable turning point in his struggle with mortality. In his own words: 'This 20-year-old girl has just changed everything for me.' Although Godfrey discusses the positive difference that his pursuit of hedonism and his varied sexual forays have made in his life, the relationships he describes are not built exclusively on sexual gratification. In his interview, he describes offering advice to his younger female partners and encouraging them to pursue their goals, and in return, becoming inspired by their youth and a renewed interest in political and social causes. While it is possible that Godfrey's fulfilling and enjoyable sexual experiences may be what lies behind his reduced fixation on mortality, it seems likely that his sense of emotional connectedness with and contributions to the women in his life plays a larger role. Godfrey himself articulates how valuable caring for others can be when it comes to building happiness and a life free from fear:

> 'I'm starting to come full circle and realise that one age-old principle is true — even though it hadn't resonated with me for years — and that is about selflessness. It's making those connections; it's giving, it's turning your energy in those directions … Being mindful, doing unto others as you would have them do unto you, caring about other people more than you care about yourself because if you just go after ego-driven pursuits, you're destined to unhappiness.'

Both Matilda and Godfrey, while coming to their respective relationships through very different paths, provide striking examples of the way that meaningful relationships can keep the spectre of mortality at bay, and transform one's life in the process.

3. Freedom

Although we may think of freedom as an entirely positive thing, Yalom and the existential philosophers argue that freedom may, in fact, be a cause of existential dread. They argue that we live in a world with nearly infinite possibilities and that our lives are inherently unstructured except for the structure that we impose on them. From this perspective, this sense of responsibility — that is, to make one's own choices, decide one's actions and life purpose — can form a core existential conflict, as we are faced with a groundless, unpredictable world, despite our own striving for structure and order. In 'The architect', Bruce appears to be struggling with this conflict after making the decision to end his architecture business:

> 'Closing the business led me to consider, more so than ever in the past, what am I here for? What am I doing? … Do any of these things coincide with the

point of geometry or structure to my life? What takes me forward from this point? ... I felt a deep sense of sadness that wouldn't go away.'

On the other hand, despite the existentialists' view that freedom can be a terrifying concept, even a quick glance through a history textbook will tell you that humans have sought and died for freedom across millennia. While too much freedom may indeed be paralysing, the lack of it can itself be a large contributor to distress. In 'The joker', Aidan tells us how he experienced regular lockdown drills at his high-security Jewish school, in preparation for a feared attack. The frequency of these events and his distress during them suggests that it's possible they played some role in his later development of anxiety. What about them did he find so terrifying? In Aidan's words: 'You couldn't leave. You were locked down. You were stuck. That's what scared me most, the fact that I couldn't move.' The physical absence of freedom, or the inability to move through this world as we would like, can be incredibly distressing.

Of course, the loss of freedom is not always imposed on us by others. Our own fears can so impair an individual's functioning that the anxiety itself becomes a prison. Across each of the 10 cases, we see the toll that anxiety can take on a human life, limiting the pursuit of their goals, of healthy relationships, of even day to day movement. We see people like Mary, who was restricted to eating all of her meals in hospital emergency departments, or Berat, whose freedom so suffered at the hands of his anxiety that he was confined to his own house for 10 years. In 'The joker', Ross points out the toll that this anxiety has taken on Aidan, noting: 'it's also restricted terribly what you've done in your life, where you've gone in your life, what you've seen in your life'. Aidan agrees, responding:

> 'Totally. I'm such a lucky privileged piece of shit that if I went to my dad tomorrow and said, 'Dad, I want to travel the world,' he'd book me a flight in an instant. That pisses me off even more, the fact that I know I can do anything, and I choose not to because I'm worried about it. That upsets me more than anything in the world. When I have all these options, everything, and I fucking choose not to do them, for one reason or another. I could go travel the world, see everything, do all these beautiful things, but I wouldn't enjoy it. It upsets me; it really upsets me.'

In Aidan's response, we see hints of the dual nature of freedom that Yalom and others discuss. On the one hand, the vast number of possible actions we could choose can in and of itself create anxiety ('I know I can do anything, and I choose not to because I'm worried about it'), as well as the distress that follows when anxiety so limits one's freedom that they are unable to pursue the things they would like to ('That upsets me more than anything in the world'). As part of our existence in this world, we must all find a balance between the two: to live as freely as possible, unburdened by the restrictive baggage of our worries, but also to navigate the overwhelming number of choices we could make and still continue to act. If we want to make the most of our time on earth, we can neither succumb to the terror of our paralysing freedom nor can we inadvertently lock ourselves into prisons of our own making.

4. Meaninglessness

How do we find meaning in an inherently meaningless world? How do we create a purposeful life while knowing full well that it one day must end? Many writers in this space emphasise the importance of building a sense of purpose and pursuing meaningful achievements, both in the broader context of mental health, as well as being a specific shield from death anxiety. Recent experimental findings support the notion that having a sense of meaning can protect us from the dread of death. One study found that reminders of death *only* increased fears of death among individuals who reported very little meaning in their life. On the other hand, participants who described having a strong sense of purpose in life showed no change in their levels of death anxiety after being asked to reflect on their own mortality (Routledge & Juhl, 2010). This association between the dread of death and meaninglessness is echoed in the words of Godfrey: 'I could just always remember thinking everything ends, there's no meaning to anything.' If meaninglessness can exacerbate one's dread of death, can building a meaningful life alleviate it?

Across the ten cases, we see many individuals experience the classic existential dilemma of how to find meaning in the face of their inevitable impermanence. One such example is that of Bruce, whose struggle to see purpose in his lifetime of professional achievements is described in 'The architect'. Bruce's depression is characterised by feelings of futility and pointlessness, common features of depressive episodes. He describes being highly goal-directed in his earlier life and notes that his previous work as an architect did indeed give his life a sense of purpose. It is understandable, then, that his depression and existential distress began to set in after his decision to close his business: 'In closing my practice and finishing work, I was closing down that meaning.' For many people, work can be a huge source of meaning in their life. For men, in particular, retirement is associated with an increased risk of depression, arguably due to this sudden loss of purpose and sense of fulfilment. Bruce's story provides a clear example of this experience, as he becomes overwhelmed by the absence of meaning at this point in his life:

> 'What am I here for? What's it all about? Does it have a meaning? Is there any meaning to life?... It somehow saddened me to think that one could lead one's life to the point of no purpose. And then I started to look around and think, well, is there a purpose in my life? Does it mean that I've done all this for zero?'

For Godfrey, his extensive activism work earlier in his life gave him a similar sense of purpose. In line with Terror Management Theory's perspectives on cultural worldviews offering symbolic immortality, such activism not only provided Godfrey with purpose but likely gave him a sense that he would exist after death by leaving his mark on the planet through the various environmental campaigns he actively engaged in. Godfrey himself describes deliberately pursuing activism as a solution to the lack of meaning he saw in life, which he attributed to his disbelief in the afterlife:

> 'That's partly what prompted my activism. I didn't feel there's any intrinsic meaning to anything; therefore I'm going to make some meaning. I'm going to care about something. I threw myself into that, and it was very successful as a distraction from the existential dilemma.'

However, for one reason or another, this activism at some point stopped fulfilling this need. Godfrey later finds himself plunged into a depressive episode, with his concerns about meaninglessness at the heart of it. What helps draw him out of this crisis, in part, is his insightful realisation that his belief in utter meaninglessness is doing him more harm than good:

'What I believe is that the ultimate meaninglessness is that you think everything is meaningless! That's the most meaningless thing you can do — to believe everything's meaningless. There is nothing in that space. There is nothing of any value whatsoever to be got from that space or that belief system'.

Ultimately, Godfrey rediscovered meaning through his interactions with women. Not only did these relationships give him a sense of purpose as he shaped the lives of the younger women around him, they also reignited his passion for social and environmental causes; causes which were once such a source of meaning for him. Like Godfrey, Melissa also describes getting a sense of meaning from her close relationships. Although she endorses the inherent meaninglessness of life, she acknowledges that her family relationships offer a sense of purpose: 'I don't believe in a plan, or anything that I do has any greater meaning. I just think we all exist on a rock hurtling through space, as the saying goes. But I guess for things that are personally more meaningful … It's my family — my mum and my dad — they are the only things that still have meaning to me personally.'

While meaninglessness can clearly create crippling existential dread, one clear message woven throughout the ten cases is the idea that finding purpose can be life changing. In 'Eating in emergency', Mary describes a two-year period in her teenage years when, like Matilda's remarkable recovery discussed above, her fears suddenly left her completely. For the first time in her life, she was able to sleep in her own bed, and even caught a plane alone — a remarkable achievement given her history of anxiety. Mary explicitly attributes this miraculous recovery to her sudden sense of meaning after entering the workforce: 'I think for the first time in my life, I had a purpose. I had a job at 13 and felt real purpose.' In 'The joker', Aidan similarly finds meaning through his work, and his projects as a filmmaker appear to serve as a kind of legacy. When asked to comment on what helped assuage his fears of death, Aidan responds with:

Doing things that will slowly get me towards the goal of, in my head, being remembered, I guess. When I make my film, when I'm working on my film, I'm still worried about dying, but I'm like, 'I'm almost there, I'm closer to not having any regrets.'

The creation of some form of legacy or, in the words of Ernest Becker, our 'immortality project', is a powerful way of shielding oneself from the dread of death, by giving one the feeling that they will live on after death through one's work. Aidan's filmmaking may well prove effective at calming his fears of death.

There may be many barriers to building a purposeful life. Anxiety can not only limit one's sense of freedom, as we've discussed, but it can also cripple one's ability to pursue meaningful activities. In 'Dinosaurs are Hiding', Rose's realisation that her fears would get in the way of her living a meaningful life became a significant turning point for her:

> I think the main thing was me wanting to find purpose. So, I knew I wouldn't get anywhere in life if I lived in my house without going outside ever. Just washing my hands all the time would mean that I wouldn't ever contribute to society, and my life would be a waste. I think that's still a bit of fear, because that's something that I try to live my life by — purpose. I need to have purpose in my life … It motivates me.'

Rose's desire to contribute meaningfully to the world, and her thirst for purpose, seemed to drive her to overcome her anxiety. And, in the end, she was able to find that sense of purpose, through her volunteer work at a veterinary clinic. She recounts a recent incident in which she helped rescue an elderly cat: 'Knowing that I made a difference, albeit a small one for a very small portion of his life, makes me feel good. I think, even though he's just a cat, he has fulfilled a life that he needed to fulfil'. Rose's words here are significant. Each of us, no matter who we are, has a life that we 'need to fulfil'. Our ability to pursue satisfying and enjoyable activities, to connect with greater causes, and to create a legacy, can all bring us closer to the ultimate goal of building a meaningful existence in our short time on this planet.

Confronting and Accepting Death

In the face of our mortality, building a sense of meaning, and pursuing solid relationships seem to be two strong defence mechanisms against the dread of our own inevitable death. But the ten cases in Part Two offer one final clue about how we may improve our relationship with death.

The attitude towards death that has been shown to predict the lowest levels of death anxiety is what is referred to as 'neutral acceptance'.

Neutral acceptance involves viewing death as a simple fact of reality and natural process, which is neither celebrated nor feared. Individuals who have cultivated this perspective on death have been shown to be significantly less distressed by death, even compared to those who view death as an escape, or as a gateway to a better afterlife.

The journey towards acceptance of death features across many of the ten interviews. For many of the individuals, their choice to accept the inevitable has proven a major turning point for them and shifted the course of their treatment and life. In 'Bring me back', Michael had previously been visiting hospital emergency departments on a near-daily basis so that he could be resuscitated if he collapsed. It was only when he witnessed his uncle die in hospital, unable to be saved by the medical team, that he finally learned to accept death in all its inescapability: 'He had everyone there, and they could do anything they wanted. But they didn't. And I watched him die … I think that stopped me racing to hospital all the time. Acceptance.' Similarly, 16-year-old Rose learned to acknowledge the universality and inevitability of death. When asked what has most helped allay her fears of death, she responds: 'I think it has been me just accepting the fact that death is inevitable … coming to terms with it and knowing that it'll happen regardless, so there's not a big reason to be fearful of it because it's going to happen to everyone eventually.' In 'Eating in emergency', Mary is living proof of the transformative power of accepting death. Despite suffering from so many crippling mental health conditions, Mary is now travelling independently, recently married, completing a course in Fine Arts, and no longer needs to eat her meals in hospitals due to her worries about ana-phylaxis and choking. At the end of her interview, Mary sums up her changed relationship with death and her shift towards acceptance rather poetically:

> 'Before, I was running away from it, and now I feel like I'm sitting at the dinner table with death. And I can look at him, and I'm suspicious, but I'm also curious and somewhat comfortable. Every now and again, I get the impulse to run away. I don't feel like death and I are best friends. But I'm not terrified of him anymore. I'm cautious of him, but I'm moving toward acceptance.'

Mary's words beautifully encapsulate the benefits to be gained from exam-ining death and our relationship with it under a microscope. If any of us want to overcome our fears of death, we first need to invite death to the dinner table, take a seat alongside it, and engage with it in a spirit of curiosity and acceptance. It is only by doing so that we can ever hope to live a life untroubled by the shadow of mortality, and instead make the most of the time that we each have, however brief.

In the words of the Roman Stoic philosopher Seneca: 'Study death always, so that you'll fear it never.' I hope that the cases described in this book, as well as these reflections, will enrich your study of death, and in doing so, your life.

References

Becker, E. (1973). *The denial of death.* New York: Free Press.

Florian, V., & Mikulincer, M. (1998). Symbolic immortality and the management of the terror of death: The moderating role of attachment style. *Journal of Personality and Social Psychology, 74,* 725–734.

Florian, V., Mikulincer, M., & Hirschberger, G. (2002). The anxiety buffering function of close relationships: Evidence that relationship commitment acts as a terror management mechanism. *Journal of Personality and Social Psychology, 82,* 527–542.

George, A.W. (1999). *The epic of Gilgamesh.* London: Penguin Books.

Goldenberg, J.L., Arndt, J., Hart, J., & Brown, M. (2005). Dying to be thin: The effects of mortality salience and body-mass-index on restricted eating among women. *Personality and Social Psychology Bulletin, 31,* 14000–1412.

Homer. (2003). *The Homeric hymns* (J. Cashford, Trans.). London: Penguin.

Iverach, L., Menzies, R.G., & Menzies, R.E. (2014). Death anxiety and its role in psychopathology: Reviewing the status of a transdiagnostic construct. *Clinical Psychology Review, 34,* 580–593.

Menzies, R.E., Dar-Nimrod, I. (2017). Death anxiety and its relationship with obsessive-compulsive disorder. *Journal of Abnormal Psychology, 126,* 367–377.

Rosenblatt, A., Greenberg, J., Solomon, S., Pyszcynski, T., & Lyon, D. (1989). Evidence for Terror Management Theory: I. The effects of mortality salience on reactions to those who violate or uphold cultural values. *Journal of Personality and Social Psychology, 57*(4), 681–690.

Strachan, E., Schimel, J., Arndt, J., Williams, T., Solomon, S., Pyszczynski, T., & Greenberg, J. (2007). Terror mismanagement: Evidence that mortality salience exacerbates phobic and compulsive behaviors. *Personality and Social Psychology Bulletin, 33*, 1137–1151.

Wisman, A., & Koole, S.L. (2003). Hiding in the crowd: Can mortality salience promote affiliation with others who oppose one's worldview. *Journal of Personality and Social Psychology, 84*, 511–527.

Yalom, I.D. (1980). *Existential psychotherapy*. New York: Basic Books.

www.ingramcontent.com/pod-product-compliance
Lightning Source LLC
Chambersburg PA
CBHW020342270326
41926CB00007B/290